Proactive PPM with
Microsoft Project 2013
for Project Server and Project Online

*A practical approach
to building and managing
schedules with Microsoft Project*

AUTHOR:
KENNETH STEINESS, PMP/PMI-SP MCP MCT

EDITOR: STEVE CASELEY
CONTRIBUTORS: CHAD OLSON, WALT NICKEL, TERRY KNEEBURG

Proactive PPM with Microsoft Project 2013 for Project Server and Project Online
By Kenneth Steiness

Copyright © 2014 Sensei Project Solutions

Printed in the United States of America
Published by Sensei Project Solutions, 8607 S 29th St, Phoenix, AZ 85042
Library of Congress Control Number: 2013921468
ISBN: 978-0-9912464-0-3

Printing History
First Edition – January 2014

Sensei books can be purchased directly from Sensei Project Solutions
(www.senseiprojectsolutions.com/books) or from Amazon.

About Sensei Project Solutions

Sensei Project Solutions is a Gold certified Microsoft Partner specializing in Project and Portfolio Management (PPM) deployments with Microsoft Project, Project Server and Project Online. With extensive experience on hundreds of PPM deployments and with thousands of users trained, Sensei Project Solutions brings a process-focused approach; and support for industry standards and best practices to all engagements. We offer a complete set of services to help an organization make their Microsoft PPM deployment successful, including full implementation and support services, training as well as pre-configured solutions, report packs and Apps.

About the Team

"It takes a village to raise a child" or so the African proverb claims. It most certainly takes a team of dedicated professionals to put together many years of project and portfolio management experience and Microsoft Project technology know-how into a practical, hands-on text book for project managers.

This book was only possible because of everyone's support and contribution. Even those who didn't directly contribute to the book helped by picking up in different areas. Here is the core team behind "Proactive PPM with Microsoft Project 2013 for Project Server and Project Online"

Author: Kenneth Steiness, PMP/PMI-SP MCP MCT
Kenneth started scheduling for the Queen of Denmark in 1995 when he was doing his national service in the Danish Royal Guards in Copenhagen. Responsibilities included scheduling security details for the Queen, Chief of Staff, Crown Jewels and special events. For the World Social Summit, he scheduled security details for Al Gore and Fidel Castro and other dignitaries when they were visiting Copenhagen. All of this was drawn out manually, by hand, in large format, ledger-style books. After leaving the military, Kenneth picked up a copy of Microsoft Project and hasn't looked back since.

Kenneth has worked in the project management and scheduling field for over 18 years, and has managed customer engagements in over 13 countries worldwide and throughout the United States. His focus is on process and the discipline of PPM and scheduling whenever he engages with clients to deploy Microsoft Project and Project Server or teaches classes on the subject. Kenneth has presented at world-wide conferences for Microsoft and PMI; and to many Microsoft Project Users Group chapters over the years.

As a co-founder of Sensei Project Solutions, Kenneth provides strategic direction to the business and is deeply involved with client relationships and deployment projects. In addition to teaching, he has a passion for App design, which has resulted in several world-class Microsoft Project Apps for iPad, iPhone, Windows Phone 8 and Android phones as well as Project Web App and the Microsoft Project client.

Editor: Steve Caseley, PMP/PMI-ACP, Scrum Master
Steve has worked in the project management field for over 25 years, and has a wealth of practical experience in successful project delivery. As a result, he has many battle scars, but none have been fatal. Over the years, Steve has helped a wide range of companies implement PPM Systems and Best Practices and has practical, hands-on PM experience in a wide range of industries, project types and sizes. Steve's passion is working with organizations to improve overall project delivery efficiency through the implementation and adaption of Industry Best Practices in Project and Portfolio management and implementation of effective PPM tools supporting these best practices. Steve has presented at international PM conferences and Microsoft Project Users Group chapters over the years.

Contributor: Chad Olson, MCTS MCSE MCP

Chad has been involved in the Microsoft Project Server platform and related products since 2001. He has focused on the technical aspects of installation, design, architecture, configuration, and customized reporting. Chad has completed over 35 different customer engagements utilizing Microsoft Project Server that has spanned across many different vertical industries. He is very involved in keeping up to date with the latest technical news of Project Server, is connected with the Microsoft Project product team, and has presented at the Microsoft Project Users Group (MPUG). He has conducted training classes for administrators, report authors, and project managers on the toolset with processes and procedures for several clients.

Contributor: Walt Nickel, MCP/MCTS

Walt brings 20+ years of Information Technology experience to the team at Sensei Project Solutions. For the past 12 years he's focused on Project, Portfolio, and Process Management with emphasis on the Microsoft Project and Project Server toolset. Walt has assisted customers domestically and internationally to achieve success with regards to Project and Portfolio Management initiatives across a variety of industries including Engineering, Oil and Gas, Financial Services, as well as Local and Federal Government. Walt's passion when working with customers is to attain consistent and reliable results in Project and Portfolio Management through the use of improving and evolving processes to fit industry best practices standards.

Contributor: Terry Kneeburg, PMP MCITP MCTS

Terry has more than 25 years combined experience in product development, project management, and consulting. He has been working with the Microsoft Project Server platform since 2004. At that time he led his mobile phone development organization in the deployment of EPM. Terry is passionate about helping clients achieve success in managing their project portfolios, delivering to companies in a variety of industries including Healthcare, Transportation, State and Local Government, Energy, Technology, Insurance, and Pharmaceuticals. He has conducted training classes for project managers, administrators, portfolio managers, and team members.

TABLE OF CONTENTS

Introduction

Proactive PPM is a philosophy and a set of best practices to help project managers and organizations be successful with Project Portfolio Management (PPM) utilizing Microsoft Project, Project Server and Project Online.

Proactive PPM Analogy

The concept of Proactive PPM might be best introduced through an analogy. When I was a 'road warrior' early on in my career, I would print directions on MapQuest before leaving for a trip. Upon arriving in a new city and getting to the rental car center, I would pull out my printed directions and start the drive to the client office. These directions, however, did not account for wrong turns, weather or detours. As a result, my map would quickly be outdated and useless. The static nature of the printed map did not meet my 'real-time' needs. As a result, I eventually purchased a GPS system, which always tracks my actual progress, reroutes me on detours and accurately forecasts my arrival time.

Printed Directions

Static; out of sync after detour or wrong turns; no update to arrival time or distance

GPS System

Tracks actual progress; reroutes on detours; provides accurate forecast of arrival time

Much like printed maps are outdated when construction sends us on a detour, static project schedules cannot only be outdated, but can actually send us down the wrong path with incorrect information for decision making.

Too many schedules are built to sell a project or show a pretty picture of how we plan to execute the project, but are never updated after that. The problem, of course, is that things don't always unfold the way we planned them, which means a reactive schedule is hard-coded with artificial dates, no forecasting ability and is not actionable. It is nothing more than a snapshot of a point in time.

What is needed today is the equivalent of a GPS system for our PPM solutions.

Reactive Schedule

Hard coded with artificial dates;
no forecasting ability; unreliable;
inaccurate actuals; snapshot of a
point in time; not actionable

Proactive Schedule

Shows actual progress to date;
reflects estimates to completion;
predicts completion dates and total
cost estimates; enables corrective
action and decision making

The purpose of Proactive PPM then is to:

- Build and maintain a schedule that reflects the true intention (scope and time) AND actual progress to date for the project
- Plan and track costs on the project
- Continuously identify and manage staffing needs
- Clearly communicate work and priorities to team members
- Provide accurate forecasting of remaining effort and durations
- Identify variances BEFORE it is too late for corrective action

In other words, we want to move away from reporting that emphasizes what happened historically (reactive) on the project to an accurate forecast of what is going to happen (proactive) if we don't take corrective action. This will help ensure that detailed project schedules are of the highest quality so that portfolio status reports are accurate, resource capacity/demand forecasting is valid and decision making is based on facts and sound project management practices.

Proactive PPM is the GPS system that will show you the path you've traveled so far, as well as how to get to the destination based on the current location, remaining distance, and known roadblocks.

A Proactive Schedule lets you see farther down the road and enables better forecasting.

Philosophy of this book

This book focuses on project management best practices with Microsoft Project, enabling project managers to build solid schedules that will reflect the true scope of the project and continuously forecast status through completion.

This book is closely aligned with industry standards from the Project Management Institute® (PMI), including:

- **The Project Management Body Of Knowledge (PMBOK Guide)** – 5th Edition, by PMI
- **Practice Standard for Work Breakdown Structures** – 2nd Edition, by PMI
- **Practice Standard for Scheduling** – 2nd Edition, by PMI

The overall goal is to teach project managers a practical approach to 'how' they should be using the tools in the context of industry best practices. As such, this book emphasizes the features of Microsoft Project and Project Web App that help facilitate Proactive PPM. It is NOT a complete guide to all features and functions.

While the principles of Proactive PPM are relevant across all industries and organizations, the processes and examples outlined in this book tend to be a better fit for those organizations wishing to manage projects AND resources. That means effort-based scheduling, such as what we tend to see in most information technology organizations or any organization needing to manage resource capacity and demand.

Assumptions

There are some underlying assumptions throughout this book to help facilitate effective and practical teaching.

We have assumed basic familiarity with the modern user interface as well as rudimentary Microsoft Project skills. Even so, we will review key concepts critical to the understanding of Microsoft Project and Proactive PPM.

We are also assuming that your project schedule reflects the 'contract' and scope of work you have agreed to deliver and that your resources know how to do their jobs. Therefore, the project schedule does NOT become a checklist of every little detail that needs to be accomplished. If resources need more guidance on the work, this information can certainly be supplied in the Notes field of Microsoft Project or even on the supporting SharePoint Project Site, but checklist items or "to-do's" will not be reflected in the schedule's work breakdown structure. More on this topic is presented in Chapter 4.

Terminology

For ease of learning and readability, we will use 'Microsoft PPM' as an umbrella term to describe the overall solution comprised of Microsoft Project (on the desktop) as well as Project Server and Project Online (Project Web App). Where it doesn't interfere with the understanding, we will also use the terms Project Server and Project Online interchangeably to avoid long, complex sentences that are hard to read.

1

CHAPTER 1:

Industry Standards and Proactive PPM

The Project Portfolio Management (PPM) approach we present in this book is based on the principle of proactivity. We develop project plans for one purpose and one purpose only—to define the roadmap to successful project delivery and completion. With the roadmap (schedule) established, we define the processes to actively track progress against this plan, allowing for early identification of any delivery challenges that could impact a successful delivery. Finally, we deploy proactive remediation actions to correct these challenges and keep our projects on track. Proactive PPM allows us to continuously identify schedule, cost, scope and other project delivery challenges by comparing the current status against the 'approved' roadmap.

1.1 Alignment with Industry Standards

1.1.1 Industry Standards – Project Management Institute® (PMI)

In this book, we present the recommended approaches for using Microsoft PPM to successfully deliver both Portfolios and Projects. As such, we align with PMI's definition of Projects and Portfolios as defined in ***The Project Management Body of Knowledge (PMBOK Guide)*** – 5th Edition.

- A project is a temporary endeavor undertaken to create a unique product, service or result.
- A portfolio refers to projects, programs, sub-portfolios, and operations managed as a group to achieve strategic objectives. The projects or programs of the portfolio may not necessarily be interdependent or directly related. (Project Management Institute, 2013)

In addition to the PMBOK Guide, we also closely align with the Practice Standards that provide the next level of detail for Scope Management and Time Management. These are:

Practice Standard for Work Breakdown Structures – 2nd Edition, by PMI
This Standard does an excellent job of providing a solid foundation for Scope Management through the use of the Work Breakdown Structure (WBS) technique. The WBS technique provides the foundation for defining work as it relates to project objectives and is the backbone of any project schedule. In fact, it is considered the single most important prerequisite to a good schedule.

Practice Standard for Scheduling – 2nd Edition, by PMI
This Standard describes scheduling methods generally recognized as good practice for most projects most of the time. In addition, it describes the hallmarks of a sound and effective project scheduling methodology and provides quantifiable means for assessing a schedule against the standard.

1.1.2 Industry Standards - Gartner

Gartner, Inc. is the world's leading information technology (IT) research and advisory company. The analysts at Gartner have done a great deal of research in the area of PPM and have published extensively on the topic, especially as it relates to PPM reporting.

Consistent with the practices defined by Gartner, we define the approaches to be used for reporting against your Portfolios and Projects to ensure that you extract the needed information: 1) supporting the sub-portfolios, and 2) surfacing the items of greatest interest to your organization, whether that is schedule performance, financial measures, issue/risk mitigation, etc.

One key measure defined by Gartner is the need to track IT spending by whether a project's primary purpose is to 'run the business', 'grow the business', or 'transform the business'. This helps ensure appropriate spending on each category is consistent with the overall strategic direction.

At Sensei Project Solutions, our clients tend to align with Gartner's PPM recommendations. As a result, this book is also influenced by the principles of Gartner's research, especially as it relates to the following PPM reporting topics:

- Variances and exceptions
- Better decision making, and steering executives to where decisions are needed
- Automated project status reporting
- Dynamic sub-portfolios

The above topics are too broad to cover in detail in this book, but the principles are infused in the recommended reports you will see throughout this book.

1.2 Principles and Purpose of Proactive PPM

It is important to understand the philosophy and principles behind Proactive PPM and appreciate the connection between data quality in individual project schedules and reporting and resource management at the enterprise level.

Ultimately, the project schedule enhances the chances of successful project delivery. To be useful then, a proactive schedule should always reflect the true intention (both scope and time) AND actual progress of the project. It should clearly communicate work and priorities to project team members, provide accurate forecasting of remaining effort and durations, and identify variances before it is too late for corrective action.

The project schedule is NOT a checklist of every little detail that needs to be accomplished but, rather, it represents the 'contract' and scope of work agreed to be delivered.

The essence of Proactive PPM is closely aligned with the spirit of the book **The 7 Habits of Highly Effective People** by Stephen R. Covey. Before you can adopt these approaches, you may need to accomplish what Covey calls a 'paradigm shift'—a change in perception and interpretation. This book provides you with an opportunity to develop your 'proactive muscles' and act with initiative rather than react to your project stakeholders and the schedule.

1.2.1 The 7 Habits of Proactive Microsoft PPM Users

The great Stephen Covey has inspired so many of us. His teachings are integrated into every aspect of my personal and professional life. I recently took some time to pause and reflect on how the '7 Habits' have impacted my own career as a scheduler and project manager. Specifically, here are some thoughts on how the '7 Habits' apply to Proactive PPM and Microsoft Project users:

Be Proactive

Perhaps the most critical aspect of being a project manager/scheduler is to take complete ownership of the schedule. As project managers, we just can't accept 'hard-coded' dates given to us by the sponsor, team members or other stakeholders. In organizations with limited resources, in particular, it's critical that we change the conversation to the following:

- Ask team members for a commitment to the 'effort' (work) estimate, not delivery dates or durations. As project managers, we need to understand the true effort of the work to be performed.
  - Example: Your developer tells you that she can have the updated prototype ready in five weeks, but when asked to clarify the effort involved, we discover that it's only 40 hours of effort. The five weeks duration estimate was based on a week of vacation time (already accounted for in the project calendar), known commitments on other projects, and various support activities.
- Ask resource managers for a commitment of the allocation of resources on your project. As project managers, we need to understand what resources are available to us and at what percentage
  - Example: The developer had previously estimated the scope of work to be 40 hours of effort (work). The resource manager now allocates this individual to your project at 50 percent.

Figure 1.1 Changing the Conversation

As project managers, we should only ever commit to dates based on: 1) effort estimates received from team members, and 2) the allocation percentage of assigned resources from resource managers. So, armed with the effort estimate of 40 hours from the team member and 50 percent allocation from the resource manager, we can now calculate the true duration (two weeks) of the task. We can also see the resulting schedule impact based on the complete dependency network and the supporting calendars. If the result is a missed deadline, then we can have an intelligent conversation with our sponsor about either reducing scope or allocating more of the resource's time to the project. While this example is very simple, the complexity of projects is typically much greater and, as such, Microsoft Project has more advanced calculations and factors in non-working time, lead/lag, and dependencies as well.

Any dates given to you by your sponsor or anyone else on the project should be entered as a 'deadline' only, never as a 'start' or 'finish' date, as that would hard-code your schedule and take ownership away from you.

You are the 'programmer,' 'author,' and owner of your schedule, so don't make excuses or live your schedule by someone else's script.

Begin with the End in Mind

The most successful projects have a deliverable-focused WBS to represent the true scope of the project. Build your schedules with the end in mind by establishing your outcomes/deliverables. This helps you manage scope throughout execution, and ensures that the entire team is on the same page as to what the work is. Examples of deliverables could include Design Document, Test Plan, Production Installation, and Trained Staff. Notice how all of these are either a physical object (document) or an outcome. What they have in common is that we can: 1) describe the end state when a deliverable is complete, and 2) explain to a team member what it means to produce that deliverable. A good test to see if you have true deliverables in your schedule is to put 'The' in front and see if it works— The Design Document, The Production Installation, etc.

You can still have phases in your project schedule, but the most important portion of the WBS will always be the deliverables and their supporting work packages/activities/tasks.

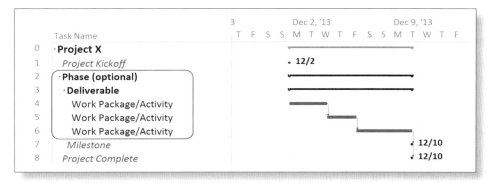

Figure 1.2 Deliverable Focused Work Breakdown Structure

The entire scope of your project should be represented within the deliverables in the WBS to be in compliance with industry standards (i.e., no detailed tasks should be present outside of the deliverable structure). It's likely that the quality of your project will improve as well when using this method since there will be less ambiguity about the scope of the work.

For more details on how to build a proactive WBS, see **PMI's Practice Standard for Work Breakdown Structures** – 2nd Edition.

Put First Things First

Once you have built a solid WBS, it's time to 'walk the talk' and put first things first. Building a complete and accurate dependency network is what makes the schedule truly proactive. When building dependencies, try to think about natural relationships that exist for the scope of work and NOT about the order in which you would like to schedule things. We typically talk about the cause and effect when adding predecessors and successors. Can we install the operating system before the server has been procured and received? It's a silly question, of course, but these relationships exist throughout your schedule. So, 'Install Operating System on Test Server for Accounting System' is dependent on the milestone 'Accounting Test Server Hardware Received.' This milestone, in turn, is dependent on 'Place Order for Accounting Test Server Hardware,' which happens to have three weeks of lead time. Modeled properly, these relationships will help you automatically update the project schedule each week as the team makes progress.

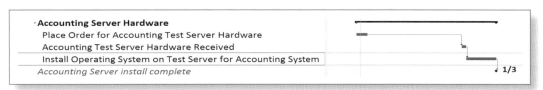

Figure 1.3 Dependencies should reflect natural relationships

The rules of dependency planning are straightforward:

1. Every detailed task and milestone in the project schedule should be included in the dependency network (i.e., no 'orphan' detailed tasks or milestones).
   That means there should be a predecessor and successor on each task/milestone, with the exception of starting points and the project completion milestone, and potentially any Level of Effort (LOE) tasks, such as Ongoing Project Management Support.
2. Lead and lag time can be used to account for softer dependencies between tasks (e.g., start testing when we're 75 percent done with coding).
3. Summary tasks should NEVER have dependencies on them.

Putting first things first also means monitoring and focusing on the critical path of the project. Showing the critical path in team meetings and status reports involves the team, and clearly demonstrates the priorities that will allow us to 'walk the talk.' If we do experience a delay during project execution, we can easily search for effort-driven tasks on the critical path to take corrective action that can help bring us back on track.

Think Win-Win
While the project schedule is an important tool for many project managers, it is often misunderstood (or not understood at all) by project team members. When building the WBS for the project, you will get a much more accurate definition of scope (and as a result, the schedule) by involving the team and letting them own the decomposition of the deliverables. It is also important to stress to the team what benefits they get from having the scope fully defined and contributing to the ongoing updates to the project schedule. For organizations that have adopted the proactive scheduling approach, these are some of the common benefits to team members:

- **Reduced over-allocation**
  - When schedules have complete dependency networks and incomplete work is rescheduled each week, the typical 'pileup' of work is avoided.
  - With resource manager commitments to allocations (see above), there are also typically fewer conflicts across projects.
- **Visibility into planned work and priorities**
  - Whether in Project Professional on the desktop or in Project Web App, project team members can get a complete list of project tasks with dates and priorities.
- **Accurate forecasting of project time availability**
  - Organizations, that choose to capture all time quickly and identify how much work is spent on projects vs. ongoing support activities, develop better forecasts.
- **Push prioritization decisions back on management**
  - Frequent interruptions by senior executives with urgent requests for support can be better managed when team members are able to show a list of scheduled work and priorities.
  - Stephen Covey's famous dialogue with a team member: "I'm happy to help with your request, Stephen. Which of these existing project tasks would you like me to postpone? Would you like me to notify the project manager or will you do that?"
- **Managers can now see how hard team members actually work**
  - If resources work 60+ hours each week to get all the work done, there's usually a long-term impact and potentially high employee turnover.

The above will help answer the "What's in it for me?" question and should get you more participation from team members when updating the status of the project schedule. It's a win-win if project managers get the input they need from the team to build the best possible schedule, and team members get a more structured working environment with visibility and reduced over-allocation.

Another win-win is between project managers and the project sponsor and key stakeholders. All too often, we neglect to ask what the success criteria are for the project and whether time, quality or cost is more important. Managing the triple constraints and reporting against key performance indicators will enable senior management to make better decisions and provide guidance for corrective action. This, in turn, gets the project manager buy-in on the project schedule and commitment to a formal project management approach.

Seek First to Understand, Then to Be Understood
In just about any situation, it's much more important to listen and understand than it is to be immediately understood. Certainly, when faced with a problem on your project, it is important to act as a facilitator and get all the right people involved in the conversation. The team members or subject matter experts on the project will often have a very good understanding of the issues and will be in a good position to provide input on how to best resolve them. By listening to their concerns, understanding the situation and their suggestions, you will be armed with all the right information to make key decisions to move forward.

When we fully understand the situation, we're better able to ask the right questions to get to a resolution. After having gathered the facts, try to provide options for the key stakeholders to review. You can accomplish this by modeling each scenario in Microsoft Project and even use the Inactive Task feature to show what the schedule would look like with and without the proposed solution.

Task Name	Start	Finish
Solution Design Document	**Aug 21**	**Sep 9**
Begin Solution Design	*Aug 21*	*Aug 21*
Develop Database	**Aug 21**	**Aug 28**
Create Entity Relationship Diagram	Aug 21	Aug 27
Create Data Dictionary	Aug 21	Aug 27
Review and Approval of Database	Aug 27	Aug 28
Database Complete	*Aug 28*	*Aug 28*
Develop System Design	Aug 28	Sep 4
Create Security Design	Aug 28	Sep 3
Create Class Design	Aug 28	Sep 3
Create Navigation	Aug 28	Sep 3
Create Screen Design - Standards	Aug 28	Sep 3
Create Workflow	Aug 28	Sep 3
Review and Approval of System Design	Sep 3	Sep 4
System Design Completed	Sep 4	Sep 4
Develop Infrastructure Design	**Aug 28**	**Sep 4**
Create Application Deployment Architecture	Aug 28	Sep 3
Review and Approval of Infrastructure Design	Sep 3	Sep 4
Infrastructure Complete	*Sep 4*	*Sep 4*

Figure 1.4 Use Microsoft Project to facilitate effective communications

As project managers, we're often the hub of communication and will experience much better results if our stakeholders feel understood before we report status or propose changes to the project. In your next team meeting, try letting team members take the lead on reporting status to the group instead of repeating what they told you prior to the meeting. You will find that they are much more open to being influenced if they feel understood first.

Synergize

What is synergy? "Simply defined, it means the whole is greater than the sum of its parts. It means that the relationship, which the parts have to each other is a part in and of itself," (*from **The 7 Habits of Highly Effective People:** Habit 6 Synergize – Stephen R. Covey*).

Once all the pieces of the schedule have been put together properly and are in line with industry standards, the schedule becomes greater than the sum of its parts. It will now truly represent the actual project and will enable the project manager to be proactive and provide executives with critical information for decision making.

If a project experiences delays or overruns, a proactive schedule will give early warning and help identify the best options for corrective actions, including the critical path, high-cost tasks, and quality issues on key deliverables.

Synergy on the project team will also allow team members to participate actively in any corrective action required. Techniques such as Crashing and Fast Tracking are much more successful with a synergistic project team and easier to apply in a proactive project schedule.

Sharpen the Saw

No doubt you know the story of the man in the forest who's too busy sawing to stop and sharpen the saw?

Every day we come across project managers who are too busy updating their schedules and running their projects to stop and learn new techniques and disciplines that would greatly increase their chances of success.

Consider these five simple changes you can make in your interaction with the schedule in Microsoft Project that would provide many-fold returns on your time investment:

1. **Options**
   Carefully review and understand the detailed options, as these have a direct impact on the calculations, dates and behavior of Microsoft Project. For example, your default Task Type will determine how tasks are calculated when they are updated, such as whether the date/duration changes or the work effort goes up.

2. **Deadlines**
   Start using the Deadline feature for dates you've committed to rather than entering a start or finish date or setting a constraint on your tasks. This approach gives you the best of both worlds. You can see what the commitment date is, but also recognize whether that date is being met or corrective action is needed.

3. **Remaining Work**
   In addition to tracking Actual Work against tasks in the schedule, also ask your team members to validate the Estimate to Completion through Remaining Work. Not only does this ensure better data quality, but it also helps team members buy into the estimates on a weekly basis, and think about effort instead of duration.

4. **Status Date**

   Utilize the Status Date feature to clearly communicate the date to which the schedule is up to date. There should be no incomplete work or milestones prior to the status date nor any actual work after the status date. Use the Update Project feature (below) to move work forward.

5. **Update Project**

   During project execution, it's quite common for things to progress at a different pace or even in a different order than originally planned. In order to ensure that the project schedule stays relevant, we must make sure that the schedule is updated each week to move any incomplete work forward of the status date. The Update Project feature does this very nicely and forces the project manager to work with resource managers and team members on how to adjust to the new reality.

Each of these will be reviewed in much more detail throughout this book.

Project managers who take time to sharpen the saw and adopt scheduling best practices, such as Sensei's Proactive PPM, typically go from spending 4–6 hours each week maintaining their project schedule to 30–60 minutes. Proactive PPM incorporates all the principles of the '7 Habits' and also aligns with industry standards and best practices. The up-front time investment during the planning phase is greater, but the ROI is significant in both time savings and quality improvements.

1.3 Project Life Cycle

The Project Life Cycle we describe follows a traditional project life cycle with Initiation, Planning, Executing and Closing phases. The modules are aligned with each of the major activities within each of these phases.

- **Initiation** is all about submitting the project proposal (Charter) complete with project details and resource plan, but no schedule yet.
- **Planning** begins when the project proposal has been approved and focuses on building the baseline schedule.
- **Executing** is the ongoing collaboration and tracking of updates for team members; approving status, taking corrective action, and reporting for project managers.
- **Closing** covers how to close out a project schedule properly.

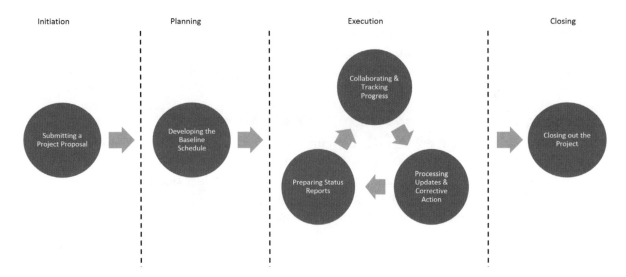

Figure 1.5 Project Life Cycle

1.3.1 Submitting a Project Proposal

The Project Proposal is important, as the information in it is used by senior management to validate and approve the project. However, as not all project proposals will be approved, it is also important to put just enough work into developing the proposal to ensure it reflects the high-level requirements (time, cost and resources) to support management approval (or rejection) without investing the effort required to develop a full project plan. Similarly, generic resources, as opposed to named individuals, should be used for long-term planning and proposals to allow for tracking overall delivery capacity. The Project Proposal provides senior management with the information needed to validate the project's objectives, business impact, costs, and delivery capacity, allow for the approval and scheduling of projects consistent with corporate objectives and, more importantly, the cancellation of projects that are not feasible based on costs, capacity or direction. The Project Proposal effectively develops the 'contract' for how the project will be delivered.

1.3.2 Developing the Baseline Schedule

Once the Project Proposal is approved, a project manager should be assigned to the project and the full detailed project plan should be developed. Where possible, the key/senior team members that will be working on the project should be involved in the creation of the plan to increase the level of accuracy and overall commitment to the plan. While we will cover the development of the Baseline Schedule in much more detail in Chapter 4, the key activities are highlighted below:

- Deliverable-based Work Breakdown Structure
  The best way to manage the overall scope of the project (reduce scope 'creep' and misunderstanding) and to ensure a consistent outline for schedules across the portfolio is with a deliverable-based WBS. A deliverable-based WBS defines the scope by defining each deliverable that will be produced by the project. The sum of the deliverables defines the total scope of the project.
- Fully resource-loaded schedule
  Work that is not assigned to anyone doesn't get done! The project should be resourced with Enterprise Resources at the approved allocation level whenever possible. As well, the project should only include work that you have direct control over. All other external

dependencies should be modeled as a milestone to allow for tracking, but no work/resources (team members) should be assigned (finish date only).

- Effort-based estimates
  Estimates that are based on when work can be completed have slack and contingency built in by committing to a completion date. Proactive project plans are developed using effort-based estimates, which define the actual effort (or work) required to complete each task, ensuring that the plan is developed based on realistic estimates.
- Complete dependency network
  Defining the predecessor/successor relationships between the tasks in the schedule helps to ensure an accurate schedule and decreases the amount of maintenance during execution. The dependency network should reflect the natural relationship of cause and effect that exists between tasks and reflect reality.
- Baseline Schedule to measure progress against
  The Baseline Schedule should always reflect the most recent agreed-upon or approved schedule, even if it includes multiple change requests. It is required to track variance and will form the basis for measuring project health with such things as 'traffic-light' health indicators.
- No hard-coded target dates
  As a matter of principle, any given target dates should be entered as Deadlines and NOT hard-coded into Start and Finish cells.
- No action items or to-do lists in the schedule
  Finding the right level of detail in the schedule is critical to manage scope and ensure a realistic status reporting cycle. Only tasks/activities needed to produce deliverables are allowed in the schedule. All action items and to-dos should be kept in SharePoint lists or in the task notes.

1.3.3 Managing the Schedule

With the schedule developed and the baseline created and approved, the project moves into execution where the focus of the team is on completing the WBS deliverables. The project management focus changes to managing the schedule by tracking actual progress against the approved baseline.

- Actuals and estimates to completion are collected each reporting period
  In addition to tracking Actual Work against tasks, team members' timesheets also need to review and validate the Estimates to Completion (Remaining Work) to produce an accurate forecast.
- Schedule is updated with accurate status each reporting period
  For the best results, and to facilitate resource capacity/demand management, status input should be processed weekly, including approval of task updates, manual updates on milestone status, risk/issues, and project status on the SharePoint Project Site.
- No Planned Work in the past
  No incomplete work can exist in the past (i.e., prior to the status date), so this must be moved forward as part of the weekly status cycle.
- Accurate representation of progress
  Accurate timesheets and realistic estimates for remaining work allow for ongoing schedule maintenance in order to maintain predictability in meeting project milestones.
- Ongoing resource requirements forecasting
  Realistic schedules allow for accurate resource forecasts.

- Effective stakeholder communication
  Stakeholder communication is always based on accurate, up-to-date, and realistic facts on project delivery to date and validated forecasts for completion.

1.3.4 Closing

Closing is a brief, but very important, phase of a project where final acceptance of the results is obtained, signifying that the project has achieved the stated objectives and the business is satisfied with the results delivered. A project review should also be completed at this time to document 'lessons learned,' to ensure that successes are repeated and mistakes are avoided.

2

CHAPTER 2:

Introduction to Microsoft Project and Project Web App

You are most likely familiar and very comfortable with Microsoft Project on the desktop. This chapter will focus on putting in context the overall Microsoft PPM solution; explain how the scheduling engine works; and highlight key features and functions of Microsoft Project and Project Web App (PWA).

2.1 The Building Blocks of PPM™

Microsoft Project has evolved from a task management application into a complete end-to-end Project Portfolio Management (PPM) solution.

The building blocks of PPM represent the common business objectives and process areas that are the business drivers behind most deployments. Sensei's philosophy is that the focus should be on solving a business problem—not on the technology—when deploying Microsoft Project and Project Server.

Within these building blocks lie the processes, procedures, tools, techniques, configuration options and training that make up Sensei's recommended approach to PPM and the heart and soul of Proactive PPM.

Project Status and Portfolio Reporting
Track actual progress to date and reforecast based on Estimates To Completion; status against key performance indicators and roll-up portfolio reporting

Project Planning and Collaboration
Plan the detailed scope of work with key deliverables, milestones and resource assignments. Collaborate on project artifacts

Budgeting and Cost tracking
Load budgets & cost estimates in project schedules; then track progress and report variance during execution

Resource Capacity/Demand Management
Establish resource capacity baseline and capture work demand to identify staffing bottlenecks

Project Intake & Prioritization
Capture project proposals with supporting business cases and prioritize against business drivers and existing workload

Figure 2.1 The Building Blocks of PPM™

2.1.1 Project Intake and Prioritization
Successful organizations manage their project intake and prioritize initiatives to ensure the best return on investment.

Microsoft PPM allows organizations to easily capture incoming project proposals through an online business case form, including high-level staffing needs, cost information, and supporting documentation.

Throughout the budgeting cycle (and at other strategic times of the fiscal year), organizations can review the incoming project proposals against the overall strategic direction of the business and prioritize them based on budgets and existing workloads to ensure a realistic portfolio of projects that provides the most value and can be successfully executed.

This prioritization process also helps the organization understand what the long-term resource needs are and where bottlenecks may exist.

2.1.2 Resource Capacity/Demand Management
During the budgeting/planning cycle and throughout the year, resource capacity and demand need to be carefully managed.

First, resource capacity should be fully mapped to ensure the organization understands how roles, skills and departments are staffed to do project work.

All incoming project proposals are required to capture high-level resources needed, typically by role, to help understand the full picture of demand on resources.

When evaluating capacity/demand, the organization is better able to determine what long-term hiring needs are and where bottlenecks exist on current projects.

2.1.3 Budgeting and Cost Tracking

Organizations frequently allocate a budget to a project before planning is complete. This 'approved funding' is captured in the project schedule for comparison to the cost estimates derived from the detailed scoping exercise. When approval is obtained, the project baseline is set and locked down.

Throughout the project, actual costs are tracked and remaining costs are re-forecasted to allow for accurate Estimates to Completion and identify variances from the original baseline.

2.1.4 Project Planning and Collaboration

Proper project planning will carefully document the full scope of work as well as assumptions, budgets, resource requirements, supporting documentation, deadlines and constraints. When all of these are integrated successfully, the project schedule can reflect reality and serve as a GPS during project execution.

A proactive schedule reflects what was originally agreed upon and is continuously updated to show progress, variance, and an updated forecast.

2.1.5 Project Status and Portfolio Reporting

Under ideal circumstances, each project is updated weekly with status on actual progress as well as an assessment or validation of the remaining effort to identify variances and produce an accurate forecast for the remainder of the project.

The individual projects roll up into portfolio reports and dashboards for an enterprise view of performance against key performance indicators. Resource bottlenecks can be identified by role, team and department.

Proactive schedules provide visibility and insight, and facilitate better decision making in a portfolio of projects.

2.2 Microsoft PPM

In an enterprise deployment, there are three major pieces to the Microsoft PPM puzzle.

1. Microsoft Project Professional (desktop)
2. Project Server or Project Online (back-end database)
3. Project Web App (Web front-end)

When transitioning from using Microsoft Project Standard (desktop only) to using Microsoft PPM, perhaps one of the most important concepts is that project schedule and resources are no longer saved in a local .MPP file, but rather directly into an SQL Server database. This is the key difference from a technology perspective that facilitates Portfolio Management and Resource Capacity/Demand Management. We now have all of our data in a single location that we can report against.

The graphic below shows how all the pieces work together (simplified for ease of communication).

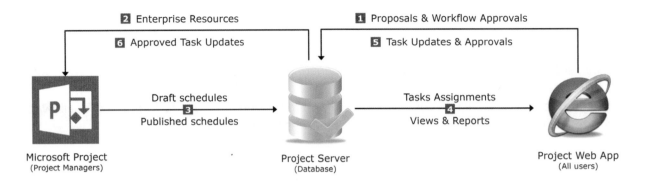

Figure 2.2 Microsoft PPM Overview

2.2.1 Proposals and Workflow Approvals

A proposal is initiated from PWA, where the user enters the business case and justification for the proposed project. This will typically include the problem statement, expected benefits, proposal costs, and high-level resource estimates. The goal with this exercise is to provide just enough information to allow executives to make a decision on whether the project should be approved. The detailed Work Breakdown Structure (WBS) and scoping comes later, so try not to spend too much time here as it may be wasted if the proposal doesn't align with the strategic direction of the organization.

Each proposal is submitted through the appropriate governance workflow and executives can review and approve all incoming proposals directly in PWA.

2.2.2 Enterprise Resources

Once a proposal has been approved, the project manager is assigned and will start the detailed planning. To this end, enterprise resources are loaded from the Enterprise Resource Pool into the schedule in Microsoft Project to ensure that all work can be evaluated against the resource capacity of the organization.

2.2.3 Draft and Published Schedules

The project manager builds out the detailed schedule in Microsoft Project, including the WBS, resource assignments, effort estimates, dependencies, deadlines and constraints.

Saved schedules are sent to the Project Server database as Draft schedules that are only available through Microsoft Project. Only when the project manager publishes the schedule will it be available in the Published database and thereby accessible in PWA.

2.2.4 Task Assignments, Views and Reports

With the schedule published and resources committed, team members will now see their task assignments in the Tasks list and Timesheet in PWA.

Published schedules are also available in Project Center views and reports.

2.2.5 Task Updates and Approvals

On a weekly basis, team members will need to update their task assignments. This can be done either through the Tasks section or the Timesheet in PWA. Regardless of method, the team member should track both Actual Work and review the Estimate to Completion (Remaining Work). This is a critical step in the process to help validate the estimates each week and identify problems early.

Project managers will then review and approve the task updates.

2.2.6 Approved Task Updates
Once approved, the task updates are now incorporated into the project schedule. Now, the project manager gets to update milestones on the project and take corrective action, if needed, and the weekly cycle starts over.

2.3 Microsoft Project

Whenever I start teaching a new group of project managers, I am reminded of this quote:

"The loftier the building, the deeper must the foundation be laid." —Thomas Kempis

For some organizations, Proactive PPM can be a lofty goal from a project management maturity perspective, and our proposed use of Microsoft Project is more advanced than most users attempt on their own. A deep foundation in the technology and project management discipline is important to achieve success with Proactive PPM.

2.3.1 Working with Enterprise Projects
If you haven't already connected your Microsoft Project Professional to your corporate Project Server environment, follow the instructions in Appendix A to establish this connection.

You will make your decision to work with the enterprise solution as soon as you launch Microsoft Project, as you will be presented with a login dialog where you will select whether you want to work locally or against Project Web App. If you choose Computer, you will be operating in local mode and none of the enterprise features discussed in this book will be available.

Select your PWA Environment from the login dialog to connect this Microsoft Project session to your corporate server; the server name(s) shown will be specific to your organization (in our example, our Enterprise Server is called 'Sensei Jumpstart'). This will activate the checkbox 'Load Summary Resource Assignments.' We recommend you leave this unselected. Selecting it will result in all the resource assignments from other projects for all resources working on your project to be loaded into Microsoft Project. While this is necessary if you are doing enterprise resource leveling at the project level, we recommend that enterprise resource leveling take place in PWA as part of Enterprise Resource Management and, therefore, you do not need this option selected. Next, depending on your organizational security policies, you may get prompted for your User ID and password.

**Figure 2.3 Microsoft Project
Login dialog**

You access projects stored in PWA the same as local projects; select File, to go to the Backstage, select Open, and then the name of your Enterprise Server (Sensei Jumpstart).

Figure 2.4 Backstage - Open projects from your PWA environment

You then get a familiar, although slightly different, Open dialog. The key difference is this Open dialog gives you the option of going directly to the Server by selecting 'Show me the list of all projects' or alternatively, immediately below it, provides you the list of the files you have been working with recently and are available in your cache.

This concept of cache is very important to understand, as while the projects are actually stored locally in your cache, Microsoft Project also connects to the server to validate that the plan you are selecting (from your cache) is in fact current and, if not, it will automatically refresh before opening. This way, you have confidence that you are always getting the most current copy, while still enjoying the efficiencies of using local cache.

At the bottom of the Open dialog, you have two radio buttons where you can control whether you will be opening your plan Read/Write or Read Only, and whether the display should show Working plans or Published plans.

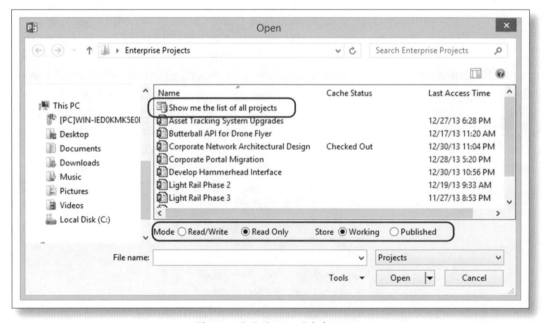

Figure 2.5 Open Dialog

If you selected Read/Write, the plan is opened, checked out to you and available for editing. If, however, you selected Read Only (or forgot to check Read/Write), the plan is opened and a large banner is displayed at the top of the plan reminding you that the plan is Read Only, and provides you an option to Check Out if needed.

Figure 2.6 Check Out Option when plan is opened Read-Only

Assuming you've opened the plan for Read/Write and make some changes, upon Save/Close, you will be prompted as to whether you want to Save and/or check the plan back in. Typically, you would check the plan back in so that others in your organization can make further updates to the plan. This saves the plan back to the Enterprise Server and removes the Check Out option on the file, allowing others to make changes. If, however, you will be going off-line for a period of time, you would say only Save. This saves the changes back to the server AND your cache, but preserves the checkout lock that you have on the file, preventing anyone else in the organization from making any changes until you return from your business trip and check the file back in by opening it and then saving it by including the Check In option.

2.3.2 Features and Navigation

Even seasoned Microsoft Project users discover new features and navigation options on a regular basis, so we thought it would be important to recap key functions here to allow us to focus more on the processes in the subsequent chapters.

Ribbons

The Ribbons offer an efficient method of navigation and access to the key features of Microsoft Project. Four of the ribbons—**Task**, **Resource**, **Report** and **Project**—provide access to the majority of the functionality and will likely be used on a daily basis, when you work with your schedule.

**Figure 2.7 Microsoft Project ribbons -
Task, Resource, Report and Project**

The names of each Ribbon are very self-explanatory and define the type of actions supported.

The **Task** ribbon contains the actions that you need to manipulate the individual task lines (rows) in your schedule.

Figure 2.8 Task Ribbon

The **Resource** ribbon contains the commands that you need to create and maintain the resources working on your project.

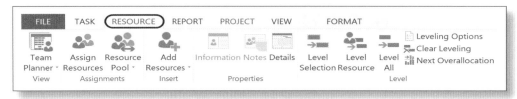

Figure 2.9 Resource Ribbon

The **Report** ribbon is new for Microsoft Project 2013, as Microsoft has improved the reporting functions and, therefore, the ribbon now supports creating and using these new, powerful reports.

Figure 2.10 Report Ribbon

The **Project** ribbon contains the commands that you need to maintain overall project information.

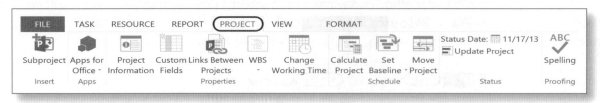

Figure 2.11 Project Ribbon

The **View** ribbon allows you to customize the information you see on your screen, providing powerful features like highlights, filters and groups.

Figure 2.12 View Ribbon

The **Format** ribbon allows you to change the look and feel of the data on the screen.

Figure 2.13 Format Ribbon

The ribbons are further divided into sections that contain related actions. For example, the **Task** ribbon has a Schedule section, which contains the commands you will be using to create and maintain the project schedule. Throughout the book, we will be referring to these ribbons and sections for specific actions, such as 'View ribbon > Data section.'

Figure 2.14 View Ribbon Data Section

As we will be referring to the ribbons and their specific actions throughout the book, we will leave the details of what each command does until it is referenced in subsequent chapters. Now, you should have enough familiarity with the ribbon to be comfortable with using this key Microsoft Office interface. In my experience, many Microsoft Project users experienced somewhat of an adoption curve when the ribbon was introduced in the 2010 version, but I think most will also agree that once you get comfortable with the ribbon and the mind-set that you select the Ribbon based on the actions you want to do (Task, Resource, Project, etc.) you won't want to give it up.

Timescale
The Timescale is the visual representation of the tasks in the WBS. As you scroll through your schedule, the timescale may slip out of focus. To ensure that you are seeing exactly what you want to focus on, use the Zoom feature to view the entire project, scroll to a specific task, or view selected tasks. You can also set the exact measure to use in the Timescale, such as Days, Weeks or Months.

As most projects will be delivered over several months (or years) Microsoft provides features for manipulating the screen display to support effectively managing the schedule, whether you're focused on the daily tasks to be completed over the next week or getting a high-level view of the entire project over a six-month time window. Management of timescale is done on the 'View ribbon > Zoom section.' The most effective way to manage the timescale is to select the tasks you are interested in and then select the Selected Tasks feature from the ribbon. This will do two things for you, first it will scale the granularity of the timescale display (Days, Weeks, Months) to ensure all the tasks you have selected can be displayed within the available space on your screen, and it will adjust the actual dates displayed to match the start date of the first task in your selected range.

TIPS & HINTS:
    Put 'Zoom > Selected Tasks' on your Quick Access toolbar—this is a real time saver, as you will be using this feature on a very regular basis

You can also directly control the granularity of the Timescale using the dropdown list to define the level of detail needed for specific purposes; for creating status reports and other management reports where you may need a weekly view for Project Status reports and a monthly view for a Project Management Office (PMO) status report. And finally, the Timescale option at the bottom of this dropdown list provides you total control over both the granularity and format of the Timescale, allowing you to control the precise information displayed, for example, making the Timescale generic (Week 1, Week 2) during the Proposal stage, and then actual (June 3) during Delivery.

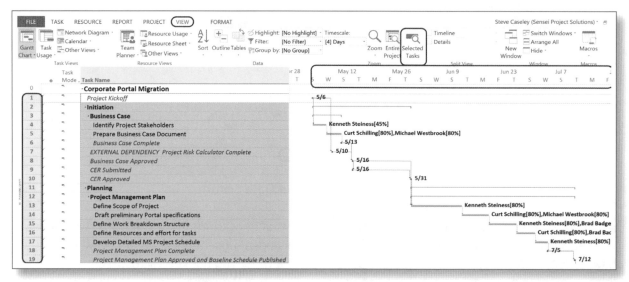

Figure 2.15 Control Timescale Zoom

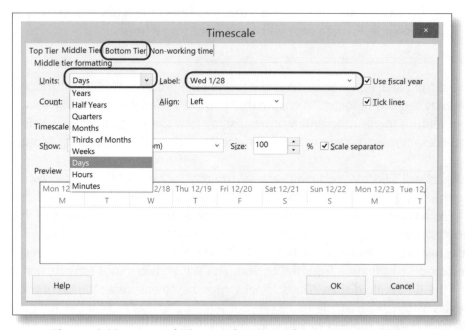

Figure 2.16a Manual Timescale Control - Set Bottom Tier

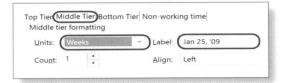

Figure 2.16b Manual Timescale Control - Set Middle Tier

Figure 2.16c Manual Timescale Control - Set Top Tier

Scroll Bars and Outline Levels

Since most projects have hundreds of lines of tasks and months of duration, Microsoft has provided a number of features to make screen navigation easy and efficient.

But first, let's talk about the basic composition of most views in Microsoft Project. Most, but not all views have two parts, a Table Area and a Time Phased Area.

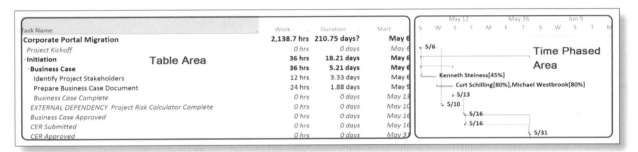

Figure 2.17 Definition of Table Area and Time Phased Area of a View

Microsoft Project synchronizes vertical scrolling of both parts so that Data and the Timescale are always aligned, while still allowing you to horizontally scroll either part independently. As well, there are keyboard shortcuts for scrolling in both directions. The left/right arrows will horizontally scroll the data part of your screen, while Alt + left/right arrows will horizontally scroll the Timescale part of your screen, and Alt + Page Up/Page Down will horizontally scroll the Timescale one screen width per push. And as if all those combinations aren't enough to remember, Ctrl + Page Up/Page Down will fast-scroll the Data Area to the far left and far right of the displayable information. Unless you're a real shortcut guru, you don't have to memorize any of this, as there is also scrolling assistance from a mouse right-click in any of the horizontal or vertical scroll bars.

Figure 2.18 Scrolling Assistance Context Menu

I find the most effective method of working in the views is to use some additional scrolling features provided on the ribbons. The first of these is Scroll to Task, available on the 'Task ribbon > Editing section.' Clicking this button will automatically reposition the Timescale to display the schedule for the task you have selected. I personally use this command so much that I have it on my Quick Access toolbar.

Figure 2.19a Scroll to Task – Task ribbon

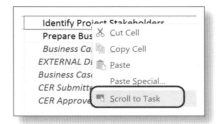

Figure 2.19b Scroll to Task – Shortcut Menu

The other feature provided by Microsoft to facilitate effective scrolling management is the ability to manage the level of detail displayed. From the 'View ribbon > Data section,' you can select the Outline level to be displayed to expand or collapse the total project plan as needed, showing only phase, deliverables or detailed tasks, depending on the Outline level selected.

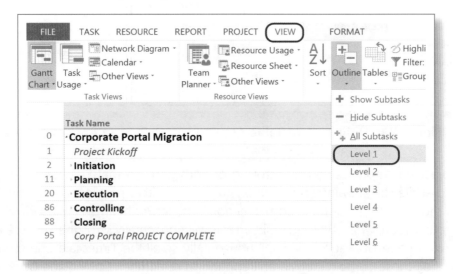

Figure 2.20a Outline Level 1

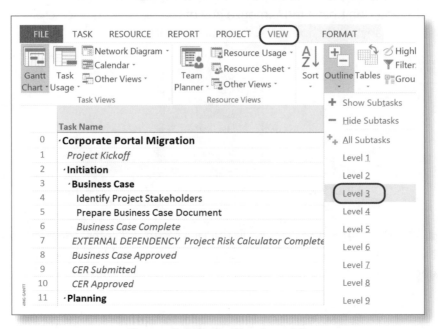

Figure 2.20b Outline Level 3

Change Highlighting

Change Highlighting allows you to view the impact of making a change on the overall project plan. For example, a simple change to a single task can have an impact on subsequent tasks, as well as potentially on the overall project finish date.

If we were to increase the work effort of the 'Prepare Business Case Document' from seven hours to 45 hours, this not only changes the finish date for this task, but also the task's duration and the Work and Duration of all the Summary Tasks. Change Highlighting shows all impacted information by changing the task background to light blue until the next change is made or the schedule is saved.

Figure 2.21 Change Highlighting

TIPS AND HINTS:

Change highlighting is a temporary display and only highlights the latest change made. Therefore, it is important that you review the Change Highlighting (when appropriate) for each change made.

If you wish to see the impact of several changes at once, we recommend using the Inactivate command to first inactivate all tasks, and then immediately Reactivate them. This will ensure that Change Highlighting is shown for all selected tasks and any other schedule impacts from these tasks. We will demonstrate this later in the book when processing Project Change Requests.

Task Inspector

The Task Inspector helps a project manager understand what is driving the tasks in the schedule. It provides on-screen guidance about the selected task and any issues, warnings and suggestions for corrections. To access the Task Inspector, use the 'Task ribbon > Task section' and select the Inspect option.

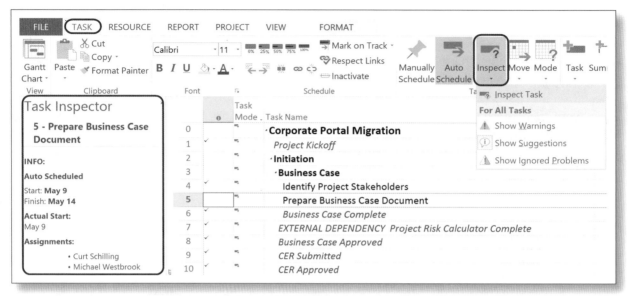

Figure 2.22 Task Inspector

Most project managers new to Microsoft Project find the Task Inspector very useful, while more seasoned users will often leave it turned off as they have become tuned to the information that the Task Inspector provides and get the information directly from the selected views.

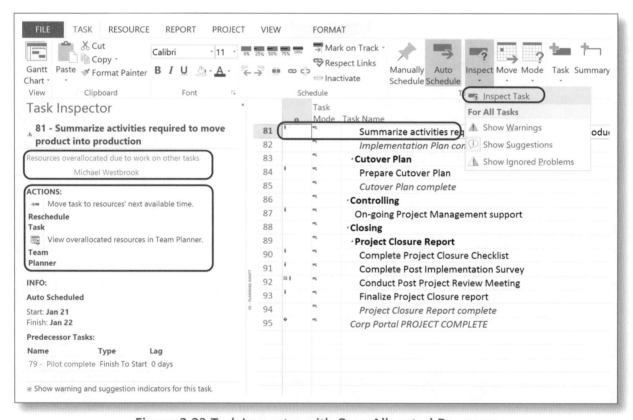

Figure 2.23 Task Inspector with Over Allocated Resource

Filters/Highlights/Auto-Filter

Filters and Highlights work very much the same in Microsoft Project as they do in other Office tools, specifically Excel, so if you're an experienced Excel user, you will be very comfortable with this aspect. You access Filters and Highlights from the 'View ribbon > Data section.'

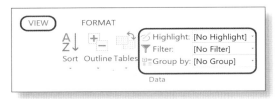

**Figure 2.24 Highlights,
Filters, and Groups**

TIPS AND HINTS:
    Before you apply a Filter or Highlight, ensure that you are showing all tasks as Filters and Highlights are only applied on viewable tasks—specifically, ensure the Outline level fully expanded to show ALL subtasks.

Microsoft provides a large number of filters that can be used for a wide variety of project management purposes. I encourage you to explore these filters further against your own schedule, as you will likely discover powerful new ways of interacting with your data. We will take a look at the Using Resource filter to allow you to get a feel for how the filters work. Once you select this filter, you get a dialog, which prompts you for a specific resource and then displays only the tasks (and summary tasks) this resource is assigned to. You can always clear any filter at any time by pressing the F3 key on your keyboard.

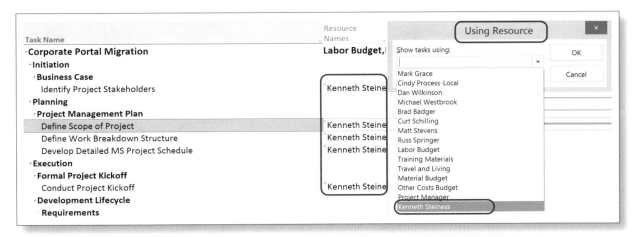

Figure 2.25 Using Resource filter

While Filters are very useful to allow you to find specific information, such as all the tasks assigned to a resource, the results of the Filter are shown without the larger context of the total project plan. Highlights provides very similar functionality as a Filter, except that the results are shown with highlighting in context of the total plan. And F3 also clears the Highlights.

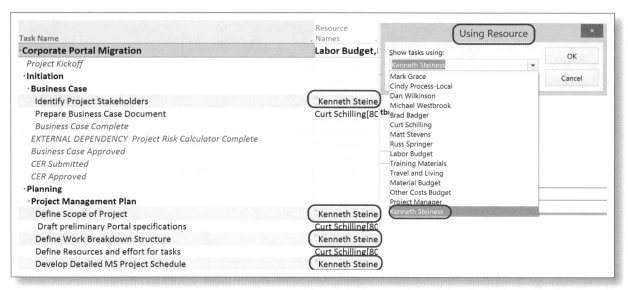

Figure 2.26 Using Resource highlight

And for those of you who are used to the ability to filter specific values in a column, Microsoft Project also provides that with AutoFilter for each column. The AutoFilter feature is turned on in 'View ribbon > Data section' by selecting Display AutoFilter from the Filter dropdown list.

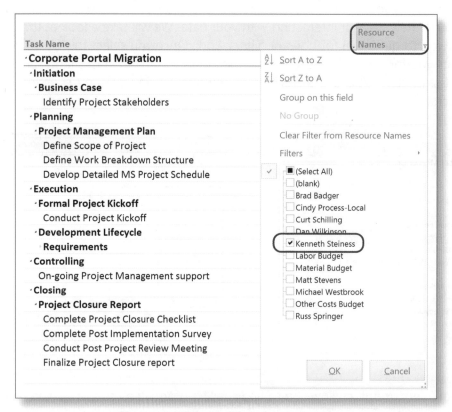

Figure 2.27 Auto Filter by Column

Depending on the Filter rules defined, you can get identical results using Filters and AutoFilter. For example, selecting AutoFilter on the resource column and selecting Johnny will give the identical results obtained earlier with the Using Resource filter. Plus, with the AutoFilter, you have the option of selecting more than one value.

Figure 2.28a Select
Multiple Resources using
the Auto Filter

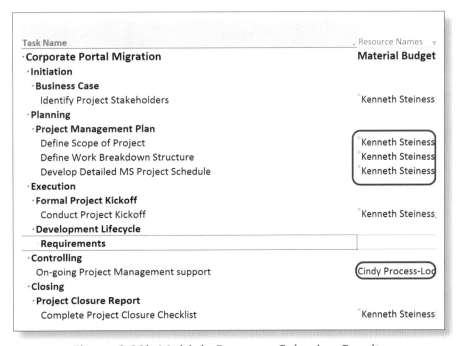

Figure 2.28b Multiple Resource Selection Results

Default Task Mode Selector

At the very bottom left-hand side of your screen, the Default Task Mode Selector let's you set whether new tasks are Auto Scheduled or Manually Scheduled. While Microsoft Project will allow you to use both scheduling options, Proactive PPM does not and, therefore, this book will be focused on using Auto Scheduled tasks. Clicking on this part of the screen will allow you to change the setting to 'New Tasks: Auto Scheduled' if it is not already set that way.

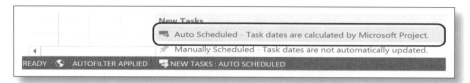

Figure 2.29 Default Task Mode Selector

Mini Toolbar and Shortcut Menu

The Mini Toolbar and Shortcut Menu allow you to quickly and easily access commands you might need to manipulate the individual tasks in your plan. The Mini Toolbar and Shortcut menu are accessed by a mouse right-click while your cursor is positioned on any task in the plan.

Figure 2.30 Mini Toolbar and Shortcut menu

The Mini Toolbar gives you easy access to the most commonly used commands in the 'Task ribbon, Font and Schedule Sections,' and the Shortcut Menu similarly provides efficient access to many of the commands commonly used to maintain the detailed information about a task. Whether you use these features will be a matter of individual usage preference, but we do encourage you to give them a try, as we find them to be good productivity improvement features in Microsoft Project.

Project Summary Task

On the 'Format ribbon > Show/Hide section,' there is an option to turn on and off the Project Summary Task. We strongly recommend that you check this option to show the Project Summary Task in your project plan. This is a better practice than inserting your own summary task in the plan, as the built-in Project Summary task is a true summary of the project, is always visible in all views independent of the Outline levels you have selected for display, and it will always contain an accurate roll up of the project details. Additionally, as will be discussed in Chapter 4, Microsoft Project provides advanced budget management with Budget Resources, which can only be used with the Project Summary Task.

On this same area of the toolbar you also have the ability to NOT display summary tasks, which removes all summary tasks from the display and shows only the detail tasks (which have schedule and resource details). This option is especially useful during analysis of the plan where the structure of phases and deliverables contained in the outline levels can make viewing the detail tasks more difficult. For example, if you wanted to sort the plan to show the tasks with the longest duration, leave the summary tasks displayed, and the sort order is constrained within the groups. We will demonstrate this in Chapter 6.

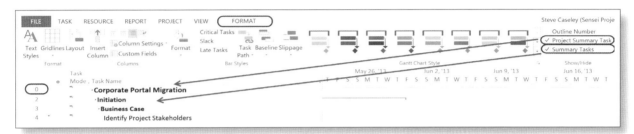

Figure 2.31 Show/Hide Project Summary Task and Summary Tasks

Additional Display Formatting

Also on 'Format ribbon > Bar Styles section,' you have the option to specifically format and highlight your views to support specific analysis or display requirements. For example, if you select the Critical Tasks checkbox, the Gantt bars turn red for all tasks on the Critical Path; the Late Tasks checkbox turns the Gantt bars gray; and the Slack checkbox extends the Gantt bars to show the slack for each task.

You can control the color and format of how these items are displayed by selecting the Format dropdown list and then selecting Bar Styles.

Figure 2.32 Gantt Chart Formatting

EXCEPTION:
> Format changes made to Enterprise Views are reset each time the schedule is loaded into Microsoft Project. Format changes made to Local Views are preserved as part of the project plan.

A new format/viewing feature added in Microsoft Project 2013 is Task Path, which is also accessed from the 'Format ribbon > Bar Styles section.' Selecting Task Path and then Predecessor, Driving Predecessor, Successor or Driving Successors will add color to your Gantt chart, identifying the appropriate Predecessors/Successors. This is a useful addition, as it allows you to very quickly identify the upstream and downstream tasks to review and validate impact. This is a significant improvement, as in the past we had to manually trace the successor/predecessor path through the schedule. And while the Network Diagram view did provide this information in the past, this is a much more screen real estate conserving way to get at this much needed information.

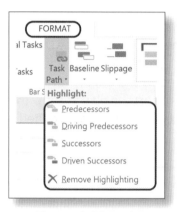

**Figure 2.33 Task
Highlighting**

Reports

New in Microsoft Project 2013 is a very powerful reporting module. These new reports are particularly valuable for project managers who need to build a status presentation for a single project. Later in this book, we will focus on the portfolio-level reports available in PWA supporting enterprise and project level requirements. What follows is a short introduction to the desktop reporting, as it will likely add some value to specific project management activities you will be undertaking as you manage your individual projects.

From the 'Report ribbon' there are a number of report groups: Dashboards, Resources, Costs, and In Progress. As all of these new reports follow a common approach; for the purpose of discussion, we will select the Project Overview report from the Dashboard group.

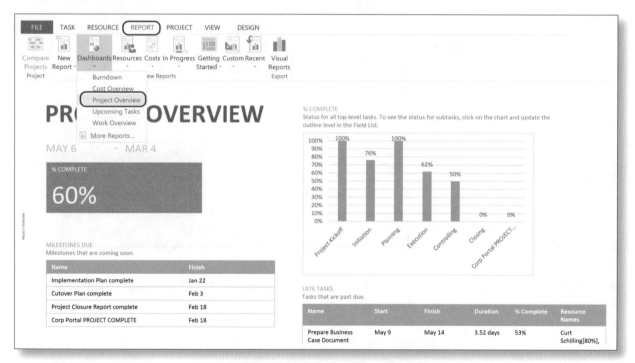

Figure 2.34 'Project Overview' report

As seen on the screenshot above, this is a substantial change in reporting from previous versions. It provides a powerful tool for creating reports that are easy to share outside of Microsoft Project. Selecting any of these areas in the report opens the Field List on the right, where you can easily adjust the Fields, Filters and Outline Level of details presented in the report.

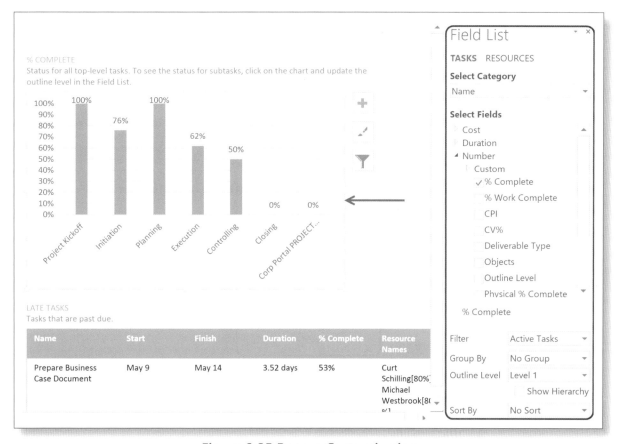

Figure 2.35 Report Customization

Once you have customized the report to suit your requirements, the report can be saved, exported and included in PowerPoint presentations or project status reports.

Views

Views are used in Microsoft Project to manage the style, format and information that is presented on your screen. As schedules contain hundreds of individual data points (Name, Start Date, Finish Date, Work Effort, Duration, Resources, Predecessor, etc.) for each task, and hundreds of tasks per project plan, it is impossible to have all information visible on a screen at any point in time—views are how we manage what information is visible to support the project management function we are currently undertaking.

Microsoft provides many views as part of a standard installation of which you are probably already familiar. Views are changed using the 'Task ribbon > View section,' and selecting the view most appropriate for the work you are about to do — Gantt Chart view for planning, Resource Usage view for understanding each resource's workload, and Tracking Gantt view for determining the impact of the current status updates on the overall project.

While these 'out-of-the-box' views are very good, we have provided a series of focused views to allow you to further fine-tune the data shown to support the activities we will be reviewing in this book. These custom views are accessed in the same way, 'Task ribbon > View section' and are visible in the Custom section of this dropdown, rather than the Built-In section. We will be referencing which custom views to use throughout this book and a complete description of our custom views and where/how we expect them to be used is available in Appendix B. These views are also available in your download package, so you can copy them to your environment.

**Figure 2.36 Microsoft
Project Views**

2.3.3 Options

In this section, we're going to review the key options that should be set to allow for Proactive PPM.

You get to Options by selecting File from the ribbon, which launches the Backstage. From there, you select Options from the bottom of the Backstage list.

**Figure 2.37 Microsoft
Project Options**

General Options

The default settings require little explanation and we leave you to explore which settings will work best for you. However, we recommend that you select a concise Date Format, such as MMM DD 'YY, as many of the views we will be exploring throughout this book will have many date fields, so to maximize the amount of information that can be shown on a screen, a small date format works best.

Display Options

Similarly, these default settings are self-explanatory, although we will specifically call your attention to the last checkbox for Entry Bar. This is just to alert you to where you can turn on/off the Entry Bar, as it's our experience that those who prefer the Entry Bar like it a lot and, those who prefer 'in-place' editing, dislike it a lot. The Entry Bar in Microsoft Project works identical to Excel, providing the option to make changes to the current selected cell in a common place near the top of the screen, rather than in-place in the cell.

Schedule Options

There are several important settings in this area to ensure the development of a proactive schedule. The first setting controls whether the changes made will be saved just for the current project or whether your changes will apply to All New Projects. The key point here is that changes you make will not be applied to existing projects—therefore if you have a significant change to make, you will have to apply it to all existing active projects you are managing. If new projects are always created from PWA, you don't need to worry about this, as the default settings are already in place from the schedule template.

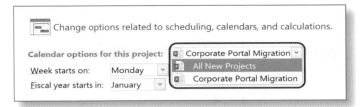

**Figure 2.38 Schedule Options - Defining the scope
of the changes made**

In most instances, you should not change the remaining fields in the calendar options section unless your organization doesn't work eight-hour days. These values are not used in calculating the schedule, but rather are used when Microsoft Project needs to change a timescale from days to weeks or months for a management report, for example. The Project Calendar, which we will discuss later, is used for calculating the schedule.

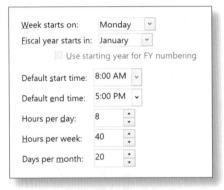

**Figure 2.39 Schedule Options -
Define Working Time**

In the Schedule section, there is an option to Show Assignment Unit as a Percentage or Decimal. While changing this option doesn't change the functionality of Microsoft Project, it certainly allows you to tailor it to suit your work patterns, specifically if you have a resource who will be working on your project half of their time—do you consider this to be .5 (decimal) or 50% (percentage)? It is a viewing preference more than anything else.

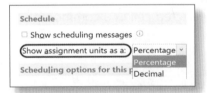

**Figure 2.40 Schedule
Options - Show
Assignment Units**

The next dropdown list, 'New tasks created,' should be set to Auto Scheduled. All new tasks should be Auto Scheduled, as this allows you to take maximum advantage of the advanced scheduling features available.

The next dropdown list, 'Auto scheduled tasks scheduled on:' provides two options: Project Start Date or Current Date. Generally, we select the Project Start Date option when doing initial planning and then change this to Current Date when the project is underway. If you forget to change the setting, it isn't an issue, as the task will be automatically scheduled as dependencies and resources are assigned. This setting is more a convenience feature, as it controls the point in the timeline where tasks are entered.

The next two dropdown lists, 'Duration is entered in' and 'Work is entered in,' can be changed to match how you work with these fields, but we will be assuming that 'Duration' is entered in days and 'Work' is entered in hours throughout this book. What these two settings do is simply allow you to enter the number two into the Duration field and Microsoft Project will make it two days and, similarly, entering 16 into the Work field, Microsoft Project will make it 16 hours. You can override and/or change these at any time with no consequences should you change how you manage these fields.

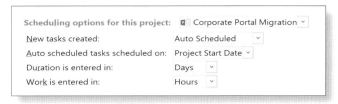

Figure 2.41 Schedule Options -
Task Definition Settings

Now we come to the MOST important option in Project—Default Task Type. We will discuss the three options: Fixed Work, Fixed Units, and Fixed Duration later in this chapter, but for now, please ensure that your option is set to Fixed Work. Selecting the task type here will set the default that is applied to each task as you build out the WBS, but each task can be changed individually, as needed.

Figure 2.42 Schedule Options –
Default Task Type

Next, we will review the functionality of the next eight checkboxes.

'New tasks are effort driven'—this is selected automatically when you select Fixed Work above and cannot be changed

'Autolink inserted or moved tasks'—while this is a personal usability preference, we recommend you leave it unchecked. If checked, Microsoft Project will automatically create a predecessor dependency with the task immediately above the inserted task and a successor dependency with the task immediately below. And while this sounds like a tremendous time saver, it's our experience that it takes more effort to change and correct these auto-linked dependencies than to set the right dependencies manually. Plus, manually creating all dependencies eliminates the risk that some of the auto-linked dependencies are wrong and are not caught at the time of creation.

'Split in-progress tasks'—this option needs to be selected to allow Microsoft Project to split a task during the weekly update cycle. If a resource did some work on a task early last week and was pulled off in a different direction after that, the project manager can use the Update Project feature to reschedule the remaining work, but only if this option is set to allow a split in the task.

'Update manually scheduled tasks when editing links'—since we are not going to create Manually Scheduled tasks, this option should be left unselected.

'Tasks will always honor their constraint dates'—this should be selected to ensure that a constraint date (such as 'Must Finish On the Date of the Annual Shareholder Meeting') is met, even if it means over-allocating the resources working on the task. In essence, we're telling Microsoft Project that it's OK to have our resources working 18-hour days, as needed, to complete this task on time. We will discuss Constraint Dates more in Chapter 4.

Both 'Show that schedule tasks have estimated durations' and 'New scheduled tasks have estimated durations' are recommended to be left unchecked as Proactive PPM does not endorse estimated durations as our focus is on work/effort based estimating.

And finally, 'Keep task on nearest working day when changing to Automatically Scheduled mode'—again, since we will be using ONLY Auto Scheduled tasks, this can be left unselected.

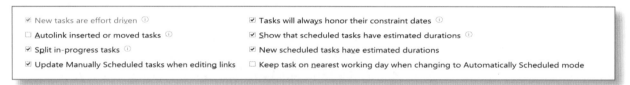

Figure 2.43 Schedule Options – Additional Scheduling Options

You can set the options under Schedule Alerts Options, based on personal preference for how verbose you want Microsoft Project to be as it updates the project schedule

The 'Calculate Project after each edit' should be turned on to ensure the schedule is always up to date as changes are made.

We recommend that you leave all three options on under the 'Calculate options for this project' to take maximum advantage of the features of Microsoft Project.

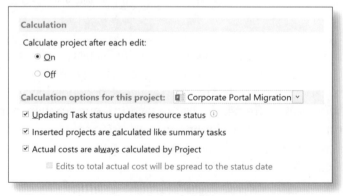

**Figure 2.44 Schedule Options –
Final Schedule Options**

Proofing Options

These are your default options for spell-check. Select Spelling from the 'Project ribbon > Proofing section' to run spell-check on your schedule.

Save Options

Similar to other tools, you can select the directories and locations where files will be saved. Assuming that you will be using the Enterprise version, all files are saved in Project Server so you do not need to be concerned with these settings.

If you prefer to 'Auto save' your project schedule, please consider also setting the 'Prompt before saving' option. When you save a schedule, the Undo history is cleared, as is Change Highlighting, which means any recent updates will have to be manually undone, if you decide not to keep them.

Advanced Options

The main 'Advanced Option' we need to discuss is PWA and the checkbox for 'Allow team members to reassign tasks.' Selecting this option provides the option for individual team members to make recommendations for reassigning tasks to other team members that are currently assigned to them. These are recommendations only until you, the project manager, accept them. Typically, organizations will make an enterprise decision on the use of this option to ensure that the policy is consistent with the organization's overall resource management policies.

2.4 Project Scheduling

Inexperienced Microsoft Project users often report frustration when the tool makes unexpected updates (or makes no updates) when the user changes one parameter. This frustration can be eliminated by a proper understanding of what the tool is doing behind the scenes.

The Microsoft Project scheduling engine uses an algorithm to calculate one of three values: Work, Units, and Duration. A brief definition follows:

- **Work** is the effort a resource spends on a task
- **Duration** is the number of business days to perform a task
- **Units** is the number of resources or materials

The algorithm uses the Task Type (Fixed Work, Fixed Units, and Fixed Duration) to determine which of the three values to leave alone and which ones to calculate. For Proactive PPM, Fixed Work is the default Task Type, but you can still have some exceptions in the schedule, where tasks are Fixed Duration or Fixed Units.

Fixed Work—the recommended default, and the Task Type we expect you will use for the majority of the tasks in your project plan. Fixed Work tasks have the total effort for the task defined by the estimator. For example, we estimate that it is going to take 24 hours to paint one side of a house. The Fixed Work (Effort) is 24 hours of focused work to complete the task. If you have three painters, you could complete the task in one eight-hour day—or if you were doing this part time on Saturday mornings by yourself, it would take six weekends to get the side of the house painted. As Fixed Work tasks truly represent the focused 'heads down' time on the task, allowing for resourcing flexibility,

I hope that you can see why it is the best way to create a proactive schedule, as the Fixed Work is what will actually complete the tasks.

Fixed Duration—these tasks always complete in the defined amount of time; it doesn't matter how many, or how few resources you assign, each task is always completed in the defined time. Sending your team on a technical training course is a good example of a Fixed Duration task, where the training course will take five days. It doesn't matter if you send a single person or five people, the course still takes five days.

Fixed Units—these tasks always require the same number of resources. In this instance, you have a controlled resource pool assigned to a task, let's say 'Create Analytical Reports,' and you have three resources. Therefore, the amount of work that these Fixed Units can get done will be dictated by the number of days available.

With these definitions behind us, let's now focus on the relationship between Work, Duration and Units. It is important to know how this relationship affects how Microsoft Project calculates tasks.

$$Work = Units * Duration$$
$$Duration = Work/Units$$
$$Units = Work/Duration$$

Based on Task Type you use, Microsoft Project will 'freeze that value' and never change it. You can always change it manually by entering a new value into the field, but Microsoft Project will never automatically change it. If you change either of the other values, it will automatically change the third value. For example, carrying on with our house-painting example where Fixed Work is 24 hours.

Fixed Work (Effort)	You Change:	Microsoft Project Calculates:
24 hours	3 units (resources)	1 day duration
24 hours	1 unit (resource)	3 days duration
24 hours	0.5 unit (resource)	6 days duration
24 hours	0.5 day duration	6 units (resources)
24 hours	1.5 days duration	2 units (resources)

So, now let's revisit the original scenario with three resources getting the house painted in eight hours, and explore what Microsoft Project will do if we change the Fixed Work estimate. For example, we've been watching TV infomercials and we purchase a fancy sprayer, guaranteed to cut our time in half.

Original Scenario	You Change:	Microsoft Project Calculates:
24 hours, 3 resources and 8 hours (1 day)	12 hours Fixed Work estimate	Maintains Resources (at 3) and recalculates Duration to 4 hours

EXERCISE – HOUSE PAINTING PROJECT

It will take 24 hours to paint one side of a house and each resource works 8 hours per day. Given the following scenario, determine the value that that Microsoft Project will calculate.

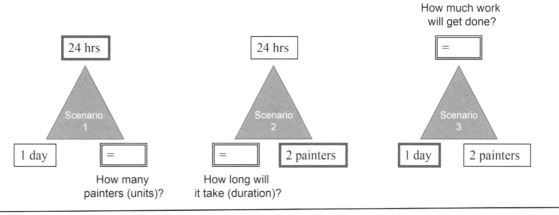

House Painting Project

Solutions

Units = Work/Duration

Work is 24, Duration is 1 day

Units = 24/1 (8 hours)

Units = 3 FTE Painters

Duration = Work/Units

Work is 24, Units is 2

Duration = 24/2

Duration = 12 hours

Work = Duration * Units

Duration is 1 day (8 hours)
Units = 2

Work = 8 *2 (16 hours)

2.5 Local vs. Enterprise

Another key concept in the Microsoft PPM solution is the distinction between Local and Enterprise items. In the past, when you used Microsoft Project Standard on the desktop, all projects, resources, views, and custom fields were stored locally (i.e., in your individual MPP files and/or in your Global MPT file, which stores the preferences for your local installation.

The key benefits of the Enterprise Microsoft PPM solution are the standardization of views and custom fields, as well as storing all projects and resources in a central location. Enterprise views, custom fields, projects, and resources are loaded from Project Server when you launch Microsoft Project Professional and connect to the server.

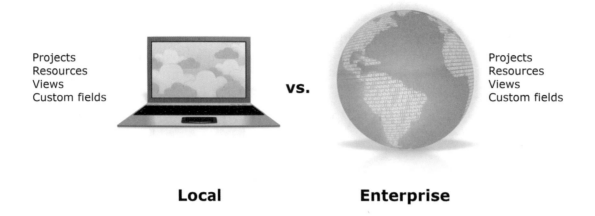

Figure 2.46 Local versus Enterprise

As a general rule, you should always work with Enterprise projects, and no longer work with Local projects. The only valid exception might be exporting a schedule to an MPP file to share with someone outside your organization—but certainly, any updates and editing should always be done in the Enterprise project schedule. Even if you want to work off-line, you can still take your Enterprise schedule with you. A Local schedule will NOT be available to anyone else in the organization nor will it be included in Enterprise reporting. Keep in mind that nobody will see your schedule updates in PWA until you Publish, so you can continue working on updates in the Draft mode and only share when you are ready to do so.

You should also strive to use enterprise resources most of the time. Enterprise resources are maintained on the Server, with availability, calendars, rates, etc. maintained globally, while Local resources are maintained only by you and are specific to your project. If a resource is available in the Enterprise Resource Pool, you must use it rather than create a Local resource. In fact, you should only use local resources if you have external contractors, or perhaps business users, who are not in the Project Server database. Just be aware that any local resources you assign to effort-based tasks, you will now have to status those tasks for them, which can create a substantial amount of work for you. At Sensei, we recommend that you minimize the use of Local resources and, instead, add a milestone task to your schedule that marks the completion of a scope of work by someone outside the core project team. Local resources are not subject to true resource Capacity/Demand Management across the portfolio of projects.

Similarly, views and custom fields should be Enterprise, whenever possible. If you find that you use a Local view frequently, talk to your administrator about adding it as an enterprise view. Chances are that others may benefit from your view also.

2.6 Project Web App

Project Web App (PWA) is the Web front-end to the Microsoft PPM environment. This is where the majority of end users operate on a daily basis to create proposals, view project status, submit task status, collaborate on project artifacts, and process approvals.

PWA is accessed via your Web browser using the URL for your organization's Project Server deployment. Depending on your organizations configuration, you may be prompted for credentials before landing on the PWA home page.

Figure 2.47 PWA Main Screen

It's been our experience that while you will use this home page a lot when you are new to PWA, you will very quickly develop your own shortcuts to go to directly to Project, Resource, Task, Timesheet and Business Intelligence, either directly from browser favorites or through the Quick Launch menu on the left-hand side.

2.6.1 Projects
Selecting Projects gives you access to the Project Center, which provides access to the published projects in your environment. It will always default to the last view you accessed (so my view may be different than yours). The ribbon auto hides to preserve screen real estate, so you will get very used to clicking on the Projects ribbon to activate the ribbon.

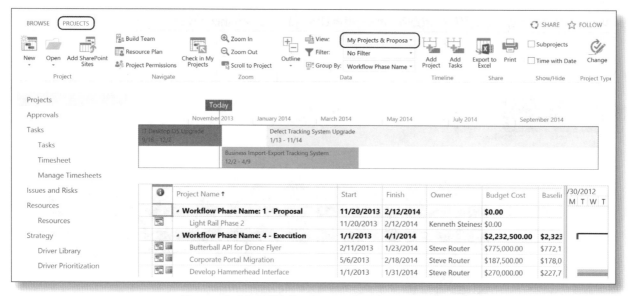

Figure 2.48 PWA Project Selection Screen

If you wish to change the view from the 'Projects ribbon > Data section,' you can select the view you wish to use. For project managers, we like the 'My Project and Proposals' view, which shows us all the projects we own as well as those where we are status managers or have been assigned work. The Proposals view is where we will typically access a new project when it has first been assigned to us. The Active views show us all the in-flight (approved) projects in various groupings. Your organization's views may not match exactly, but the important thing here is to understand the navigation between views in the Project Center.

The Project Center is where new project proposals are submitted (see Chapter 3 for details). From the 'Project ribbon > Project section,' users can submit a new proposal from the new dropdown list.

**Figure 2.49 PWA
New Project
Dropdown**

PWA acts much like Microsoft Project in that many commands operate at the Line Level. For example, to select a row, you would click in the most left-hand column (much like selecting a row in Excel). This allows you to select further actions from the ribbon … for example, Project > Navigate > Resource Plan to build the team and enter high-level resource estimates.

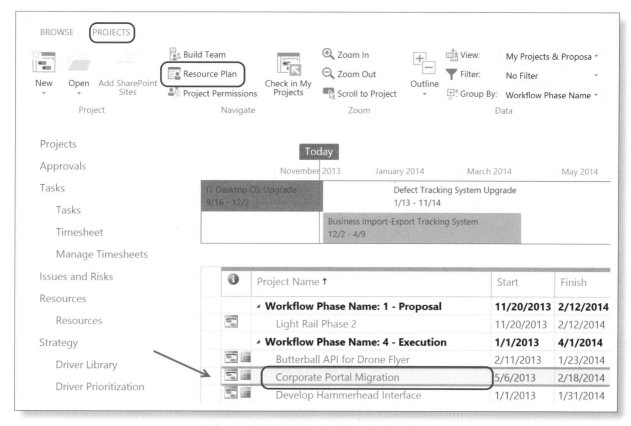

Figure 2.50 PWA Project Selection

If, however, you directly click on the project name, you are opening the actual project within PWA and are presented with the Project Workflow Status page.

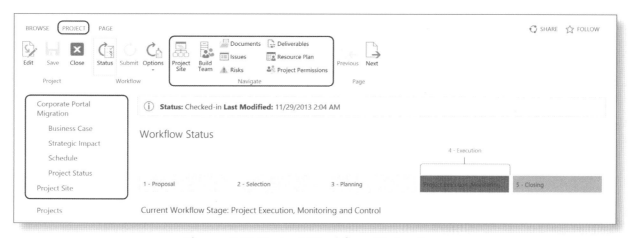

Figure 2.51 Project Workflow Status Page

The Project drilldown on the left allows you to select the other relevant Project Details Pages (PDP) for your project. The exact information displayed will be controlled by the project type and the governance process defined by your organization.

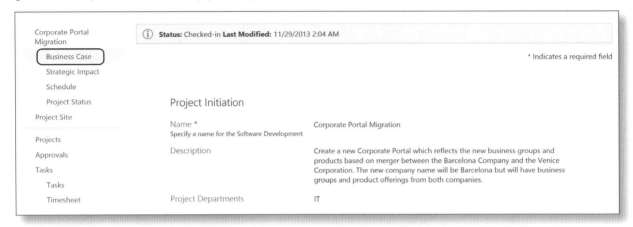

Figure 2.52 Project Business Case

The Project Site link brings you to the project collaboration site, where users can manage documents, risks, issues, action items, and much more.

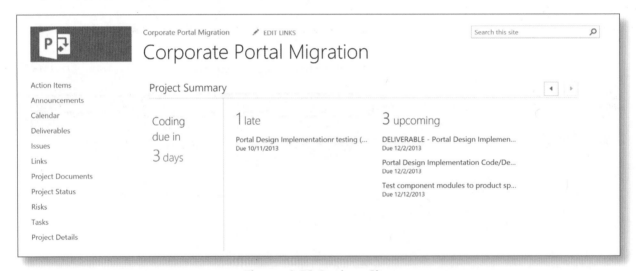

Figure 2.53 Project Site

To return to PWA, simply select the Project Detail link or use your browser's back button.

2.6.2 Approvals

Approvals is used to approve project status and timesheets from your team members. This will be covered in more detail in Chapter 6.

2.6.3 Tasks and Timesheets

Tasks is used primarily by team members (remembering you are likely a team member on your own projects with assigned tasks and timesheet requirements). Team members will use:

- **Tasks** to review the tasks they are assigned to
- **Timesheets** to create and submit their weekly timesheets, tracking the time spent on tasks and updated estimates to complete each task
- **Manage Timesheets** to submit future timesheets for vacation periods or adjust existing timesheets. We will review this functionality in more detail in Chapter 5.

2.6.4 Issues and Risks

Issues and Risks display all the issues and risks assigned to you. All project issues and risks can be viewed from the individual Project Sites, but PWA provides a summary of all of them here.

2.6.5 Resources

Resources allows you to view the resources in the Enterprise Resource Pool. Selecting a resource activates the Resources ribbon, giving you access to the commands to view assignments and availability. We will review this functionality in more detail in Chapter 6.

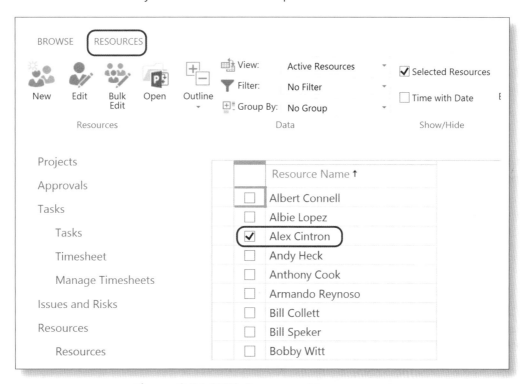

Figure 2.54 PWA Resource Management

2.6.6 Reports

Selecting the Reports options will launch you into the Business Intelligence Center where you can access the reports that your organization has put in place.

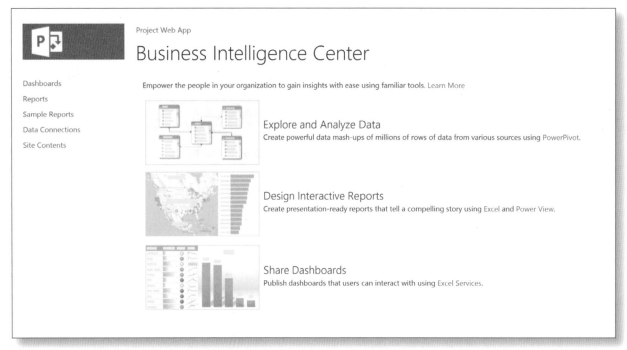

Figure 2.55 PWA Reports - Business Intelligence Center

At Sensei, we recommend using a standard set of PPM reports and dashboards that are aligned with Gartner's PPM recommendations and PMI's industry standards. We will use these reports and dashboards for the walk-through here and also throughout the book as examples of good project management practices.

We have identified five primary Dashboards: Summary, Projects, Resources, Timesheets, and Issues and Risks.

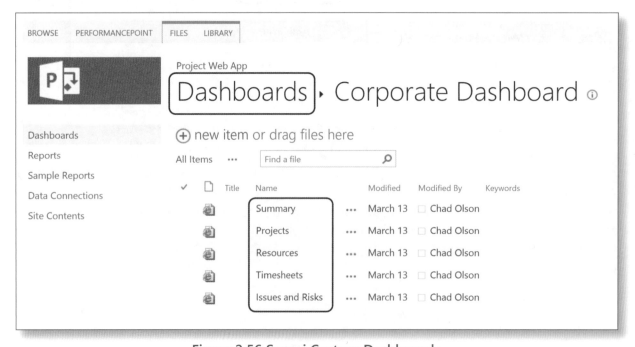

Figure 2.56 Sensei Custom Dashboards

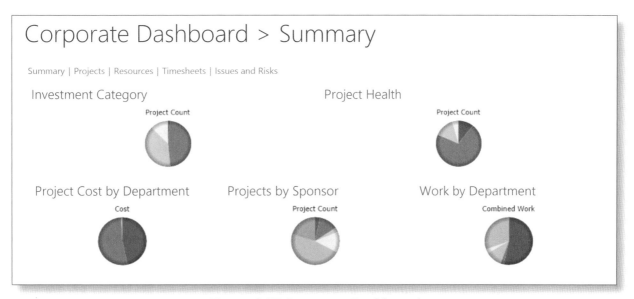

Figure 2.57 Summary Dashboard

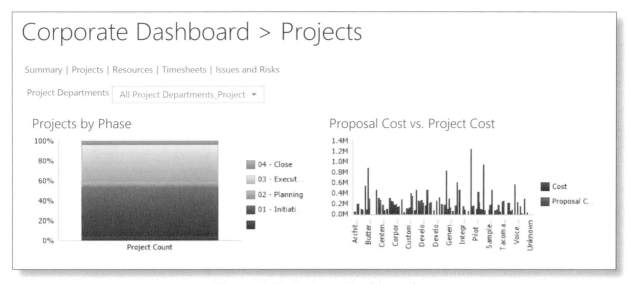

Figure 2.58 Projects Dashboard

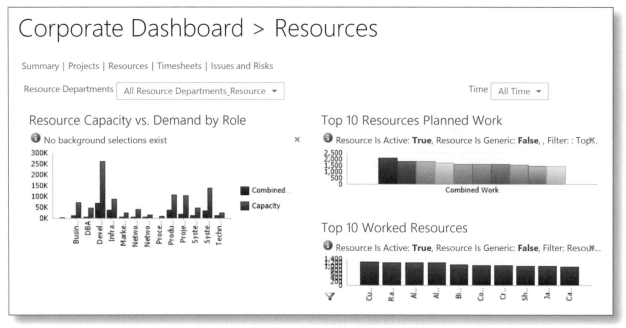

Figure 2.59 Resources Dashboard

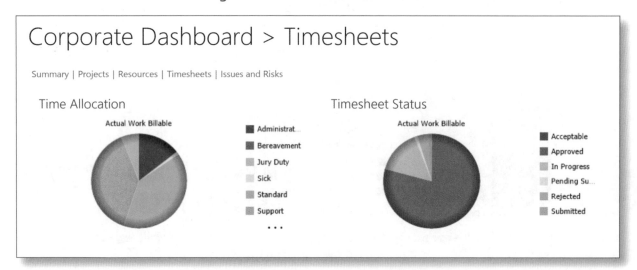

Figure 2.60 Timesheet Dashboard

Figure 2.61 Issue and Risk Dashboard

We have also identified six key reporting areas: Project Intake & Prioritization, Resource Capacity/ Demand Management, Budgeting and Cost Tracking, Project Planning and Collaboration, Project Status and Portfolio Reporting, and PMO Governance.

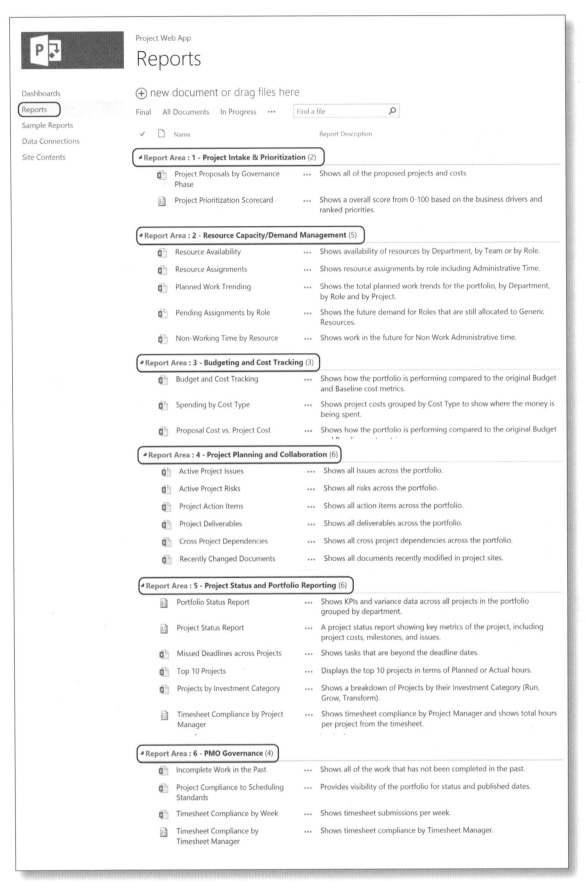

Figure 2.62 Sensei Custom Reports

The PWA reports are interactive and allow for filtering of specific project and resource data to dynamically select the specific details needed to suit your information and reporting requirements.

These reports provide you with the information you need to keep control of a large and ever-changing portfolio of projects.

2.6.7 Shared Documents

Shared Documents provides a repository for storing key documentation for your deployment. We recommend loading your organization's procedure documents that define how Microsoft Project and PWA are to be used in your organization. In the sample below, you can see the Procedures defined by Sensei Project Solutions.

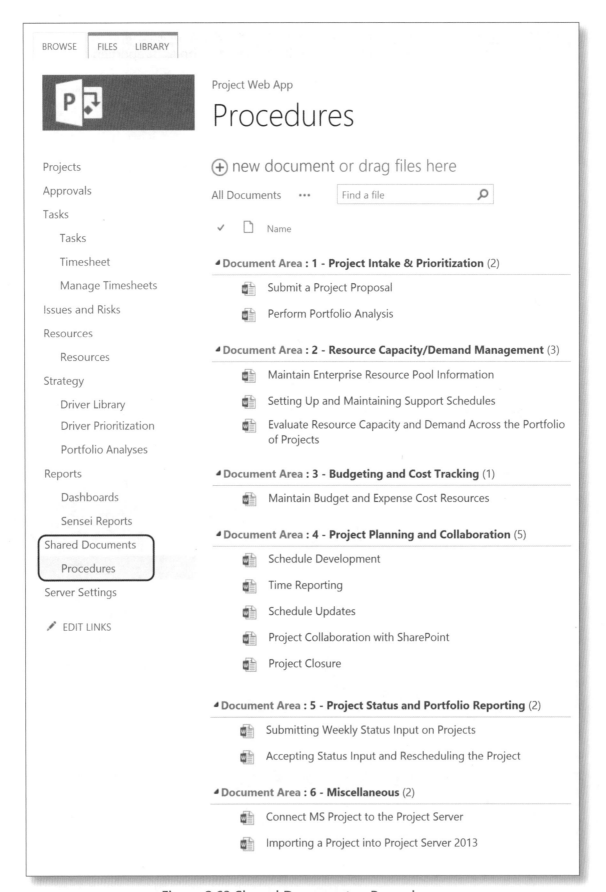

Figure 2.63 Shared Documents - Procedures

3

CHAPTER 3:

Submitting a Project Proposal

Proper project governance process includes project intake and prioritization to ensure that all projects are approved before work takes place, and more importantly, that only appropriately justified projects are approved. Project intake is the process by which new project proposals are submitted with a business case, cost estimates, resource demand, and strategic impact. This information is utilized in the project selection and prioritization process to ensure that the organization executes the set of projects that return the most strategic value within the available cost and resource constraints.

In this chapter, we will review the steps to create and submit a project proposal in Project Web App (PWA). If you are not using PWA, the material discussed is this Chapter is still relevant, as securing approval for the project is important; you would just follow existing organizational policies.

Each project proposal is typically subjected to a governance workflow that guides the portfolio approval process. In this chapter, we assume that such a governance process is in place, but the detailed discussion of setting this up is beyond the scope of this book.

3.1 Completing a Project Proposal

Proactive Project Portfolio Management (PPM) ensures that all project proposals are captured and submitted for review and approval and that the organizational governance process is followed. This is accomplished by completing the project proposal in PWA. From the Quick Launch toolbar, select Projects.

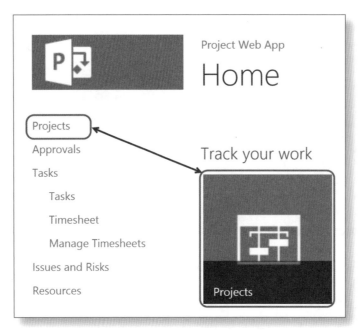

**Figure 3.1 Select 'Projects' from
Quick Launch or Home Page**

From the Projects ribbon > Projects section,' select the New button, and the category of proposal you are going to create from the dropdown list.

**Figure 3.2 Select the
Proposal Category**

Once the project proposal dialog is displayed, enter all the details currently known about the project. It is very important to complete this information as accurately as possible, as this will be used by management to determine which projects should be approved (and not approved).

As obvious as it may sound, pay particular attention to the project name, as in most cases, this will become the name that will describe the project until completion, and a descriptive name helps ensure that everyone who sees dashboards, reads status reports or even hears about the project name in the hallway will have a clear understanding of what is being accomplished.

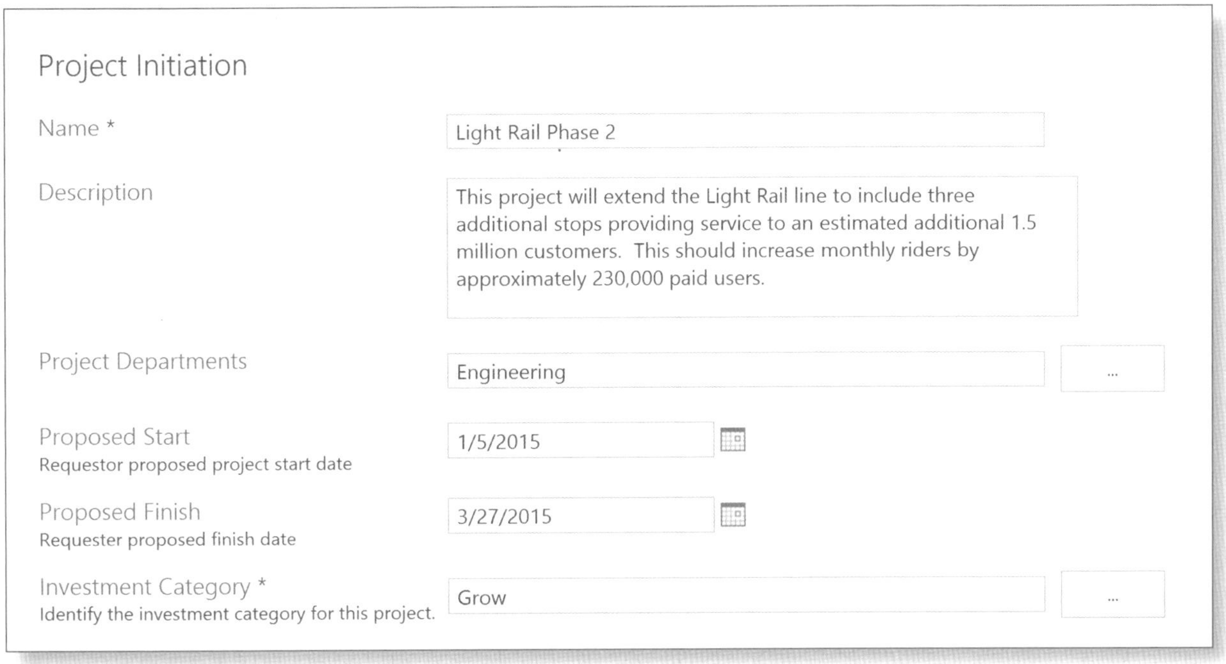

Project Initiation

Name *

Light Rail Phase 2

Description

This project will extend the Light Rail line to include three additional stops providing service to an estimated additional 1.5 million customers. This should increase monthly riders by approximately 230,000 paid users.

Project Departments

Engineering

...

Proposed Start
Requestor proposed project start date

1/5/2015

Proposed Finish
Requester proposed finish date

3/27/2015

Investment Category *
Identify the investment category for this project.

Grow

...

Figure 3.3 Project Information Dialog

TIPS & HINTS:

I still remember an urgent, high-priority project that was fast-tracked through the approval process so fast that the project name was entered as Project X, as no one wanted to take the time to give it a meaningful name. And, unfortunately, that stuck with me for the next 18 months, resulting in many, many, many explanations ("no this isn't top secret, this is to accomplish A, B and C"). But by the time we realized that our cryptic name was causing some issues, it had also been reported on the corporate dashboard for enough months that changing it was also going to be an issue.

Also, pay attention to the Owner field on the Project Proposal Form, as PWA will use this field to assign permissions to the appropriate owner. If this field isn't set properly, the owner will not be able to access the proposal/project. While the Owner can be changed once the project proposal is submitted, it is always easier to set it first and ensure the project proposal gets assigned appropriately to allow for email notifications and queue management. Other project-level custom fields are also important from a reporting perspective. For example, the Sponsor field will need to be populated in order for the reports to allow filtering and grouping on projects by the sponsor. Your organization's custom fields may be different from what we show here, but as a best practice, you should consider including the Sponsor field.

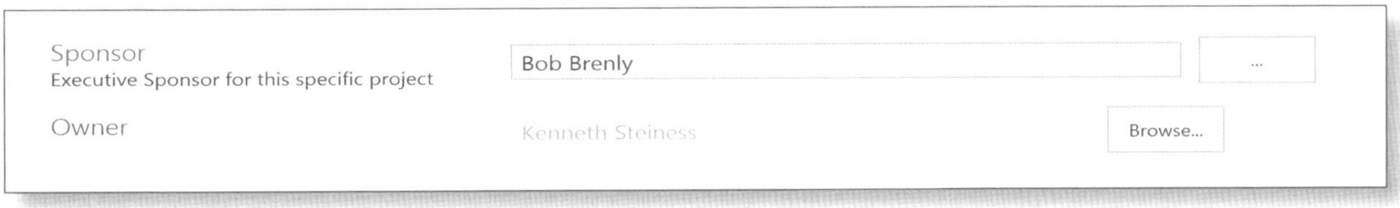

Sponsor
Executive Sponsor for this specific project

Bob Brenly

...

Owner

Kenneth Steiness

Browse...

Figure 3.4 Project Sponsor and Project Owner Section of the Project Information Dialog

Once all the information is added to the form, the project proposal is saved and the next form for Project Strategic Impact will be presented.

Project Strategic Impact

Rate the impact of this project on the business drivers below.

Expand into new markets and segments
Expand revenue growth aggressively by penetrating new markets and expanding reach to segments of penetrated markets

- ○ No Rating
- ○ None: Does not grow revenue from any markets and segments
- ○ Low: Grows revenue from new markets and segments by up to $500K
- ● Moderate: Grows revenue from new markets and segments by $500K to $1M
- ○ Strong: Grows revenue from new markets and segments by $1M to $3M
- ○ Extreme: Grows revenue from new markets and segments by more than $3M

Improve Customer Satisfaction Score
Measurably improve scores on customer satisfaction surveys through implementing standardized customer service processes, grow the number of customer service relationships, and improve the nature of each relationship

- ○ No Rating
- ○ None: Does not change customer satisfaction index
- ○ Low: Increases customer satisfaction by up to 2%
- ● Moderate: Increases customer satisfaction by 2% to 3%
- ○ Strong: Increases customer satisfaction by 3% to 5%
- ○ Extreme: Increases customer satisfaction by 5% or more

Figure 3.5 Project Strategic Impact

The Project Strategic Impact form allows you to rate the impact of your project on each of the business drivers identified in your organization. It is very important to fully and accurately complete the ranking of each business driver, as it is used in the project selection/approval process to determine which proposals should be approved or rejected.

Projects / Drivers ↑	Expand into new markets and segments	Improve Customer Satisfaction Score
Banff Database Builder	Moderate	Strong
Centennial Tool for the European Developr	Moderate	Strong
Colorado Web Site Design and Rollout	Moderate	Moderate
Create Integrated Monitoring for Light Rail	Strong	Moderate
Create Marketing Collateral for the New Cr	Strong	Moderate
Custom Filters for Anti-virus Software	None	Moderate
Defect Tracking System Upgrade	Low	Strong
Deploy the Wireless Network Across the Cc	None	Low
Develop IT Inventory Bar Code Scanner	None	Moderate
Develop the Bell Milage Report	None	None

Figure 3.6 Portfolio Analysis

3.2 Building a Resource Plan

The project proposal is completed by building the Resource Plan, which identifies the estimated resource requirements. Once the Resource Plan is created, it is available to enterprise resource management and is used in the project selection/approval process to validate that there are resources available to work on all approved projects.

Select and open your project proposal and select Resource Plan from the 'Project ribbon > Navigate section.'

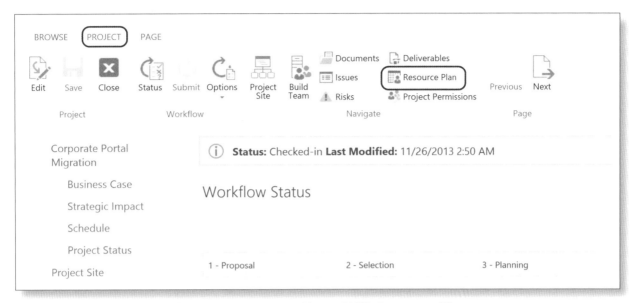

Figure 3.7 Resource Plan - PWA Resource Plan

The Plan ribbon provides the functionality needed to develop the Resource Plan. We will work from left to right on this ribbon to first build the team, then deal with entering the resource requirements.

Figure 3.8 Develop Resource Plan - Plan Ribbon

3.2.1 Build Team

The Resource Plan identifies the resources needed to complete the project. This is done by selecting the 'Build Team' button to launch the Team window, which uses a standard left/right table view where the Enterprise Resources (who have are already defined in PWA by your Project Management Office (PMO) are displayed on the left and the resources you select for your project will be displayed on the right. As we are building a high-level Resource Plan at this time, we would typically only select and assign generic resources to our plan. (In Chapter 4 – Developing the Baseline Schedule, we will change these generic resources to the appropriate named resources). To ensure that only generic resources are used for the Resource Plan, select the Generic Resources view from the Data section. This will present the list of the generic resources defined by your organization's resource management. Select the appropriate resources from the left-hand list and press Add to make them available to your project's Resource Plan.

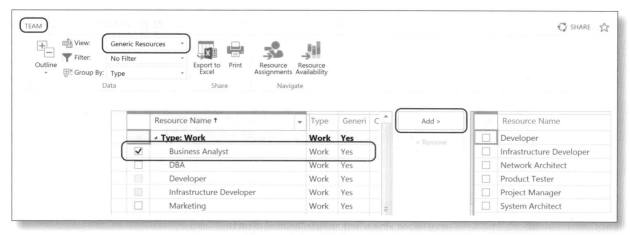

Figure 3.9 Build Team

With all the needed generic resources assigned to your proposal, you would then select Save & Close and return to the Resource Plan.

3.2.2 Identify Resource Requirements

With all the generic resources required to complete the project identified, we next define how much time you will require from each role. From the 'Plan ribbon > Resource Utilization section,' select the Calculate From dropdown list and choose the appropriate option. Setting this value tells PWA whether to calculate the resource utilization (demand vs. capacity) directly from your Microsoft Project Plan, from the Resource Plan we are about to create—(or both for rolling wave planning):

- **Resource Plan**—select this option if you are building a new proposal and want the reports and portfolio analysis to use data from the Resource Plan instead of the Project Plan (schedule)
- **Project Plan**—select this option if you want resource assignments and availability to calculate from the Microsoft Project schedule
- **Project Plan Until**—select this option if you are doing rolling-wave planning. This allows you to use the Project Plan through the end of the next iteration, where you have a detailed schedule and then use the Resource Plan from a certain date forward, where you don't yet have a detailed schedule. Depending on your processes, this could also reflect using the schedule for the current approved phase of our Project Plan and Resource Plan for unapproved phases of the project

It is our expectation that you will not have an existing Project Plan at this preliminary proposal stage and, therefore, we will assume that you will be selecting Resource Plan.

At this time, we will also adjust the Date Range, using the 'Plan ribbon > Date Range section' to customize the timeline in the data entry area in order to facilitate efficient data entry of the project's resource requirements. In the Display section of the ribbon, you can adjust the Work Units and Timescale to match your preferences. We recommend using Full-time Equivalent, as generic resources don't have specific resource availability calendars. It is also typical for all but very short projects to develop the Resource Plan using a Month timescale. You can switch between Day, Week, and Month timescales at any time and PWA will adjust the resource requirements accordingly—you are simply setting the unit you wish to use for doing the data entry.

Figure 3.10 Develop Resource Plan Timescale - Date Range and Units

With these settings confirmed, it's now time to enter the actual project's generic resource requirements directly into the planning calendar.

Resource Name ↑	Booking Type	11/26/2013	12/1/2013	1/1/2014
✔ Developer	Proposed	1	1	0.5
✔ Infrastructure Developer	Proposed	1	0.5	0
✔ Network Architect	Proposed	1	0.5	0
☐ Product Tester	Proposed	0	0	0
☐ Project Manager	Proposed	0	0	0
☐ System Architect	Proposed	0	0	0

Figure 3.11 Resource Requirements

With the resource requirements complete, you can Save and Publish the Resource Plan. It is important to Publish the Resource Plan, as that is what feeds your project's requirements into the Resource Availability and Assignment Reports.

3.2.2 Submit Proposal for Approval

The Resource plan is completed by submitting the proposal for approval. Using the 'Project ribbon > Workflow section,' select the Submit button. In order to be able to Submit the project proposal, you must have the project checked out. If you are ready to submit a project proposal, but the Submit view is not enabled (grayed out), from the 'Project ribbon > Project section', select the Edit button to check the project out. This will enable the Submit button.

Once you've submitted the project proposal, the Workflow will change to reflect the fact that the project proposal is now completed and it has passed to the next stage in the governance process.

WORK SESSION #1 – SUBMIT A PROJECT PROPOSAL

We will be using the Light Rail Phase 2 project throughout the book, and each work session builds upon the previous one. We have included completed versions of the Microsoft Project plans in the download package representing the end of each session to allow you to compare your results against ours and to ensure you always have an appropriate starting point for each exercise. Sample Project Plans are available for downloading as defined in Appendix C.

This is the first of 16 work sessions that develops and then manages the 'Light Rail Phase 2' project. Each Work Session describes the Project Management activities covered and provides screen shots depicting the expected results. Appendix D provides a consolidated set of the sixteen Work Sessions for ease of access and printing. Appendix E provides detailed step-by-step solutions for each Work Session.

This short work session aims to submit the project proposal in PWA. We encourage you to work with your PWA administrator to get access to a training area in PWA to allow you to complete these exercises. If this isn't possible and/or you don't have PWA available in your organization, we always provide adjusted Work Session instructions to allow you to complete the segments that are specific to Microsoft Project.

This exercise will be completed exclusively in PWA—if you do not have access to PWA, you can skip this exercise in its entirety.

OBJECTIVE

To initiate a project proposal including the Business Case and Resource Plan.

STEP 1   Initiate a New Project Proposal

In PWA, create a new project proposal and ensure that you select an Enterprise Project Type which is consistent with a software development project (in our environment we would select Software Development).

STEP 2   Complete the Proposal Details

Your project should be named 'ZZ_<Your Name>_Light Rail Phase 2' (Where <Your Name> is your first name just in-case others in your organization are also completing these exercises) and complete the other fields on the Project Initiation screen.

STEP 3   Create the Resource Plan

At this point, consistent with a project proposal, named resources are not known, but the resource roles required for the project are known, therefore you will select the generic resources from the Enterprise Resource Pool that are required for your project.

Assign three generic resources to your project proposal: Project Manager, Business Analyst and Procurement Specialist (or similar roles as defined by your organization).

Create a Resource Plan using January 5, 2015 as your project start date and March 27, 2015 as your end date.

Add the Project Manager to your proposal as a full-time resource for the three-month duration; the Business Analyst as a full-time resource for the first month, and then as a half-time resource for the remaining two months; and the Procurement Specialist as half time resource for the three months of the project.

Submit your Project Proposal for approval.

EXPECTED RESULTS

Project Initiation

Name *	Kenneth Light Rail Phase 2
Description	Sample Project for completing training exercises
Project Departments	IT
Proposed Start Requestor proposed project start date	1/5/2015
Proposed Finish Requester proposed finish date	3/27/2015
Investment Category * Identify the investment category for this project.	Transform
Sponsor Executive Sponsor for this specific project	Joe Gibbs
Owner	Kenneth Steiness Browse...

Figure WS.1a – Project Proposal

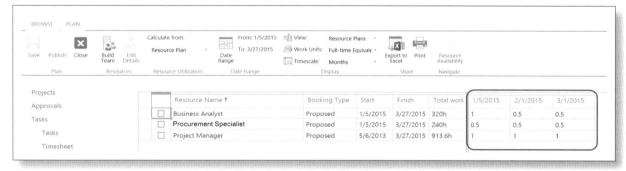

Resource Name ↑	Booking Type	Start	Finish	Total work	1/5/2015	2/1/2015	3/1/2015
Business Analyst	Proposed	1/5/2015	3/27/2015	320h	1	0.5	0.5
Procurement Specialist	Proposed	1/5/2015	3/27/2015	240h	0.5	0.5	0.5
Project Manager	Proposed	5/6/2013	3/27/2015	913.6h	1	1	1

Figure WS.1b – Resource Plan

3.3 Updating the Status Manager

If you are assigned to deliver a project where the project proposal was developed by someone else, there are two critical fields that must be set to allow you to take ownership of the plan.

STEP 1

Ensure that the Owner field is set appropriately. This field must be changed by either an administrator or the previous project manager. In PWA, select the project you are assigning to someone else and open the project for editing in PWA.

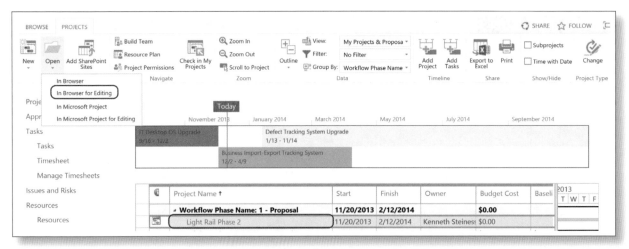

Figure 3.12 Select Proposal

Select Project Information from the Project on the left to open the Project Information dialog window.

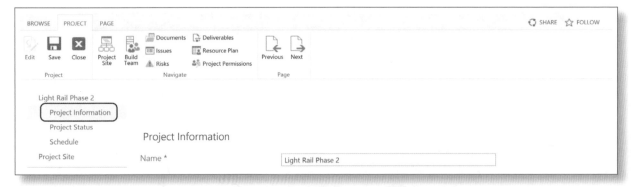

Figure 3.13 Select Proposal

Using the Browse functionality, select the appropriate owner and then Save the updates.

Figure 3.14 Update Project Owner

STEP 2

Ensure that you are the Status Manager for the project. It is critical that you are the Status Manager, as this is used by PWA to route the weekly team members' status updates. To validate this, select the project in PWA and from the 'Projects ribbon > Project section' select 'Open In Microsoft Project for Editing' from the dropdown list.

Figure 3.15 Select Project for Editing

Once the plan is opened in Microsoft Project, select a view such as '10 – Project Status,' which has the Status Manager column displayed. Then, from the 'View ribbon > Data section,' select Outline – All Subtasks to ensure that all lines in the plan are displayed.

Once you have expanded the outline level to show the complete task list, validate that you are the Status Manager. If you need to update the Status Manager go to 'Task ribbon > Editing section' and select Find/Replace to replace the existing Status Manager with yourself.

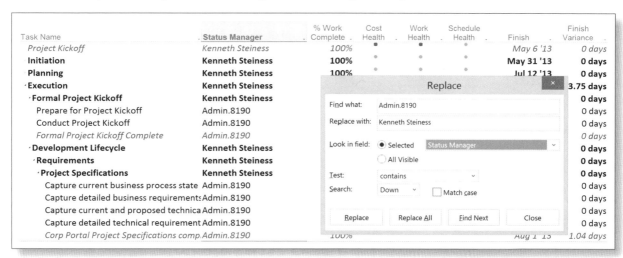

Figure 3.16 Replace all existing Status Managers with yourself

TIPS & HINTS:
When using Microsoft Project commands like Find/Replace and Filter/Highlight, it is always important to first verify that you are showing all tasks, as these commands are only executed on the tasks currently displayed on the view.

With that change made, we can exit Microsoft Project, ensuring that you select to Save the changes and Check In, and then Publish to make the results are visible to everyone in your organization.

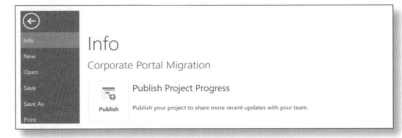

Figure 3.18 Publish Project

Figure 3.17 Save and Check In

TIPS & HINTS:

As a best practice, get in the habit of always closing the schedule and selecting Save and Check In when you are done with your changes. Remember to also Publish' the schedule if the changes need to be visible in PWA's Project Center and updated assignments sent to team members.

4

CHAPTER 4:

Developing the Baseline Schedule

Developing a good baseline schedule is the most important thing we, as project managers, can do to help ensure overall project delivery success. A realistic project schedule will:

- Identify all the work required (and only the work required) to deliver the desired results
- Document realistic estimates to complete the identified work
- Identify skills required to staff the project
- Provide a realistic project schedule based on task dependencies to ensure the work is completed in the right order
- Develop a baseline against which project progress can be tracked and monitored to validate that the project is on schedule.

A good baseline schedule will allow us to track progress and provide reliable status to the project sponsor. Without a baseline schedule, you are reporting status based on gut feel, team opinions and most likely an optimistic desire to report that your project is on-time; but this is little more than a best guess. The right solution is a status report against a project baseline which allows you to measure the exact status of all tasks planned to date; for example, at week 12, all tasks are on track (or not). In this scenario, the project baseline would tell you that the first 23 tasks in the plan should be 100% complete and the next 5 tasks should be in progress. A quick comparison of actual results versus the baseline allows you to provide a very accurate and realistic status – on schedule, ahead of schedule or behind schedule based on facts rather than intuition.

If you determine that you are in fact behind schedule, you can then immediately start remedial actions to address any and all problems. It's a far easier conversation with the project sponsor in week 12 of a 45 week project that you've detected a schedule delay and that you've started corrective actions; as opposed to the gut-feel approach where our optimistic tendency is that the project is on schedule until week 40 (of 45) at which time we have to then tell the project sponsor that the project is suddenly late and worse, it's too late to take corrective actions and that the project now won't complete until week 50.

Figure 4.1a Non Proactive PPM - No early schedule slippage indicators

Figure 4.1b Proactive PPM - Early indicator of schedule slippage

As shown in the diagram below, developing a schedule baseline is a multi-step process beginning with the development of the project Work Breakdown Structure (WBS) and concluding with a detailed project baseline with resources, assignment, estimates, dependencies and deadlines and constraints. While the exact order of completion is not critical, it is critical that all the steps are completed to develop an effective project baseline schedule.

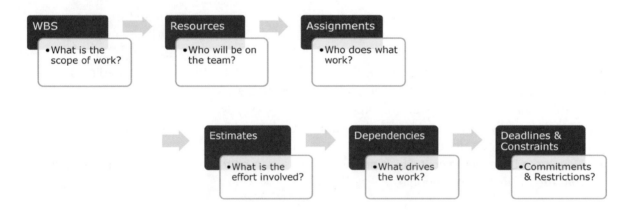

Figure 4.2 Steps to create a Proactive Project Schedule

As defined in the PMI PMBOK Guide®, the WBS defines the complete scope of the project by identifying all the deliverables (products/results) that the project is expected to deliver. 'The WBS is a hierarchical decomposition of the total scope of work to be carried out by the project team to accomplish the project objectives and create the required deliverables. The WBS organizes and defines the total scope of the project, and represents the work specified in the current approved project scope statement'. (Project Management Institute, 2013).

The first step of developing a WBS is to establish a complete definition of all the deliverables required to satisfy the requirements for the project. Project deliverables are tangible items, like 'Design Document' and 'Customer Maintenance Prototype' and should be direct contributors to project completion. If a deliverable doesn't help finish the project, we should not include it. The deliverables should then be reviewed with the Project Sponsor to ensure that the list is complete and that if the deliverables are produced as planned, that the project will be deemed successful.

TIPS & HINTS:

To validate whether you are building a deliverable-based WBS, try putting the word 'The' in front of your deliverables. For example, 'The Design Document' or 'The Trained Staff' work well. The deliverables should represent something tangible or a specific outcome, not an on-going activity.

Work Breakdown Structure (WBS)

- Phase (optional)
    - Deliverable
        - Detailed Task
        - Detailed Task
        - Detailed Task
        - Milestones

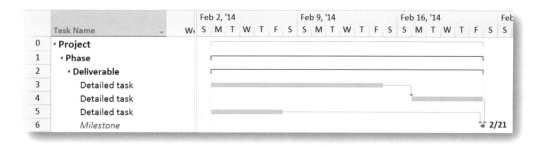

Figure 4.3 Work Breakdown Structure Elements

TIPS & HINTS:

Deliverables are typically decomposed into work packages through multiple levels; major work package (Document Chapters) thru minor work packages (Document Sections) until the lowest level work package, typically referred to as a task, is identified. Tasks are typically defined as stand-alone work assignments which can be assigned to a single resource, with an estimate that can be completed within a single reporting period.

With the deliverable list approved, the next step to complete the WBS is to decompose the deliverables into work packages where the combined results of the work packages complete the requirements for the deliverable.

TIPS & HINTS:

Some project managers find it easier to create the initial, high level WBS outside of Microsoft Project. You can use the Organization Chart add-on for PowerPoint to do so or even Visio or third party products, such as MindManager from MindJet, a personal favorite of the author. Then, simply bring the WBS into Microsoft Project when complete.

As shown on the sample WBS below, the project is initially decomposed into the project phases (design, development and testing) and then each phase in decomposed into the deliverables (design > design document and concept mockups) and then each deliverable is decomposed into the work packages required to complete the deliverable.

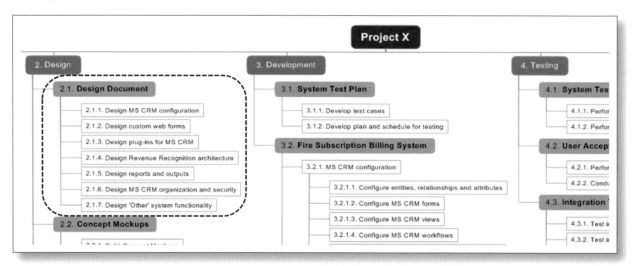

Figure 4.4 Complete Work Breakdown Structure

We recommend that you always validate the 100% rule to every branch of the WBS where the sum of the work at the child level must equal 100% of the work represented by the parent and that the WBS does not contain any work that falls outside the scope of the project or parent. The 100% rule applies upwards as well, as the deliverable must be 100% completed once all the child objects are completed.

The purpose of decomposition is to sub-divide the deliverable into manageable and estimable components. For example, it is very difficult, if not impossible, to accurately estimate the effort to create an 'Analysis Document' for an Inventory Management system (is it 4.5 months of effort or 5.2 months?). But if the 'Analysis Document' is sub-divided into work packages, the resultant task for 'Review Inventory Validation Method with Accounting' can be much more accurately estimated at 10 hours consisting of 2 hours to research validation methods, 2 hours to meet with Accounting, 1 hour to document the meeting results, 4 hours to document and prepare the recommendation and 1 hour to secure approval of the recommendation from Accounting.

The following table summarizes how to effectively develop a WBS. Work with the project team to describe each Deliverable and decompose into the detailed tasks with the supporting descriptions.

Work Breakdown Structure (WBS)	Details	Deliverable/ Outcome
<Phase>		
<DELIVERABLE1> *** Identify the major deliverables of the project	*** Write a brief, high level description of the deliverable, focused on the 'what' of the project, not 'how or when'.	
<DETAILED TASK> *** Decompose each deliverable into actionable Work Packages/Detailed Tasks. *** Each detailed task must have a name that is unique within the schedule and can be interpreted by team members without seeing the context of the WBS.	Description: *** Write a detailed description of the scope within each Detailed Task. Assumptions: ***Document any assumptions that significantly impact the scope and effort of this task. External Dependencies: *** Document any external dependencies for this task; i.e. items needed from the client in order to complete the work. Estimating Guidelines: *** Where appropriate, include information about Estimating Assumptions, i.e. what the effort estimate is based on and what assumptions are made.	*** Enter detailed effort estimate in hours.

When decomposing work packages, it is important to create manageable tasks without getting to the point of micro-management. In the example presented above, the task was defined as 'Review Inventory Validation Method with Accounting' with an estimate of 10 hours. We have an expectation that the assigned team member will do research, meet with Accounting, document meeting minutes etc. based on having experienced and qualified team members assigned to our project, but we leave it to the team member to develop their own strategy for how each task will be completed; giving the team member creative control over how they actually complete the task assignment within the 10 hour boundary you set for them. As the work packages are decomposed, it is important to ensure that each task created is appropriately named. Each task name should be self-contained and self-descriptive as team members will be assigned tasks without necessarily seeing the complete project schedule. A common mistake is to simply define the task as 'Create Test Strategy', recognizing that the task is a child of the 'Acceptance Test Plan' deliverable. A better self-contained and self-descriptive task name would be 'Create Acceptance Test Strategy' ensuring that the team member assigned the task is able to fully appreciate the expectations when it occurs on a timesheet or task list.

TIPS & HINTS:

Microsoft Project doesn't use the WBS terms just discussed – deliverables, sub-deliverables and tasks. Instead, it uses 4 generic terms – project summary task, summary task, detailed task and milestone.

The project summary task is a special task maintained by project and is created automatically as line zero in a project's WBS – Microsoft Project uses it to present a summary of the project.

Summary tasks are used to represent phases, deliverables and sub-deliverables.

Detailed tasks are the lowest level of the WBS decomposition.

Milestones are used to represent significant events (milestones) in the project for reporting and management purposes.

With the WBS fully developed, the next step is to identify the skills required to complete each of the tasks in the WBS. The resources to be assigned to the project should be based on the enterprise resource pool which identifies all resources and the level of availability they have for project work. This is typically done in partnership with a resource manager to ensure each selected resource has the availability needed to work on the project. These resources are then assigned to the project tasks, matching the resource skills to the task requirements.

In an ideal world, you would identify resources with the specific skills for each project task ensuring you have the perfect person to complete each task. However, in practical application, this would typically result in a VERY large project team with each team member completing a very small number of tasks. This is not a realistic way to resource a project as there would be a significant amount of overhead with learning curve, communications and overall co-ordination. Practical project resourcing needs to temper the desire for highly skilled resources versus having a smaller more manageable team of resources dedicated to the project. It is still important to ensure that the assigned resources have adequate skills for all assigned tasks, even if a few of the tasks will results in a skills stretch.

Figure 4.5 Effective Team Composition

With appropriately skilled resources assigned to each task, estimates are then developed for the amount of work (effort) required to fully complete the scope associated with the task. Developing realistic estimates is a considerable challenge as the only time an accurate understanding of the amount of work required will be known is after the task is complete. Recognizing that estimates are 'best guesses' it is also critical that the estimates developed use appropriate estimating techniques and are not just randomly generated numbers or the results of throwing darts at a board. As entire reference books can be, and have been, written on estimating techniques, we will simply state that sound, realistic and validated estimates should be created for each task as part of developing the baseline schedule.

As discussed in Chapter 2, for Fixed Work tasks, estimates should be based on the amount of work required to complete the task. Estimates should not be developed for the amount of elapsed time the task should take. Consider the example where an estimate is 20 hours of work; if this task is completed by a full-time project resource, the work will take 2.5 days, but if it is completed by a resource who can only spend 50% of their time on project work, the same task will take a full week. This results in a significant change in project deadlines and milestones. Work-based estimating provides the maximum flexibility for project resourcing and allows Microsoft Project to determine the project baseline based on established scheduling best practices.

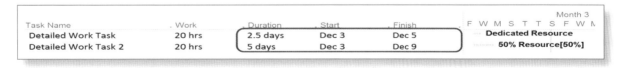

Figure 4.6 Comparison of Resource Assignment Units

The next step to develop the baseline schedule is to identify all the dependencies between the tasks, effectively identifying which tasks have predecessor relationships which must be completed to provide the necessary inputs and information for the next task to begin. At its most simplistic, using a house building example, the roof cannot be constructed before the walls are built, and the walls cannot be built before the floor is completed and so on, or put in the language of dependencies, the walls are dependent on the floor and the roof is dependent on the walls. Creating a complete set of dependencies is critical to having Microsoft Project develop an effective schedule because while it is an extremely powerful and sophisticated tool it does not yet have built in artificial intelligence, fuzzy logic or simply good old common sense to just know that the walls have to be built before the roof can be constructed. Left to its own scheduling rules, any tool, in the absence of dependencies, could well have the construction of your house in totally the wrong order.

The last step is to add any additional deadlines and constraints into Microsoft Project to ensure that the resultant schedule supports any external, non-project, requirements. Examples of these would include no code implementations in the first 2 weeks of Sept due to high business volumes of students returning to college, or the project must submit audit records to the external auditors 4 weeks prior to fiscal year end. While acknowledgement of these deadlines and constraints are critical, we as project managers should also work with the business to eliminate as many of them as possible to develop the best possible baseline schedule based on the specific project characteristics we have just discussed.

With the overview complete, we will now review the details of the process for developing the baseline schedule in the remaining sections of this Chapter.

4.1 Copy Resource Plan to Project Plan

Since the Resource Plan is not connected to the project schedule, you may want to copy the resources you just selected into the schedule. This step is entirely optional and often times is not needed if your organization uses standard schedule templates that already have generic resources associated with the plan. We recommend only copying the Resource Plan to Project Plan if you are going to start your schedule from a clean slate. This way, you will at least have the resources that were requested during the proposal process. The allocated hours do NOT come across though, only the resources themselves.

You align your schedule with the resource plan in PWA by selecting the appropriate project in the Project Center. Select the project you created previously in Chapter 3 and then from the 'Projects ribbon > Navigate section' select 'Build Team'

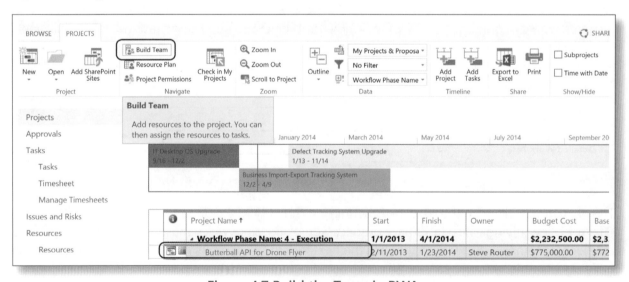

Figure 4.7 Build the Team in PWA

Next, you select to copy the 'Resource Plan' to the Project.

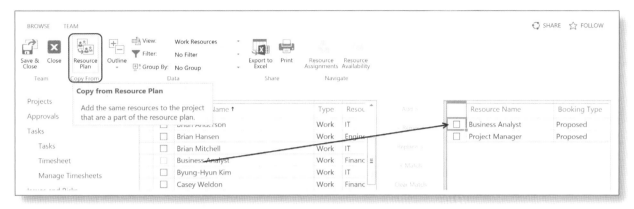

Figure 4.8 Copy the Resource Plan into the Project Plan

With these two steps completed, your schedule has been pre-populated with the resources defined in the 'Resource Plan'.

4.2 Setting Project Start Date

The project 'Start Date' is set either as part of the proposal on the Business Case page in Project Web App (PWA) or in Microsoft Project on the 'Project Information' dialog. It should never be set on the detailed tasks in the schedule as this creates a constraint.

Unless your project start date was set correctly in the proposal in PWA, you will want to make sure to set it now, before building out the detailed schedule and starting to socialize dates.

Open your schedule in Microsoft Project and from the 'Project ribbon > Properties section', select 'Project Information' to display the Project Information dialog.

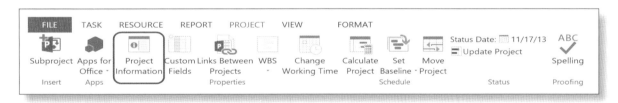

Figure 4.9 Project Information

If you do not know the project start date at this time, simply select a most likely start date and then update this field once the project is fully approved and ready to be initiated. The schedule will be automatically recalculated whenever you update this field.

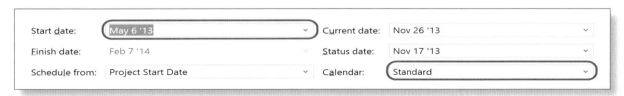

Figure 4.10 Project Information Dialog

At this time, you should also validate that the appropriate project calendar is selected for the project. The default, as shown, is the Standard calendar which defines the working days for your project, the default settings from Microsoft has 5 working days per week (Monday thru Friday) and an 8 hour work day. Your organization has likely made adjustments to the Standard calendar to suite the specific requirements for all projects delivered. If there are multiple calendars available, you should ensure that you select the appropriate calendar for your project as this may impact your dates. For tasks without resources assigned, Microsoft Project will schedule your dates based on this calendar and you would get very different results with a standard 8 hour by 5 day calendar versus a 24 hour by 7 day calendar.

If you have resources assigned to all detailed tasks, then this becomes less of an issue as Microsoft Project will first schedule work from the base calendar for each resource.

One final consideration for setting up your project information from this window is the 'Schedule from:' field. There are 2 options, the default as show is to schedule your project from the 'Start Date' and the alternative is to schedule your project from the 'Finish Date'.

Schedule your project from the 'Start Date' whenever possible, as it gives you the maximum amount of flexibility to fine-tune the project to suit delivery requirements. However, if you have an absolute MUST finish by type of project, you can have the schedule calculated from the finish date which may actually calculate a start date which is in the past. And while you can still adjust the project's dependencies, resourcing, estimates and so on to recalculate a more realistic start date, most project managers find scheduling from the finish date to be counter-intuitive.

We recommend always scheduling from the start date and then using a deadline to mark the contractual finish date. That way, you will get the best of both worlds as you can see whether the current schedule will allow us to meet the deadline and therefore take corrective action, as necessary.

WORK SESSION #2 – PREPARE THE PROJECT SCHEDULE

OBJECTIVE

This work session kicks off the development of the baseline schedule. It initiates the development of the detailed project schedule in Microsoft Project.

For PWA users, Step 1 is a preliminary step required to pre-load our sample schedule into your Project Server environment.

STEP 1   Connect to Enterprise Environment and Load a Training Schedule

Launch Microsoft Project and log into your Project Server environment. (See Appendix A if you need additional direction on connecting to your Project Server environment).

Open the 'Light Rail Phase 2' plan obtained from the download site (See Appendix C for additional details on how to connect to the download site).

From the File Menu select 'Save As' and save the file to your Enterprise environment. This will save our sample schedule into your environment and make it available for the following Work Sessions.

STEP 2   Complete Project Definition

Set the Project Start Date to January 5, 2015 and validate that the relevant enterprise custom fields project details are set correctly. Any fields with an asterisk are mandatory.

STEP 3   Save and Check in the Plan

Close and Check-in the schedule.

EXPECTED RESULTS

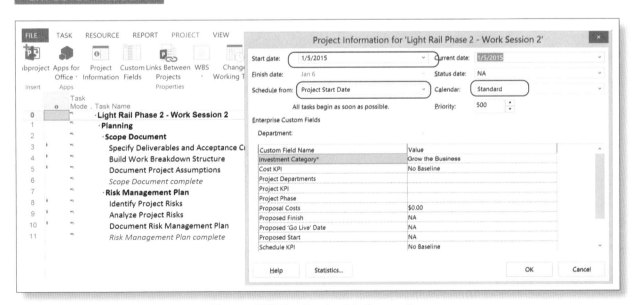

Figure WS.2 – Project Information

4.3 Completing the Project Work Breakdown Structure (WBS)

The Work Breakdown Structure (WBS) defines and organizes the total scope of a project. It should capture all deliverables and include 100% of the work defined by the project scope. In other words, any work that needs to occur to complete the project needs to be included somewhere in the WBS of the project.

A good WBS will typically have one or two levels of Summary Tasks (Phases and Deliverables) below the project summary followed by Detailed Tasks and Milestones. In Microsoft Project, these translate into one of the 4 types of tasks:

- **Project Summary Task**
  - Summarizes the entire project. Also known as 'Task 0'.
  - Budgets are assigned at this level only.
- **Summary Tasks**
  - Used to organize the WBS into phases and deliverables (and sub-deliverables and work packages on larger projects).
  - No work or duration estimates are assigned here, this is summary of the data from detailed tasks.
  - No dependencies should be created at this level.
- **Detailed Tasks**
  - Represent the level of the WBS where work is estimated and resources are assigned.
  - Some organizations refer to this level as the activity.
- **Milestones**
  - Represent beginnings and completions.
  - No work, duration or resources should be assigned here. Milestones are used to represent a state of the deliverable or phase, etc. It is either on or off, much like a light switch. A milestone is either complete or it is not.

A good, deliverable-focused WBS should follow the structure in the table below, but variances are allowed to support specific project types or unique requirements.

WBS element	Description
Phase	Identify major phases of work, e.g. Analysis, Design or Development
Deliverable	Identify the major deliverables of the project, e.g. Functional Requirements, Design Document, Test Plan, etc.
Detailed Task	Break the deliverables down to an appropriate level of task detail that identifies the work that needs to be done to produce the deliverable.
Milestone	Marks the completion of the scope of work outlined for the deliverable.

A key to successful project scheduling is to break down the project goals into phases, deliverables and detailed tasks before considering delivery dates, resource constraints, specific resources, or task dependencies. This helps to objectively identify all of the work without subconsciously leaving out real work in order to fit date or resource constraints.

Figure 4.11 Generic Work Breakdown Structure

4.3.1 Detailed Tasks

For the development of a proactive project schedule, the detailed tasks are probably the most important elements of the WBS. When project team members access tasks in PWA, they will see only a list of projects and the detailed tasks. They do NOT see the complete WBS by default, i.e. the phases and deliverables of the project. Therefore, **each detailed task must have a name that is unique within the schedule and can be interpreted by team members without seeing the context of the WBS.**

The table below contains guidance on the various elements of detailed tasks.

Elements of Detailed Tasks	Description
Task Name	The task name should be action-oriented and start with a verb. It must be unique within the schedule and accurately convey the work that is to be completed. Start with words like 'Review', 'Test', 'Perform', 'Write', etc. and write a full sentence. Try to avoid abbreviations as these can cause confusion. For example: *Conduct User Acceptance Testing*
Placeholders	Where appropriate, use placeholders to make it easy for the team lead to complete the detailed scope. Placeholders are used to ensure that repeated tasks are unique in the schedule when the team lead creates multiple iterations or instances of a task. Placeholders can identify specific products (PRODUCT), processes (PROCESS), components (COMPONENT) or other items that are replaceable in the schedule. For example: *Conduct User Acceptance Testing for PRODUCT*, where PRODUCT could be replaced by *SAP* and the task would be copied for each required instance of the task.
Notes	Enter a detailed description of each task in the notes field. This information is included in the My Tasks view for team members and conveys the detailed scope of the task.

Elements of Detailed Tasks	Description
Level of detail	Ideally, detailed tasks should be broken to a level of detail that falls within a few reporting periods (not to exceed 4 weeks as a guideline), but not so detailed that they become to-do or checklist items. For organizations trying to get a handle on resource capacity/demand management in addition to reliable project dates, a good range might be 8-40 hours, i.e. tasks shouldn't be smaller than 8 hours or larger than 40 hours (per assignment). That way, in any given reporting period a detailed task is typically either not started, started this period, finished or late (avoiding tasks that are 'in-progress' forever.) Tasks with less than 8 hours of work should be consolidated into larger tasks, where possible, or added to the template as milestones. A good measure of the level of detail is where tasks: ■ can be realistically and confidently estimated in hours of work to complete ■ have a meaningful unit of work that can be assigned to a responsible individual (or sometimes multiple) ■ cannot be logically subdivided further ■ can be completed quickly ■ have a meaningful conclusion and deliverable ■ can be completed without interruption (without the need for more information)

4.3.2 Milestones

Milestones in Microsoft Project can perform various functions in the schedule, including (but not limited to) the examples in the table below:

Milestones	Description
Beginnings or completions	Milestones can be used to mark a key kick-off event that marks the official beginning of the project or another significant point in the project (even if some work was done prior). A project completion milestone can also be used to highlight when the project is scheduled to be completed or go live (even if there are support activities after this point).
Major deliverables or key points in the project	Use milestones for major deliverables or key points on the project, e.g. business case complete, project management plan complete or formal kickoff complete.
Approval points	If gate reviews or approval points are utilized, then these should have milestones that are linked to all of the incoming (predecessor) and outgoing (successor) tasks, e.g. project management plan approved and baseline schedule published.

Milestones	Description
External dependencies	Any external dependencies (i.e. events outside the control and scope of this project), should be clearly identified in the schedule and linked to the tasks they affect. That way, any delays experienced on external dependencies will automatically move the start dates of those tasks dependent on that event. This is key to creating a dynamic project model.

Milestones are a great way of tracking overall progress on the project and also help to ensure a proactive project schedule (when combined with dependencies). The table above contains guidance and examples of how milestones may be used in a project schedule template.

To set a milestone, change the 'Duration' of the task to '0' and Microsoft Project will automatically mark the task as a milestone. Milestones should NEVER have any work or resources assigned to them.

Using these guidelines, the process of actually creating the WBS for your project begins.

4.3.3 WBS Development

Using the '01 – Detailed Scope – WBS' view, the project WBS should be created following the guidelines defined above. WBS elements are created by entering the name of the phase, deliverable, task or milestone directly into the 'Task Name' column.

Ensure that the 'Project Summary Task' is displayed. From the 'Format ribbon > Show/Hide section' select 'Project Summary Task'.

Figure 4.12 Add Project Summary to the WBS

Following the standards defined above, create a 'Milestone' to be the anchor point for all other project tasks. From the 'Task ribbon > Insert section' select Milestone and create a 'Project Start' milestone. (Alternatively, you could type the Milestone directly into the 'Task Name' column and set the 'Duration' to zero)

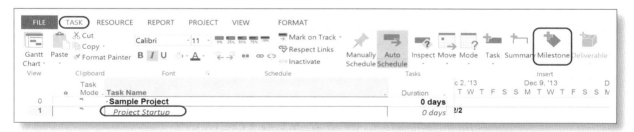

Figure 4.13 Insert a Project Startup Milestones as the first line in the plan

Continue entering tasks in the 'Task Name' column one row at a time. The structure of the WBS (outline levels) is developed using the 'Indent and Outdent' buttons from the 'Schedule section' of the task ribbon. In the example below, the Indent button was used once with the 'Customer Requirements Document' line selected to indent it, which makes the 'Analysis' line above it a Summary. The Indent was used a second time on the 'Interview Business Owner' task which indented it and made the 'Customer Requirements Document' a Summary. All subsequent lines added remain at the same indentation level.

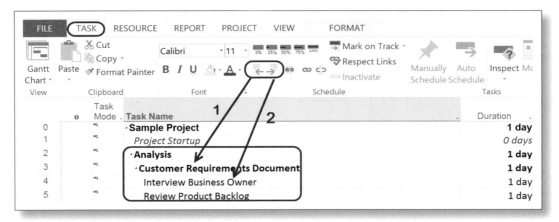

Figure 4.14 Use Indent functionality to create the WBS Structure

Once all the tasks required to complete the 'Customer Requirements Document' are entered, the deliverable is completed with a Milestone which was created by entering the milestone directly into the Task Name and setting the 'Duration' to zero (or by using the Insert Milestone as described above).

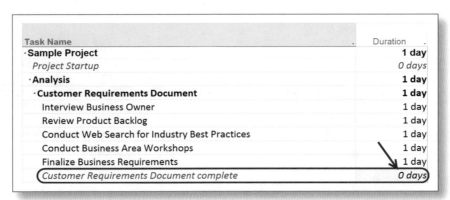

Figure 4.15 Complete each Deliverable with a Milestone

The WBS evolves as Deliverables and Phases are added until the WBS is complete. As shown below, a new deliverable; 'Current Situation Assessment', is created by first selecting it and using the Outdent to remove it from the 'Customer Requirements Document' structure and then the first task in the new deliverable; 'Review Customer Service Request' is Indented to make it part of the 'Current Situation Assessment' summary. Similarly, once the 'Analysis' phase is completed, the Outdent is used to start the new Phase, Design.

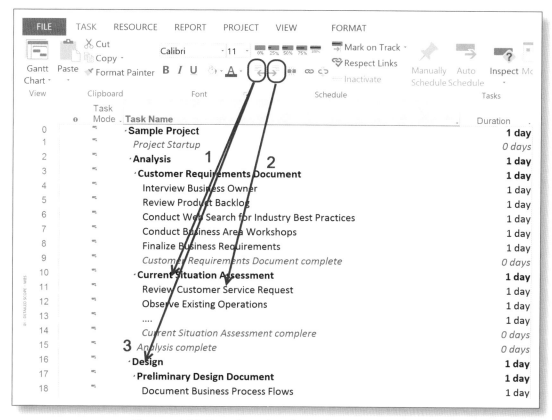

**Figure 4.16 Develop the Complete WBS using
Indent and Outdent to create the WBS structure**

Additional tasks can inserted into an existing WBS Structure (Phase or Deliverable). New lines are inserted immediately above the line that is currently selected in the WBS. The new line can be added using the 'Task Ribbon > Insert section' and selecting the appropriate type, or alternatively a new blank line can be inserted into the plan by either hitting the Insert key on your keyboard or doing a right-mouse click to activate the shortcut menu.

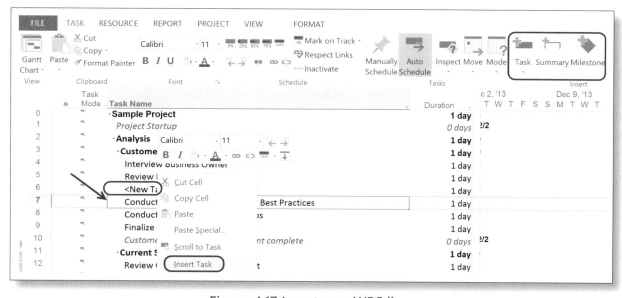

Figure 4.17 Insert new WBS lines

If a task needs to be deleted from the WBS it is important to select the whole line, not just the Task Name cell, by selecting the line number. Once the whole line is selected it can be deleted using the Delete key on your keyboard or using the 'Delete' command from the shortcut menu.

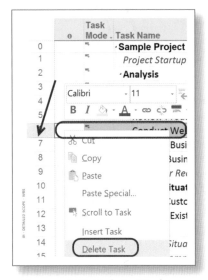

Figure 4.18 Delete Task on Shortcut Menu

Entire sections of the WBS can be moved, cut and copied in a similar manner which is to first select the entire line(s) and then select the appropriate commands from the shortcut menu (or use standard keyboard shortcut keys – Ctrl C, Ctrl V). Lines from the clipboard are inserted immediately above the selected line.

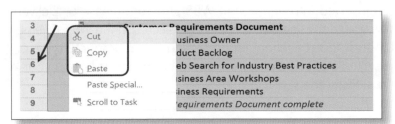

Figure 4.19 Cut, Copy and Paste commands work at the line level

Using these techniques, continue to develop the WBS ensuring that each Phase and Deliverable are properly structured and that a Project Completion milestone is the last line in the plan.

	Task Mode	Task Name	Duration
0		·Sample Project	**1 day**
1		*Project Startup*	*0 days*
2		·**Analysis**	**1 day**
3		·**Customer Requirements Document**	**1 day**
4		Interview Business Owner	1 day
5		Review Product Backlog	1 day
6		Conduct Web Search for Industry Best Practices	1 day
7		Conduct Business Area Workshops	1 day
8		Finalize Business Requirements	1 day
9		*Customer Requirements Document complete*	*0 days*
10		·**Current Situation Assessment**	**1 day**
11		Review Customer Service Request	1 day
12		Observe Existing Operations	1 day
13		....	1 day
14		*Current Situation Assessment complere*	*0 days*
15		*Analysis complete*	*0 days*
16		·**Design**	**1 day**
17		·**Preliminary Design Document**	**1 day**
18		Document Business Process Flows	1 day
19		....	1 day
20		....	1 day
21		*Project Completion*	*0 days*

Figure 4.20 A Project Completion milestone should be the last task in the plan

As each project will have a unique WBS based on the project scope and deliverables required, you will quickly develop your own rhythm and process for creating the WBS – some people like to create the complete WBS and then indent/outdent the structure, others prefer to develop the WBS one deliverable at a time. The key to successfully developing a complete WBS is to decompose the scope into deliverables, deliverables into sub-deliverables (as needed) then identify the tasks required to complete each deliverable.

We close out this section with some additional characteristics of a good project WBS

1. Always include the 'Project Summary Task (Task 0)' – it summarizes all aspects of the project and provides an excellent summary of the project.

Task Name	Work	Duration	Start	Finish	Actual Start
0 ·**Corporate Portal Migration**	2,159.7 hrs	**210.75 days**	**May 6**	**Mar 4**	**May 6**

Figure 4.21 Include Project Summary Task in all Projects

2. Include a 'Milestone' as the first line (project start) and last line (project completion) in your project. These 2 milestones should be the only tasks in your project that don't have predecessors and successors, respectively.

Figure 4.22 Include Project Start and Project Finish Milestones in all Projects

3. The project WBS levels should follow a predictable pattern. We recommend the following:
    a. Outline Level 1 should contain only project-level milestones and phases

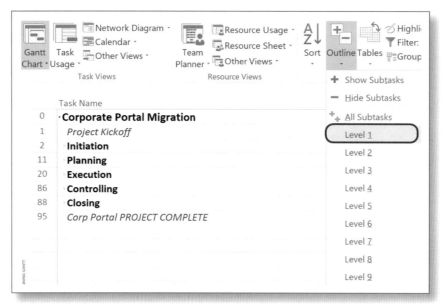

**Figure 4.23 Outline Level 1 -
Project-level milestones and phases only**

    b. Outline Level 2 should contain only the phase-level milestones and deliverables.

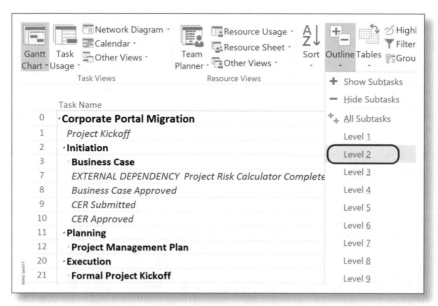

**Figure 4.24 Outline Level 2 -
Phase-level milestones and deliverables**

    c. Outline Level 3 should contain deliverable-level milestones and detailed tasks. On large projects, you may also have sub-deliverables here and then the detailed tasks at Outline Level 4.

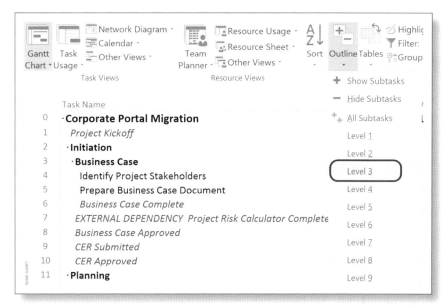

Figure 4.25 Outline Level 3 -
Deliverable-level milestones and detailed tasks

4. Milestones should be used to reflect the completion of each phase or deliverable and the names should match with the word 'complete' added to the milestone.

Figure 4.26 Milestones should reflect
completion of each deliverable

5. Blank lines should not be used in your project (some project managers like to add blank lines to separate chunks of the project). Instead, Summary tasks should be used to chunk the project.

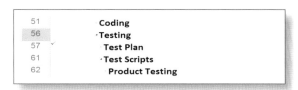

Figure 4.27 No Blank Lines -
Use Summary Tasks for chunking plans

6. Use Task Notes to add additional details to ensure the task is well defined.

Figure 4.28 Use Task Notes

WORK SESSION #3 – COMPLETE THE WBS FOR THE PROJECT

OBJECTIVE

This work session is focused on developing the WBS for the project. Over the next several work sessions, you will complete the Work Breakdown Structure for the project, build the team, assign resources, enter effort estimates, establish dependencies and set deadlines and constraints. In this work session, we will complete the development of the WBS loaded in the previous work session.

STEP 1   **Add Project Start Milestone**

Add a 'Project Start' milestone to the beginning of the project

STEP 2   **Add new deliverable**

Add the 'Procurement Plan' deliverable with detailed tasks after the scope document deliverable based on the following WBS:

> Procurement Plan
>
>> Determine Procurement Requirements
>>
>> Define & Publish Subcontractor Scope
>>
>> Identify Potential Subcontractors
>>
>> Identify Subcontract type
>>
>> Document Subcontractor Management Plan
>>
>> Procurement Plan complete (Milestone)

STEP 3   **Add completion milestones**

Add the following additional milestones:

> 'Planning phase complete' at the end of the Planning phase
>
> 'Light Rail Phase 2 complete' milestone at the end of the project.

STEP 4   **Add Task Notes**

Enter notes for one task.

EXPECTED RESULTS

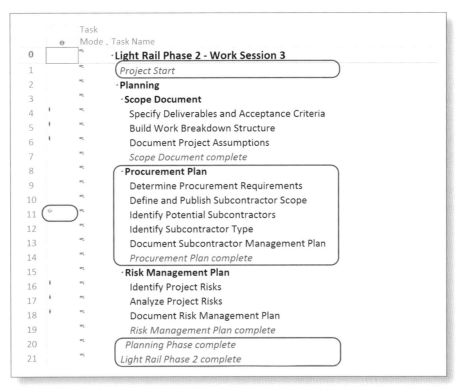

Figure WS.3 – WBS Complete

4.4 Build Team

Building the team is focused on replacing the generic resources from the schedule template or the proposal with named resources.

Typically, in preparation for this, you would have met with your corporate resource manager and negotiated for named project team members who satisfy the skills identified in the Resource Plan. This negotiation is typically done outside PWA and Microsoft Project. Once you know which resources are to be assigned to your project, you would add them to your plan, replacing the generic resources from the Resource Pool.

You do this from the 'Resource ribbon > Insert section' using the 'Add Resources' dropdown list, 'Build Team from Enterprise ...'.

Figure 4.29 Build the Team

Using the 'Build Team' dialog, you would assign resources to your project selecting them from the left Enterprise Resource list and adding them to the right Project Resource list. You will likely be using a combination of 'Replace' to change generic resources to named resources and 'Add' for new resources as part of the build team process.

This dialog provides the facility to group your resources by a number of enterprise fields, such as applications, cost type, expertise, resource department, role and skill to make finding resources easier.

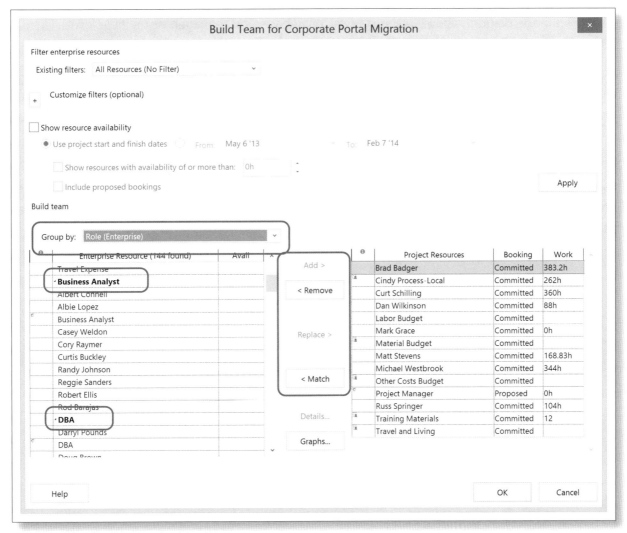

Figure 4.30 Assign Enterprise Resource to the Project

While the 'Build Team' dialog has selection capabilities to search for and select resources based on availability, you will typically not use this functionality in Microsoft Project as resource utilization and capacity is managed at the enterprise level – to be discussed in more detail below.

The second build team activity is to set the resource availability for your team.

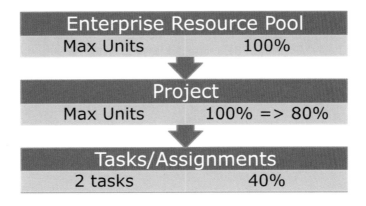

Figure 4.31 Resource Utilization

As shown in the diagram above, resource availability has to be managed at multiple levels. First, at the enterprise level, most resources will be available 100% of the time (assuming that all work is accounted for in the enterprise environment). Therefore, in PWA at the enterprise level, 'Max Units' is set to 100%. For those of you with a few years of experience under your belt, yes, we agree, no one is available 100% because of vacation, sick, and other duties and assignments, but, this is at the enterprise level, so it is appropriate to have all resources available 100%. Enterprise resource management will be managing vacation and other duties and assignments outside of direct project assignments and will in fact be managing each resource at 100%.

As project managers, we become involved at the next level in the diagram, project assignment. As shown in the diagram, a resource who is dedicated to a project, would typically at most, be at max units of 80%, and for some organizations less.

EXCEPTION:

I remember working with a military unit once where full-time project assignments were 30%, yes, I said 30%. These project team members were also full-time uniformed military personnel and therefore were expected to take part in training exercises and drills on a regular basis to maintain combat readiness, resulting in full-time project assignment of 30% (or 12 hours a week).

Individual resource allocations to a project are defined by enterprise resource management and as a project manager, we are responsible for ensuring that we effectively use each assigned resource to this allocation. For example, if we are assigned a resource at 40%, we are responsible for ensuring we effectively use them 16 hours a week, but are not responsible for the remaining 34 hours (that's enterprise resource management's responsibility).

To set each individual's max units, use the 'B – Resource Sheet' view. In Microsoft Project, from 'Task or Resource ribbon > View section' and then from the dropdown list select the 'B – Resource Sheet'. On this view, you adjust the 'Max Units' column to match the allocations provided by enterprise resource management.

Resource Name	Type	Max Units
Type: Work	**Work**	**582%**
Mark Grace	Work	80%
Cindy Process-Local	Work	80%
Dan Wilkinson	Work	40%
Michael Westbrook	Work	40%
Brad Badger	Work	80%
Curt Schilling	Work	80%
Matt Stevens	Work	80%
Russ Springer	Work	90%

Figure 4.32 Set Resource Max Units

As can be seen from the screenshot, this may result on some resource over allocations (the red resources). We will discuss how to resolve this later in this Chapter when we discuss leveling resource workload.

The final line in the diagram above, where we could further control an individual resource allocation at a task level will be discussed in the next section – Assign Resources.

EXCEPTION:

As 'Max Units' is controlled at the enterprise level, this field is reset to its default value (often 100%) each time the project is loaded, therefore, you must reset this to the appropriate project level each time you are leveling your project resources.

WORK SESSION #4 – BUILD THE PROJECT TEAM

OBJECTIVE

This work session continues the development of the baseline schedule and is focused on the identification of the named individuals who will be on the project team. This will involve both replacing the generic resources with the named resources as well as adding additional named resources to the team.

If you are not using Enterprise resources you can complete this step in Microsoft Project and create 3 project resources. If you are using Enterprise Resources, use the 'Build Team' dialog (also in Microsoft Project) to add resources to the team.

STEP 1   Build the team

Replace the 'Project Manager' with yourself

Replace the 'Procurement Specialist' with an appropriate member of your organization

Replace the 'Business Analyst' with a different appropriate member of your organization

Note: We appended the role to the end of the assigned resource name for the purpose of these work sessions to facilitate ease of knowing which named resource is filling each role – this is not a best practice for actual project delivery.

EXPECTED RESULTS

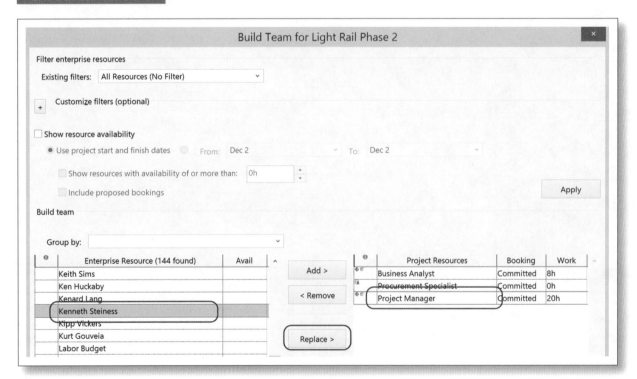

Figure WS.4 – Build the Team

4.5 Assign Resources

With the team built, we are now ready to assign the team to each task in the WBS. This is one of the instances where we are going to make very specific recommendations on using Microsoft Project effectively. While there are many ways in which resources can be assigned to tasks, we recommend using only 2:

1. 'Assign Resource' dialog
2. 'Task Details' view

Both these methods provide you the degree of control over resource allocation needed to ensure that Microsoft Project is doing exactly what you want, rather than defaulting to out-of-the-box behavior.

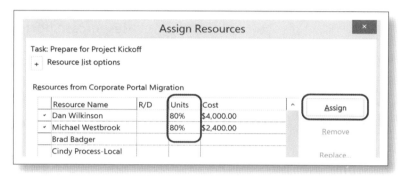

Figure 4.33a Resource Assignment Dialog

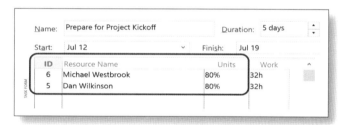

Figure 4.33b Resource Assignment Task Form

While most views can be used for assigning resources, we find a view like '05 – Planning Gantt' is very effective as it provides all the information associated with managing resource assignments.

The main method you will use, specifically during initial resource assignment will be the 'Assign Resource' dialog. It can be selected from the 'Resource ribbon > Assignment section > Assign Resources' or from the task shortcut menu - right mouse on the task and select 'Assign Resources'

Figure 4.34a Assign Resources Button

Figure 4.34b Assign Resources Shortcut Menu

A key feature of the 'Assign Resource' dialog is that it will remain open while allowing you to also select and change the information in the '05 – Planning Gantt'. For those of you technically minded windows users, or if you simply want to impress someone as the next party you attend – the 'Assign Resource' dialog is a Modal Window (it stays open while allowing you to continue to work in other windows).

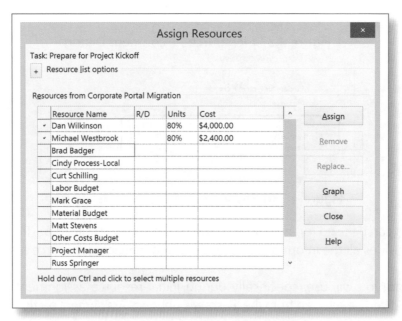

Figure 4.35 Assign Resources dialog

We are now ready to assign resources to project tasks. To do this, select each task from the '05 – Planning Gantt' view and then in the 'Assign Resources' dialog select the appropriate resource(s) who will work on the task and ensure that the units are set appropriately for the selected resource as it may need to be set differently than the default assignment units.

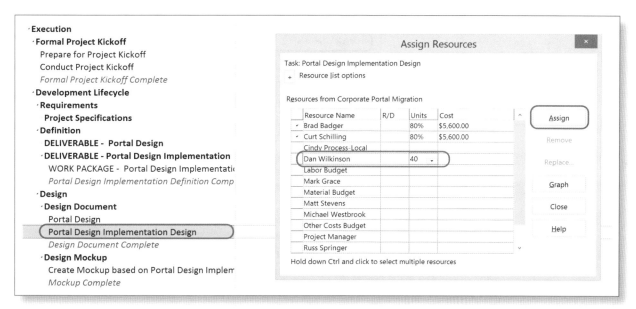

Figure 4.36 Assign New/Additional Resources to a Task

Selecting a resource and pressing 'Assign' will assign the resources at the max units previously set during Build Team, which is what you will likely want in most instances. If however, you want a resource to work on two tasks simultaneously, you would manually set the 'Assignment Units' on the appropriate tasks (as represented in the last line of the diagram presented in Build Team) and manage these individual assignments to the resource's availability level.

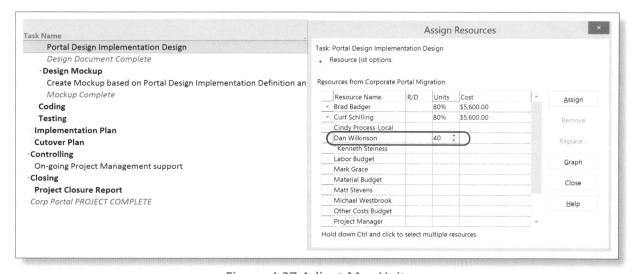

Figure 4.37 Adjust Max Units

The second method we recommend for assigning (and managing resources) is the 'Task Details' view. This is actually a split screen in Microsoft Project which is activated by selecting the window control in the lower right of your screen and dragging it up, or alternatively, you can activate this from the 'View ribbon > Split View section' and select the 'Details' checkbox and selecting the 'Task Form'.

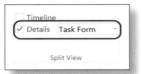

**Figure 4.38a
Launch Task
Details Split Screen**

**Figure 4.38b Activate
Split Window Drag Bar**

If the resource details does not show in this second window, the information displayed on this form can be controlled by a right mouse click and selecting either one of the Resource and Successor/ Predecessor options.

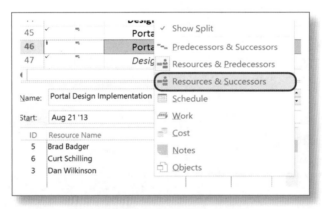

**Figure 4.39 Select the details
for the Split Screen**

With the Task Form visible, additional resources can be assigned from the pull down menus and the 'Assignment Units' set for all resources assigned to the task. In addition, the work effort can be manually divided between the resources assigned to the task.

TIPS & HINTS:

   The longest assignment on a task will always drive the overall duration of the task. Keep this in mind when planning and when trying to take corrective action and bring the project back on track.

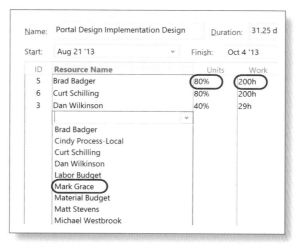

**Figure 4.40 Select Additional Resources
and/or adjust existing resources
on the Task Form**

We recommend the exclusive use of these two methods for assigning (and managing) the allocation of resources to tasks in the project as they provide the ability to explicitly set the max units.

WORK SESSION #5 – ASSIGN RESOURCES

OBJECTIVE

This work session continues the development of the baseline schedule and involves setting the appropriate project assignment levels for each resource to ensure that they are scheduled for work at the appropriate level.

STEP 1   Assign Resources to Tasks

Assign yourself to all the 'Procurement Plan' detailed tasks at 40%

Assign your colleague to 'Identify Potential Subcontractors' at 40%

EXPECTED RESULTS

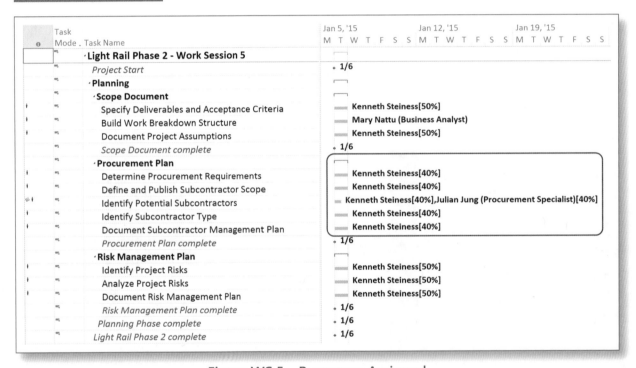

Figure WS.5 – Resources Assigned

4.6 Estimating Effort

As discussed in Chapter 2, fixed work is our default work type, which means that all estimates to be entered into Microsoft Project should be effort based (or work estimates). In other words, the estimates needed are for focused heads down, hands-on time actually required to complete the work associated with each task.

This is often a substantial mindset change for a lot of team members as most people think in terms of 'I can have this done by next Friday', rather than it will take be 32 hours of work to get it done. We describe this as 'Changing the Conversation'. As shown in the diagram, there are three parts to effectively defining the work required to complete a task. First and most important, is the commitment from the team member that the task can be completed with the estimated amount of work. Next, is the commitment from the enterprise resource mangers that the resource is committed to the project at the agreed allocation, and finally the project manager combines the effort estimate (32 hours) and the resource allocation (50%) and Microsoft Project calculates that the task will take 8 days of calendar time to complete.

Figure 4.41 Changing the Conversation

It's our job as proactive project managers to ensure that the conversation gets changed and our team members move from giving us completion date estimates to true effort based estimates. In most organizations, this transition will take time and you need to be prepared from some red projects early in the transition as everyone adapts to the change.

Entering effort estimates can be done on any view where the 'Work' column is visible, we recommend '5 – Planning Gantt', the same as used above for assigning resources. With the Work column visible, the effort based estimates are simply entered into the Work column on a task by task basis and Microsoft Project calculates the duration based on the assigned resources availability.

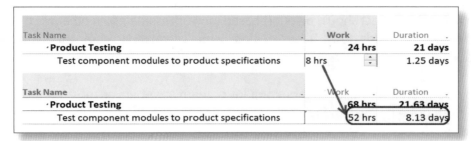

**Figure 4.42 Update Work to reflect estimate,
Duration is calculated based on assigned resources**

As our tasks are defined as effort based, and the resources are already assigned, based on the formula from Chapter 2; 'Work * Units = Duration', Project will calculate the duration as we enter the work estimates per task – '52 hours work * .8 resource units = 8.13 days duration.

While the majority of tasks should be effort based, there will be instances where one of the other task types will be needed, specifically fixed duration. To define fixed duration tasks, we first need to change the task type, and then enter the duration estimate. To do this, open the 'Task Information' dialog by double clicking on the task (or select Information from the right-mouse shortcut menu). On the 'Advanced Tab', the 'Task Type' is changed to 'Fixed Duration'. After clicking OK to commit the change, the estimated calendar days would be entered into the 'Duration' column and Microsoft Project will calculate the effort.

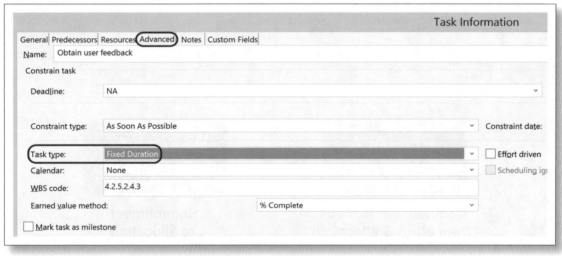

Figure 4.43 Fixed Duration Task Advanced Tab

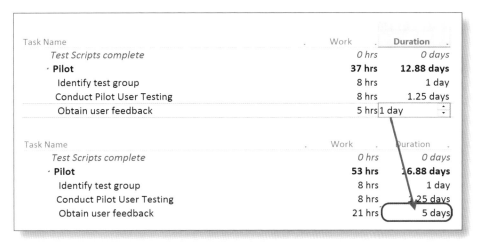

Figure 4.44 Update Duration to reflect estimate,
Work is calculated based on assigned Resources

If there is more than one resource assigned to a task, by default, Microsoft Project will spread the work evenly across each resource. If you wish to fine-tune the work distribution, the 'Split Window, Task Form' discussed in assign resources can be used.

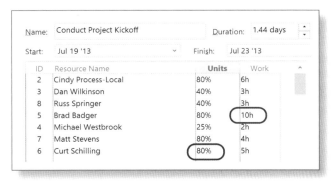

Figure 4.45 Task Form can be used to fine-tune
resource assignments to a task

WORK SESSION #6 – ESTIMATE EFFORT

OBJECTIVE

In this work session, we add the work estimates to each task in the schedule. These estimates are for the amount of effort required to complete each task. Microsoft Project will calculate the duration for each task based on these estimates and the resource assignments defined in the previous work session.

STEP 1   Add effort estimates to the plan

Enter Work estimates for following tasks

      Specify Deliverables and Acceptance Criteria – 8 hours

      Build Work Breakdown Structure – 40 hours

      Document Project Assumptions – 16 hours

      Determine Procurement Requirements – 8 hours

      Define and Publish Subcontractor Scope – 16 hours

      Identify Subcontractor Type – 32 hours

      Document Subcontractor Management Plan – 32 hours

      Identify Project Risks – 20 hours

      Analyze Project Risks – 10 hours

      Document Risk Management Plan – 10 hours

STEP 2   Add duration estimates to the plan

For the 'Identify Potential Subcontractors task', set the task type to 'Fixed Duration' and give it a duration of 1 month.

EXPECTED RESULTS

	Task Mode	Task Name	Work	Duration
		Light Rail Phase 2 - Work Session 6	**320 hrs**	**20 days**
		Project Start	*0 hrs*	*0 days*
		Planning	**320 hrs**	**20 days**
		Scope Document	**64 hrs**	**5 days**
		Specify Deliverables and Acceptance Criteria	8 hrs	2 days
		Build Work Breakdown Structure	40 hrs	5 days
		Document Project Assumptions	16 hrs	4 days
		Scope Document complete	*0 hrs*	*0 days*
		Procurement Plan	**216 hrs**	**20 days**
		Determine Procurement Requirements	8 hrs	2.5 days
		Define and Publish Subcontractor Scope	16 hrs	5 days
		Identify Potential Subcontractors	128 hrs	1 mon
		Identify Subcontractor Type	32 hrs	10 days
		Document Subcontractor Management Plan	32 hrs	10 days
		Procurement Plan complete	*0 hrs*	*0 days*
		Risk Management Plan	**40 hrs**	**5 days**
		Identify Project Risks	20 hrs	5 days
		Analyze Project Risks	10 hrs	2.5 days
		Document Risk Management Plan	10 hrs	2.5 days
		Risk Management Plan complete	*0 hrs*	*0 days*
		Planning Phase complete	*0 hrs*	*0 days*
		Light Rail Phase 2 complete	*0 hrs*	*0 days*

Figure WS.6 – Task Estimates

4.7 Establishing Dependencies

Creating dependencies is one of the less obvious aspects of using a scheduling tool as in most instances, the dependencies we enter into our plans are common sense, either because the tasks fall sequentially in the plan or anyone would know that the hardware has to be ordered and delivered before it can be installed. However, Microsoft Project doesn't understand that sequential tasks in the plan should be completed in that logical order and definitely doesn't have the artificial intelligence to determine logical implementation sequences. And that's a GOOD THING. While Microsoft Project does have a set of rules it uses when determining the project schedule, we, as project managers, definitely need to do a significant amount of work to ensure it calculates the schedule we need as opposed to the out of the box, one size fits all rules schedule that would be created by default.

Dependencies are used to identify and define the work relationships. Dependencies are used to capture the cause and effect relationships in the project, and while this directly impacts the project schedule, we should not use dependencies to define the project schedule. This is a key distinction to understand when creating dependencies, as we need to ensure we are capturing the real dependencies – the effect of completing the design document will cause the start of the work on the next deliverable, database normalization; where the schedule is simply a natural consequence of this dependency. While this may appear as a very subtle distinction, it is a key distinction as dependencies used to define the schedule often introduce many artificial or false dependencies by arbitrarily setting the order in which you think the tasks and deliverables should be completed.

Another key misconception with dependencies is attempting to use dependencies to manage resource availability, where Johnny is working on both A and B, so therefore B must be dependent on A, simply because Johnny cannot do two things at the same time. Or even worse, adding false dependencies to delay work on a task because Johnny is on vacation for a week. Microsoft Project is very good at managing resource allocations and we do not need to add any resource availability dependencies.

There are 4 types of dependencies: Finish-Start, Start-Start, Finish-Finish and Start-Finish.

Finish-Start is the default dependency and is the most common dependency used as it represents the true cause and effect relationship where Task B cannot start until Task A finishes.

Start-Start defines a relationship where Task B can start as soon as Task A starts. Start-Start dependencies are commonly used when several tasks can all start at the same time.

Finish-Finish defines a relationship where a task cannot finish until the predecessor task finishes. A common use for these would be quality assurance tasks that cannot finish until the work being validated is completed.

Start-Finish dependencies are rarely used and are included purely for the viewpoint of ensuring we provide full coverage of the dependency relationships. In a Start-Finish relationship the start of the second task ends the predecessor task. To better understand this, consider the case where you are scheduled to take an exam at a predefined date (the Successor Task) – the predecessor task – Study can continue until the minute the exam starts, but then stops.

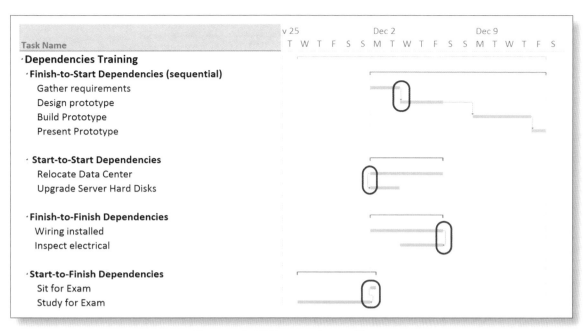

Figure 4.46 Dependency Types

Setting dependencies is straight forward, and like most things it can be done in several ways. While dependencies can be created in most views, we recommend using the '3-Dependencies' view as it has the 'Predecessor' and 'Successor' columns visible for easy validation of all dependencies. One of the most common methods is to use the 'Link Selected Tasks' icon from the 'Task ribbon > Schedule section'. Prior to selecting this icon, it is important that you have already selected the predecessor and successor tasks in the task list. The order of selecting tasks is critical as the first task selected is the predecessor and the subsequent task(s) become the successor(s). An alternative, once the tasks have been selected, you right click and select the 'Link Selected Tasks' from the mini-toolbar.

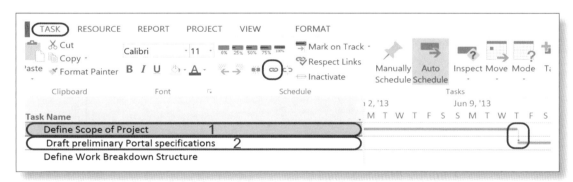

Figure 4.47 Creating Dependencies

When dependencies are created in this fashion, the default type of Finish-Start is applied. If you need to change the dependency type, double clicking on the dependency line in the 'Gantt Chart' will open the 'Task Dependency' dialog where you can then change the dependency type. Alternatively, you can double click on successor task to open the 'Task Information' dialog and use the 'Predecessor' tab to change the 'Dependency' type.

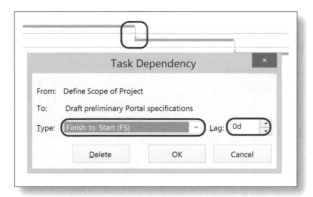

Figure 4.48 Task Dependency Dialog

CAUTION:

Do not use 'Drag and Drop' to set or modify dependencies. While Microsoft Project supports this, we have found that although this action does create and modify dependencies, it almost always creates unwanted constraints which must then be removed.

And a final method for creating and maintaining dependencies is to directly enter the appropriate task numbers directly into the predecessor and successor columns.

Figure 4.49 Predecessor and Successor Columns for Dependency maintenance

As discussed in the WBS section of this chapter, we highly recommend having milestones to record the completion of each deliverable and that the milestone would be the successor of the task paths required to complete the deliverable. This ensures that you have an effective way of tracking and managing the completion of each segment of your plan.

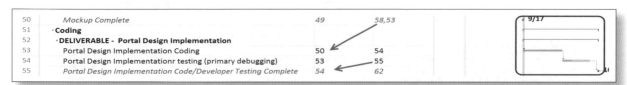

Figure 4.50 Each Deliverable should be kicked off
by the previous Deliverable Completion Milestone and conclude with a Milestone

BEST PRACTICE:

To facilitate creating a complete dependency network for your project, first create all the dependencies within a deliverable. Then link all the deliverable milestones to complete the phase milestone, and then finally link the phase milestones to complete the project milestone. Do not create dependencies on summary tasks as the milestone dependencies provide a much more effective way for managing the overall project schedule.

We have provided three highlights/filters to allow you to validate that your dependency diagram satisfies Proactive PPM standards as discussed earlier in this chapter. From the 'View ribbon > Data section' select the '2A – Dependencies on Summary Tasks', '2B – No Predecessors on Detailed Tasks/ Milestones', and '2C – No Successors on Detailed Tasks/Milestones' filters to help validate your adherence to the best practice described above.. The 2A filter should not return any tasks, the 2B filter should identify only the project start milestone and the 2C filter should identify only the project completion milestone. We find the '2C – No Successors on Detailed Tasks/Milestones' particularly effective for determining all the successors to the deliverable milestone as it quickly identifies the elements of the deliverable which are complete and therefore should be linked to the milestone.

Figure 4.51a Dependency Filter 2A -
Dependencies on Summary Tasks - should return no tasks

Figure 4.51b Dependency Filter 2B – No Predecessors on Detailed Tasks or
Milestones – should return only the Project Kickoff Milestone

Figure 4.51c Dependency Filter 2C - No Successors on Detailed Tasks of
Milestones - should return only the Project Completion Milestone

Running these filters only ensure compliance with the PPM standards, it does not validate that all the required project dependencies have been created. The only way to validate that all required dependencies have been created is a thorough and completed review of the project plan, preferable with subject matter experts.

'Dependencies' can also be fine-tuned to allow for gaps between tasks and overlaps between tasks (leads and lags). Consider an example where there is a 5 day delay between delivering a document and obtaining final acceptance. You can create a new task called 'Review and Accept Detailed Design Document' to cover these 5 days, but since this isn't a task you're managing or expecting time to be tracked against your project, this approach isn't ideal. Instead, we recommend creating a dependency with a 5 day lag between the completion of the document and the next project task. You would complete the dependency as described above, and then you would add the 5 day lag.

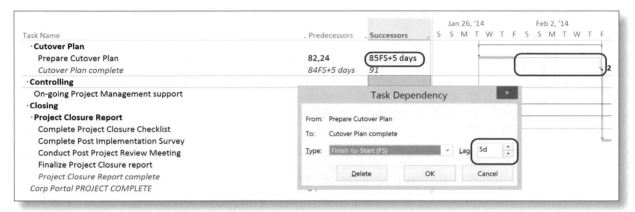

Figure 4.52 Task Dependency Dialog – Lag Time

Similarly, if you need to overlap tasks, for example, starting the preliminary testing prior to the completion of all the development activities, you would again define the dependency using the standard method, and then define the overlap (Lead or negative Lag). You can enter Lag (positive or negative) as specific timeframes (5 days) or as a percentage of the task (25% of the task duration).

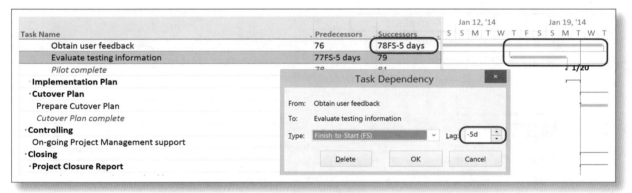

Figure 4.53a Task Dependency Dialog – Lead Time

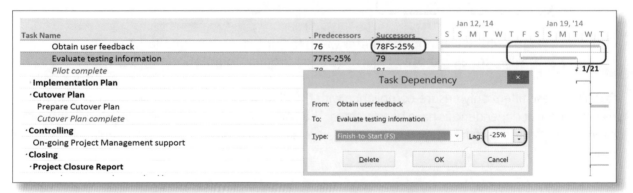

Figure 4.53b Task Dependency Dialog – Lead Time with Percentage

We highly recommend capturing the reasons for any detailed customization you do with dependencies in the 'Notes' field for the task. The reason being, a complex Finish-Start with a five day lead may make sense while you are developing the plan, but six months later when you're trying to modify the project schedule, the logic behind this dependency may not be as obvious. Double-clicking the task name will open the 'Task Information' dialog, select the 'Notes' tab and enter the reasoning for the dependency setup will greatly improve future comprehension.

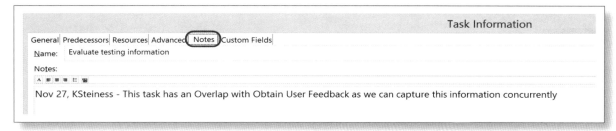

Figure 4.54 Add Notes to describe complex dependencies

TIPS & HINTS:

If you are experiencing an issue defining the dependency network for your project, consider starting at the end of the project and working upwards through the schedule. In order to complete the project, I need to complete these 2 deliverables, in order to complete this deliverable, I need to complete these 3 activities, etc.

WORK SESSION #7 – CREATE DEPENDENCIES:

OBJECTIVE

In this work session we will create the task dependencies required to develop the project schedule. Dependencies between project tasks are required to ensure the tasks are executed in the correct order.

STEP 1   Add task dependencies

Add the following dependencies to plan:

Make the first task in the scope deliverable dependent on the project start milestone

For the Scope Document deliverable:

Both the 'Build Work Breakdown Structure' and 'Document Project Assumptions' are Finish-Start dependent on 'Specify Delivery and Acceptance Criteria'.

The deliverable completion milestone is Finish-Start dependent on both the 'Build Work Breakdown Structure' and 'Document Project Assumptions'.

For the Procurement deliverable:

The first task on the Procurement deliverable should be dependent on the completion of the Scope deliverable

The first two tasks, 'Determine Procurement Requirements' and 'Define and Publish Subcontractor Scope' have a Finish-Start dependency.

The third task, 'Identify Potential Subcontractors', has a Finish-Start dependency on 'Publish Subcontractor Scope', but there is 7 day lag before it can start.

Create a Finish-Start dependency between 'Define and Publish Subcontractors Scope' and 'Identify Subcontractor Scope'.

Create a Start-Start dependency between the last 2 tasks, 'Identify Subcontractor Type' and 'Document Subcontractor Management Plan' with a lag of 2 days.

Create a Finish-Start dependency between 'Identify Subcontractor Scope', 'Identify Subcontractor Type' and 'Document Subcontractor Management Plan' and the deliverable completion milestone.

For the Risk Management Plan deliverable:

Create a serial Finish-Start dependency relationship where each task is dependent on the one immediately above it in the plan.

Create a Finish-Start dependency between the 'Project Start' milestone and the first task in the Risk Management Plan

STEP 2   Add milestone dependencies

Make the completion of the three deliverables all predecessors of the 'Planning Phase Complete' milestone

Make the 'Planning Complete' milestone a predecessor of the 'Project Complete' milestone

STEP 3   Validate dependencies

Validate that the dependency diagram is complete by running the following filters:

- '2a – Dependencies on summary tasks',
- '2b – No Predecessors on Detailed Tasks/Milestone' and
- '2c – No Successors on Detailed Tasks/Milestones'.

EXPECTED RESULTS

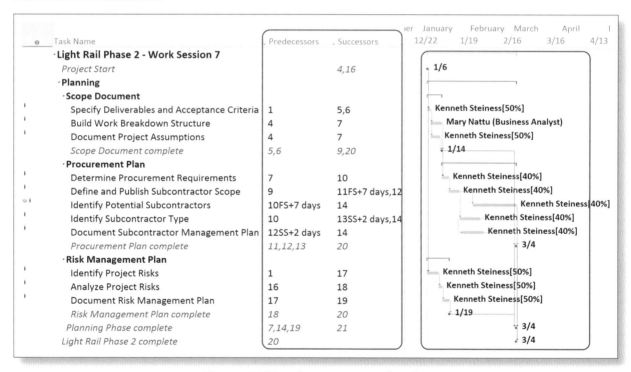

Figure WS.7 – Create Dependencies

4.8 Setting Deadlines and Constraints

Often, dates are given or set before a project is planned out fully or starts execution. Some of these dates are contractual in nature or set by executives or the client. We tend to think of these types of dates as 'commitment' dates, i.e. a stake in the ground. Other dates are based on a real 'restriction' to scheduling, such as delivery of materials, a scheduled training class with an external instructor or planned maintenance windows.

The key is to understand which dates are commitments and which ones are restrictions and apply the appropriate technique. As a principle, arbitrary commitment dates given to the project manager should never be entered as anything other than a deadline in Microsoft Project. Dates that carry restrictions, on the other hand, can often be entered as constraints.

You want to avoid constraints as much as possible and use deadlines instead to ensure a proactive schedule.

4.8.1 Deadlines

While most projects will have deadlines defined by management "this has to be done by the end of June", in a lot of instances, these are desired dates and often are negotiable. Recognizing this, deadlines provide a better alternative to setting constraints on your project. Unlike constraints which will impact the schedule and can create resource allocation issues, deadlines allow us to develop the best possible schedule based on the WBS, resources, estimates and dependencies while at the same time reporting on whether this schedule will achieve the deadline.

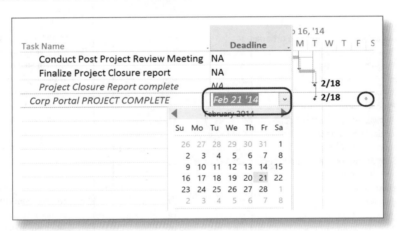

Figure 4.55 Setting the Deadline Date

Deadlines can be entered directly on View '4 – Deadlines and Constraints' or set using the 'Task Information > Advanced Tab' dialog (double click on the task name or from the shortcut menu). Once a deadline is set, an indicator is added to the Gantt Display providing a visual clue as to whether the current schedule will meet the deadline.

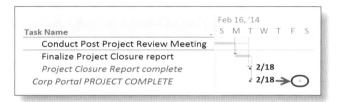

Figure 4.56 Deadline Icon in the Gantt Chart

If the deadline date will be met, we have nothing more to do. But if the deadline will not be met, Microsoft Project will create an alert in the Indicator column to let us know we have a problem and then we can work on the schedule to adjust the resourcing, dependencies, etc. to change the schedule and bring the project back on track.

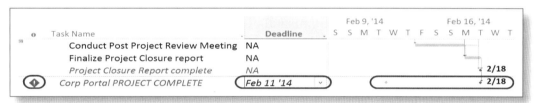

Figure 4.57 Missed Deadline Indicator

4.8.2 Constraints

Microsoft Project provides the ability to directly control the project schedule through setting specific constraint dates to control when a task starts or finishes. While you can set both soft constraints (Start/ Finish No Earlier or Later Than) and hard constraints (Must Finish/Start On), we recommend not using constraints of any type, leaving this field to the default 'As Soon As Possible', except when you have a restriction to your scheduling.

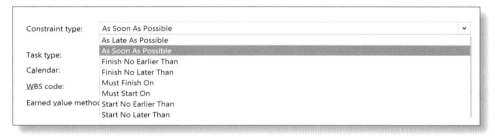

Figure 4.58 Task Constraint Types

Setting constraints effectively limits Microsoft Project's ability to manage the schedule as it is constrained by these dates and as a result may over or under-allocate the resources to satisfy the required dates are met.

We do acknowledge that there will be some tasks where a constraint absolutely makes sense, such as 'Deliver Project Overview to Annual Stakeholders Meeting' where a 'Must Start On' is appropriate, but strongly recommend you limit the use of constraints and instead use deadlines (as discussed above) for tasks where a specific deadline is important.

Constraints can be set using the '4 – Deadlines and Constraints' view or from the 'Task Information Advanced Tab' dialog. First select the appropriate task, and then select the required 'Constraint Type and Date'. Project will put an icon in the Indicator column to indicate that a constraint has been added to the task.

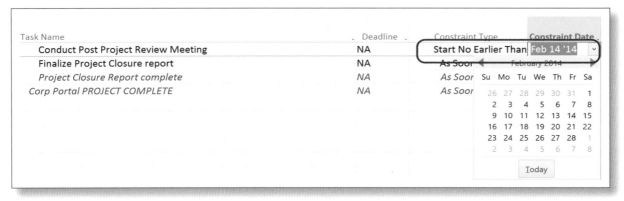

Figure 4.59 Setting Constraints – 04 Deadlines and Constraints View

In order to assist in validating that any constraints in your project are appropriate we have created a filter '3A – Constraints' to allow you to specifically review all tasks in your plan that have a constraint and confirm that the constraint is valid.

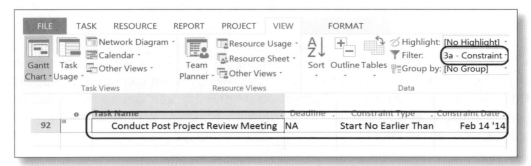

Figure 4.60 Constraint Filter 3A - Constraints -
Validate all Tasks with Constraints are appropriate

Setting constraint dates using other methods such as directly changing the start or finish date or dragging and dropping Gantt Chart bars should be avoided as these methods do not allow you to define the 'Constraint Type' field.

Contrast the difference – with Constraints, Microsoft Project will ensure the constraint is met by moving dates forward, while with deadlines we have the entire feature set of the scheduling engine available to adjust the project and find the best way to meet the deadline.

When a deadline is not going to be met, Microsoft Project will help you determine where you can adjust the schedule by identifying 'Slack' (add the Slack column to your view) based on the deadline (as opposed to the calculated end date). Then, using the standard project management principles for managing and reducing the Critical Path, the project can be adjusted to meet the deadline. Or, once all possible actions are taken, and the deadline still cannot be achieved, you are armed with the facts to negotiate with management to have the deadline moved.

Task Name	Finish Slack
· Closing	**-4.5 days**
· Project Closure Report	**-4.5 days**
Complete Project Closure Checklist	9.13 days
Complete Post Implementation Survey	2.88 days
Conduct Post Project Review Meeting	-4.5 days
Finalize Project Closure report	-4.5 days
Project Closure Report complete	*-4.5 days*
Corp Portal PROJECT COMPLETE	*-4.5 days*

Figure 4.61 Slack indicates
which tasks are on the Critical Path

WORK SESSION #8 – SET DEADLINES AND CONSTRAINTS:

OBJECTIVE

This work session concludes the development of the baseline schedule and consists of setting the required deadline and constraints on the project to satisfy the stated business and organizational milestones.

STEP 1 — Add deadlines

Add deadline to 'Light Rail Phase 2 complete' milestone and set it to Friday, 6 weeks after the project start date (Feb 13, 2015)

STEP 2 — Add Constraint

Add Start No Earlier Than constraint to 'Identify Potential Subcontractors' task and set it to Tuesday, 3 weeks after the project start date (January 20, 2015).

EXPECTED RESULTS

	Task Name	Deadline	Constraint Type	Constraint Date
	Light Rail Phase 2 - Work Session 8	**NA**	**As Soon As Possible**	**NA**
	Project Start	*NA*	*As Soon As Possible*	*NA*
	Planning	**NA**	**As Soon As Possible**	**NA**
	Scope Document	**NA**	**As Soon As Possible**	**NA**
	Specify Deliverables and Acceptance Criteria	NA	As Soon As Possible	NA
	Build Work Breakdown Structure	NA	As Soon As Possible	NA
	Document Project Assumptions	NA	As Soon As Possible	NA
	Scope Document complete	*NA*	*As Soon As Possible*	*NA*
	Procurement Plan	**NA**	**As Soon As Possible**	**NA**
	Determine Procurement Requirements	NA	As Soon As Possible	NA
	Define and Publish Subcontractor Scope	NA	As Soon As Possible	NA
	Identify Potential Subcontractors	NA	Start No Earlier Than	Jan 20
	Identify Subcontractor Type	NA	As Soon As Possible	NA
	Document Subcontractor Management Plan	NA	As Soon As Possible	NA
	Procurement Plan complete	*NA*	*As Soon As Possible*	*NA*
	Risk Management Plan	**NA**	**As Soon As Possible**	**NA**
	Identify Project Risks	NA	As Soon As Possible	NA
	Analyze Project Risks	NA	As Soon As Possible	NA
	Document Risk Management Plan	NA	As Soon As Possible	NA
	Risk Management Plan complete	*NA*	*As Soon As Possible*	*NA*
	Planning Phase complete	*NA*	*As Soon As Possible*	*NA*
	Light Rail Phase 2 complete	Feb 13	*As Soon As Possible*	*NA*

Figure WS.8 Set Deadlines and Constraints

4.9 Level Resource Workload

Resource Leveling in Microsoft Project is probably one of the most misunderstood features available, yet it is one of the most important tools in the proactive project manager's tool kit. We will provide a very comprehensive review of resource leveling in this section to help you get over any concerns you may have about it, and to hopefully convince you that it really does help develop a very effective project schedule (that doesn't burn out your team from over-allocation).

4.9.1 Pre-requisites to resource leveling

Before using the automated feature, you will need to ensure that each resource has the appropriate project allocation set and that there are no manual over-allocations.

EXCEPTION:

   The automated resource leveling will NOT adjust tasks where the resource assignment is above Max Units nor will it change assignment level to resolve over-allocations.

Using the 'A – Resource Usage' view, you will be able to adjust the project allocation, check for manual over-allocations and view the peak assignments for resources:

- **'Max Units'** is assigned at the resource level and is reset each time the plan is loaded from the enterprise database. Therefore, if your project resource allocation is less than the enterprise resource load, this field needs to be adjusted to the appropriate project allocation each time you are working with resource leveling.
- **'Assignment Units'** is set for each task assignment. This value is set by you when resources are assigned to a task (as discussed in Assigning Resource above). This field can NOT be changed by the leveling process, so it is important to ensure the no individual assignment is greater than the max units the resource has for this project. Adjust these manually, as needed, if they do exceed max units.
- **'Peak'** for each resource is calculated as a rollup of all the overlapping assignments. When the peak is greater than max units, the resource will need to be leveled or assignments moved to other resources.

If adjusting max units and assignment units still leaves you with over-allocations, it is time to use the automated resource leveling functionality.

4.9.2 Resource Leveling Options

At its most simplistic form, resource leveling ensures that the project's resource demand does not exceed the resource availability. And when it does find an instance where the demand is greater than availability, it will attempt to correct the over-allocation primarily by changing the schedule to move tasks to a date when there is available resource capacity.

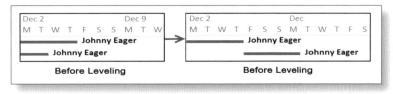

Figure 4.62 Resource Leveling

Before leveling, Johnny was over-allocated on Monday and Tuesday and scheduled to work 16 hours on each of these 2 days. The leveling process moved the second task forward to the next week when Johnny has capacity to complete the task.

While this example is based on full-time allocation of 8 hours a day, the same principles apply for any level of allocation (max units), it's just that the number of hours available for allocation are reduced accordingly. It is our job as project managers to ensure that we develop project schedules that support each team member's allocation. Specifically, if enterprise resource management tells us that a resource is available to a project 40% of the time, we must ensure that the resource allocation doesn't exceed 16 hours a week (40% of 40 hours). Enterprise resource managers are responsible for ensuring that the overall allocation of the resource across multiple projects does not exceed 40 hours, not the project manager – a subject that is outside the scope of this book.

TIPS & HINTS:

Before leveling resources, remember that 'Load summary resource assignments' on the login screen should be deselected. Otherwise, you will be competing with other schedules for resources and your dates will likely be pushed out as a result. If you want to level resources across multiple projects, simply open all the projects you want to work with and then perform resource leveling.

While it is definitely easy to spot Johnny's over allocation in the simplistic example above, it's not so straight forward in a real project plan with hundreds of tasks and dozens of resources. This is where the automated resource leveling functionality shines and can help us recognize issues even in very large schedules.

Figure 4.63 Resource Overallocation

In any resource view, over-allocated resources can be identified by the warning icon in the 'Indicator Column' as well as the resource name listed in red.

The 'Resource Graph' view also provides a good overview of where resources are over-allocated and by how much.

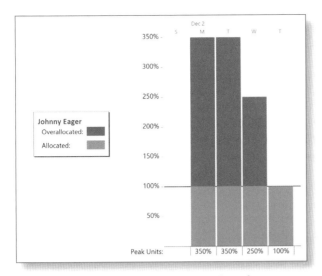

Figure 4.64a Resource Graph

Figure 4.64b Resource Usage

The 'Resource Usage' view will highlight not only the resource itself, but also any specific assignments on the days they are over-allocated (or the summary allocation, as is the case here).

While typically, resource leveling will create a very effective schedule, there will be instances where it doesn't give you the exact results you want, specifically when there are multiple independent tasks assigned to the same individual but the order of the schedule developed by Microsoft Project is different than desired. For example, you have 2 tasks assigned to Johnny, one to 'Develop Training Materials' and the other to 'Develop Operational Documentation', and resource leveling schedules the Operational Documentation first, but we would prefer that the Training Materials is completed first. While we could accomplish this using Dependencies, it is not recommended as this would introduce an artificial dependency based on Johnny's availability, something we want to avoid as a future resource changes (getting Betty to do the documentation, for example) would still be impacted by this artificial dependency. Instead, we recommend setting the 'Priority' on the task higher than the default 500 to achieve the desired results. We enter the 'Priority' from the 'Task Information' dialog. With the 'Priority' set, the tasks will be rescheduled as desired the next time we level the resources.

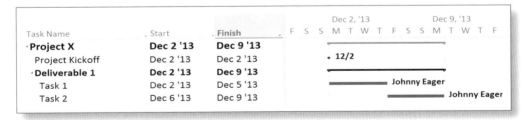

Figure 4.65a Schedule After Leveling

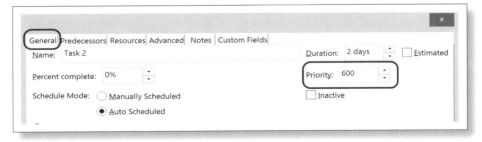

Figure 4.65b Task Priority

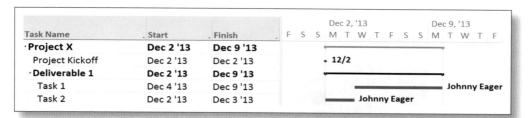

Figure 4.65c Schedule After Priority and Leveling

From the 'Resource ribbon > Level section', there are a number of options related to leveling. We start with 'Leveling Options', which brings up the 'Resource Leveling' dialog.

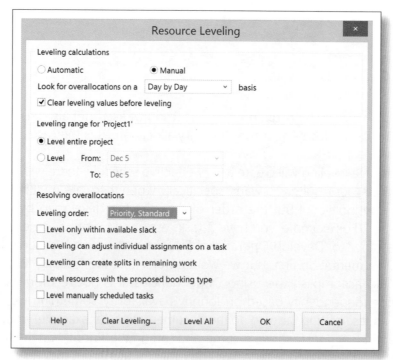

Figure 4.66 Figure 4.66 Resource Leveling Dialog

We recommend always using 'Manual' calculations. Otherwise, resource leveling would run each time the schedule is changed.

'Look for over allocations on a day by day basis' will highlight where resources are working more than their daily maximum and level accordingly. 'Week by Week' will highlight where resources are working more than their weekly maximum, which could be problematic, if 40 hours of work is scheduled on Monday (then it might not recognize a problem).

'Level entire project' will level all tasks regardless of date range, which is typically what we are looking for.

As discussed above, there will be instances where we will want to set priorities, so the Leveling Order should be set to 'Priority, Standard'. During the planning process, we recommend unselecting all the remaining checkboxes as that provides the most flexibility when leveling resources and the most realistic schedule. This may change the project's end date as it ensures that no resources are working greater than their assigned max units.

To demonstrate resource leveling, we deviate from the project plan used so far and will use the Resource Leveling file which you can access from the download area.

With new plan downloaded and the '06 – Leveling Gantt' view selected (this view is particularly effective for validating the results of leveling as the changes made by leveling are clearly visible in the Gantt area), from the 'Resource ribbon > Leveling section', select 'Level All'.

Figure 4.67a Project Schedule prior to leveling

Figure 4.67b Project Schedule after Leveling Pass 1

As shown on the screenshots above, Microsoft Project has addressed the resource over allocation on Johnny, but in doing so, has moved the project end date. We will review these results in considerable detail as it is important that you understand how this works to develop trust in this feature.

First, notice the amount of 'Change Highlighting' visible, all but Tasks 2, 3 and 4 were impacted by leveling. The most significant change made was rescheduling Task 1 to a future date where Johnny has availability. As a result of this change (to Task 1), the project overall schedule was also impacted as all successor tasks to Task 1 had to also be rescheduled – which ended up moving the project end date by 1 day. If this change to the end date is acceptable, we declare leveling a success as all resources are scheduled to work within the assigned max units. If, however as it is in most instances, the end date is not movable, we explore some of the levelling options we turned off on our initial leveling pass – most specifically the first option in the third section – 'Level only within available slack'.

By selecting this option, we're effectively telling Microsoft Project that the finish date is not movable, and that leveling should only make use of available slack in non-critical path tasks.

Before we do this, we must 'Clear Leveling' taking the project back to the original state where Johnny is over allocated on Tasks 1 and 2. Next, we select the 'Level only within available slack' checkbox, save the changes and then 'Level All' again. You may get a pop-up message informing you that Microsoft Project cannot resolve all resource over-allocations. As this is expected, you should 'Skip All' and allow leveling to complete. This time the results are in-between the original and the previous attempt. Task

1 is still rescheduled, but not as significantly which resolves some of the over allocation on Johnny, but not all, and, most importantly, the finish date was not changed. Better, but not perfect.

Figure 4.68a Leveling Informational Message

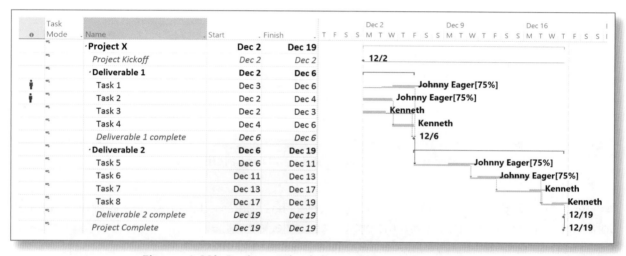

Figure 4.68b Project Scheduling after Leveling Pass 2

Continuing to explore the next 2 leveling options:

- 'Leveling can adjust individual assignments on a task' – this option defines that on tasks with more than one assigned resource, the individual assignments can be changed between resources (while preserving the total task effort estimate). Since we don't have any tasks with multiple resources, in this specific example, there would be no change, but this option could have a significant improvement on projects where this situation exists.
- 'Leveling can create splits in remaining work' would allow project to split tasks to reschedule tasks, again with the goal of reducing resource over allocation. In our example, this option would not reduce the remaining over allocation for Johnny – but on your projects, again, it could have different results. If you have tasks where the assignments can be done independent of each other, you may want to consider creating separate tasks to support maximum scheduling flexibility.
- 'Level Resources with the proposed booking type' would also perform resource leveling for those resources that are not yet 'committed'.

- 'Level manually scheduled tasks' will have no impact on a Proactive Project Schedule as we do not recommend using 'Manually Scheduled Tasks'.

Back to our example, since we have exhausted all the automated leveling options, we have the option of accepting the reduced over-allocation and asking Johnny to work overtime for the one remaining day or to review the estimates, resource assignments or task dependencies to remove the over allocation and preserve the end date. Resource leveling can do a lot for us but as we have seen, there will be instances where, given the project plan we have created, that over-allocations cannot be fully resolved by the automated feature.

EXCEPTION:

While the resource max units will be reset to the enterprise resource level every time you load the plan into Microsoft Project, typically you do not need to change this each time the project is loaded as the assignment units are preserved and in most instances, this is adequate for weekly tracking and status updates (to be discussed in Chapter 6 and 7). However, you will need to reset it every time you are doing a significant replan and resource level to ensure that both the assignment within tasks (assignment units) and between tasks (max units) do not create any resource over allocations.

WORK SESSION #9 – RESOURCE WORKLOAD LEVELING

OBJECTIVE

This work session is focused on ensuring that the resources assigned to the project are being effectively utilized up to their assigned levels. The process of developing the schedule in the previous work sessions will often result in resource over and underutilization. This work session will resolve these and develop a project schedule that honors each resource's allocation to the project.

STEP 1   Set Max Units

Set max units for yourself at 80% and set the max units for the person assigned to the 'Procurement Specialist' tasks and the person assigned to the Business Analyst tasks to 40%

STEP 2   Validate Assignment Units

Validate and correct any instances where any resources are assigned to a task where the Assignment Units is greater than that resource's max units (Hint, there should be one instance of this for the assignment to the 'Build Work Breakdown Structure' task)

STEP 3   Validate Peak Assignment

Validate and correct any instances where any resources' peak assignment exceeds their max units (Hint, there are none of these in this example, but completing this step is critical as this may occur on your projects).

STEP 4   Resolve over-allocations

Correct the over-allocation of yourself on all assigned tasks that are being executed in parallel to be 40%. This is needed as a result of changing your project allocation from an unrealistic 100% to a more realistic 80% - as a result individual parallel task assignments need to change from 50 to 40%

STEP 5   Level Resources

Level the project by setting the leveling options to be Day-by Day and unselect all checkboxes in the 'Resolving over allocations' section and validate the results using '06 – Leveling Gantt' and 'A – Resource Usage'. Result - Task 13 'Develop Subcontractor Management Plan' should be moved to resolve the resource over allocations

Figure WS.9a – Set Resource Project Allocation

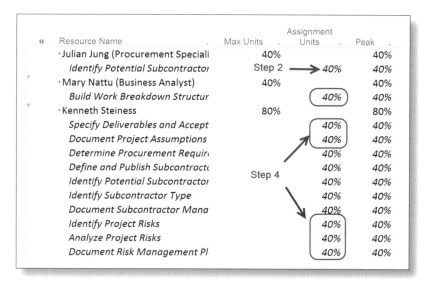

Figure WS.9b – Resource Assignment Units

Task Mode	Task Name	Work	Duration	Start	Finish
	Light Rail Phase 2 - Work Session 9	**320 hrs**	**49.5 days**	**Jan 6**	**Mar 16**
	Project Start	*0 hrs*	*0 days*	*Jan 6*	*Jan 6*
	Planning	**320 hrs**	**49.5 days**	**Jan 6**	**Mar 16**
	Scope Document	**64 hrs**	**15 days**	**Jan 6**	**Jan 26**
	Specify Deliverables and Acceptance Criteria	8 hrs	2.5 days	Jan 6	Jan 8
	Build Work Breakdown Structure	40 hrs	12.5 days	Jan 8	Jan 26
	Document Project Assumptions	16 hrs	5 days	Jan 8	Jan 15
	Scope Document complete	*0 hrs*	*0 days*	*Jan 26*	*Jan 26*
	Procurement Plan	**216 hrs**	**34.5 days**	**Jan 27**	**Mar 16**
	Determine Procurement Requirements	8 hrs	2.5 days	Jan 27	Jan 29
	Define and Publish Subcontractor Scope	16 hrs	5 days	Jan 29	Feb 5
	Identify Potential Subcontractors	128 hrs	1 mon	Feb 16	Mar 16
	Identify Subcontractor Type	32 hrs	10 days	Feb 5	Feb 19
	Document Subcontractor Management Plan	32 hrs	10 days	Feb 19	Mar 5
	Procurement Plan complete	*0 hrs*	*0 days*	*Mar 16*	*Mar 16*
	Risk Management Plan	**40 hrs**	**12.5 days**	**Jan 6**	**Jan 22**
	Identify Project Risks	20 hrs	6.25 days	Jan 6	Jan 14
	Analyze Project Risks	10 hrs	3.13 days	Jan 14	Jan 19
	Document Risk Management Plan	10 hrs	3.13 days	Jan 19	Jan 22
	Risk Management Plan complete	*0 hrs*	*0 days*	*Jan 22*	*Jan 22*
	Planning Phase complete	*0 hrs*	*0 days*	*Mar 16*	*Mar 16*
	Light Rail Phase 2 complete	*0 hrs*	*0 days*	*Mar 16*	*Mar 16*

Figure WS.9c – Fully Leveled Schedule

4.10 Budgeting and Cost Planning

Microsoft Project supports project level budgets as well as detailed cost planning at a task level. The budget number is a high level amount that is frequently given to the project manager prior to detailed cost planning (although the ideal situation is the reverse) and the cost details are managed at the task level.

4.10.1 Budgeting

The budget for project might be a single number for the overall project budget or it could be broken down to a more granular level of software budget, hardware budget, travel budget, internal labor and external labor or other categories your organization may have defined.

Microsoft Project supports this using a resource defined as a 'Budget Resource'. To create a budget resource, using the 'B – Resource Sheet' view, create the new resource by entering the name and assign it a type of 'Cost, then using the 'Resource Information' dialog (which is launched by double clicking on the resource or right mouse clicking in the resource and selecting 'Information' from the 'Context Menu') select the 'Budget' checkbox to set the resource as a 'Budget Resource'.

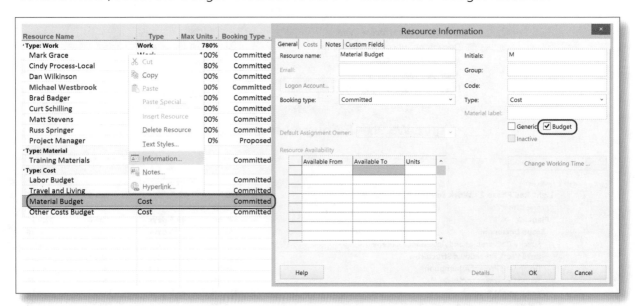

Figure 4.69 Define Budget Resources

Budget resources are special resources and can only be assigned to the 'Project Summary Task' and are meant to record the project budget (as sub-sets of the original 'Project Summary Task'). These budget resources are assigned to the 'Project Summary Task' the same way other resources are assigned to non-summary tasks – using the 'Assign Resources' dialog.

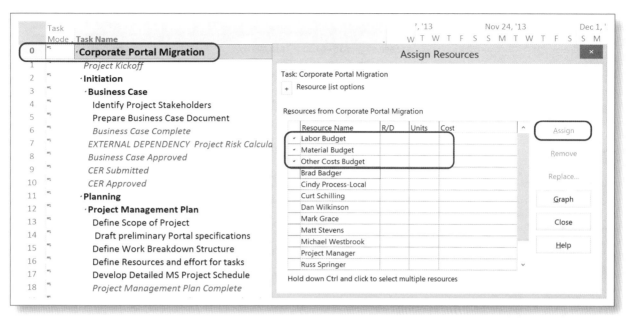

Figure 4.70 Assign Budget Resources to the Project Summary Task

The final step is to allocate the budget costs to each assigned budget resource. Using the '02 – Budgeting and Cost Planning' view, enter the budget amounts into the 'Budget Cost' column. The costs will be evenly spread over the project duration, but you can manually adjust the costs per time period if the costs should be distributed differently.

Figure 4.71 Allocate Budget Costs to Budget Resources

4.10.2 Cost Planning

On many projects, the most significant cost component is the resources assigned. The costs for resources is automatically calculated based on the resource rates and the number of work hours planned for each.

Using view '09 – Cost Tracking', resource costs (work resources) can be viewed.

Task Name	Actual Cost	Baseline Cost	Total Cost	Remaining Cost	Cost Variance	Details	4th Quarter Oct
Definition	$12,600.00	$12,600.00	$12,600.00	$0.00	$0.00	Cost	
						Act. Cost	
Design	$26,800.00	$26,800.00	$26,800.00	$0.00	$0.00	Cost	
						Act. Cost	
Design Document	$14,800.00	$14,800.00	$14,800.00	$0.00	$0.00	Cost	
						Act. Cost	
Design Mockup	$12,000.00	$12,000.00	$12,000.00	$0.00	$0.00	Cost	
						Act. Cost	
Coding	$17,013.34	$22,400.00	$22,400.00	$5,386.66	$0.00	Cost	$10,506.67
						Act. Cost	$5,120.00
DELIVERABLE - Portal Design Implemer	$17,013.34	$22,400.00	$22,400.00	$5,386.66	$0.00	Cost	$10,506.67
						Act. Cost	$5,120.00
Portal Design Implementation Coding	$12,800.00	$12,800.00	$12,800.00	$0.00	$0.00	Cost	$906.67
						Act. Cost	$906.67
Brad Badger	$6,400.00	$6,400.00	$6,400.00	$0.00	$0.00	Cost	$453.33
						Act. Cost	$453.33
Curt Schilling	$6,400.00	$6,400.00	$6,400.00	$0.00	$0.00	Cost	$453.33
						Act. Cost	$453.33
Portal Design Implementationr testing (	$4,213.34	$9,600.00	$9,600.00	$5,386.66	$0.00	Cost	$9,600.00
						Act. Cost	$4,213.33
Brad Badger	$2,106.67	$4,800.00	$4,800.00	$2,693.33	$0.00	Cost	$4,800.00
						Act. Cost	$2,106.67
Curt Schilling	$2,106.67	$4,800.00	$4,800.00	$2,693.33	$0.00	Cost	$4,800.00
						Act. Cost	$2,106.67

Figure 4.72 Resource Cost Planning

In addition to the costs for these work resources, there are two other ways to allocate costs to project tasks in the form of material resources and cost resources. These are added to your schedule using the same processes defined in the Build Team section of this Chapter where we added the work resources.

If your enterprise resource pool contains material and cost resources, you would select and assign them to your project the same as we allocated the team in the above sections Defining the Team and Assigning Resources. If, however, your enterprise resource pool only contains work resources, you can assign material and cost resources as local resources. From the 'B – Resource Sheet' view, enter the appropriate resource name and select 'Material' or 'Cost' as the 'Resource Type' following the same process defined above for local resources.

TIPS & HINTS:
Differences in Resource Types

Work resources (the default) have finite availability as defined by the resource calendar. A human is the traditional work resource and has 40 hours per week available to complete the work assignments on tasks. Machinery and equipment are also typically managed as work resources as they also have finite availability and can be managed by calendars.

Material resources have an infinite availability based on the assumption that the required material can be purchased to satisfy task requirements. Material resources has a unit charge associated with them and are consumed as tasks are completed, for example a task to build the wall of a house would consume 2X4 Lumber as the walls are constructed. The consumption of these materials allocates the cost of the material to the task.

Cost resources provide the ability to allocate other costs to a task. Costs resources are not automatically allocated as the task is completed and must have actual costs incurred entered during delivery – more on this in Chapter 6 – Processing Updates and Taking Corrective Action.

When you create a material resource you define both the 'Material Label' and the unit charge for the material in the 'Standard Rate' column (the same field used to define the resource rates). Cost resources do not require either of these as part of resource definition as this information is set when the cost resource is assigned to a task.

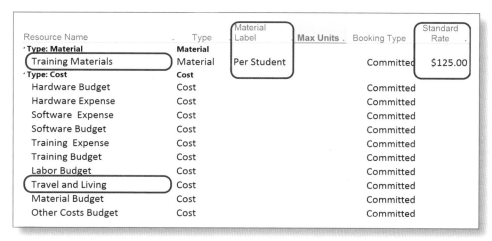

Figure 4.73 Define Material and Cost Resources

Both material and cost resources are assigned to tasks in the same way that work resources are assigned, from the 'Resource ribbon > Assignment section > Assign Resources' button to launch the 'Assign Resources' dialog. When material resources are assigned, you define how many units of the material the task will require and for cost resources you directly define the costs to be allocated to the task.

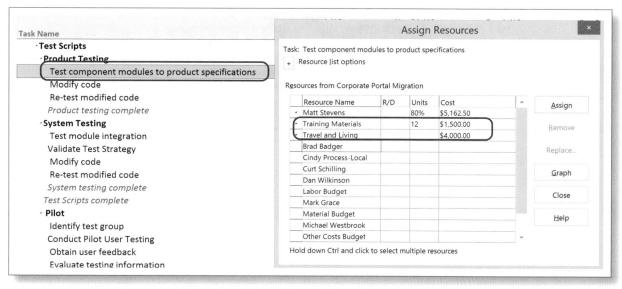

Figure 4.74 Assign Material and Cost Resources to the Plan

All task costs, work, material and cost, are managed within the plan and summarized at the task, summary and project summary.

Task Name	Budget Cost	Cost	Details	Oct	Qtr 4 Nov	Dec
Corporate Portal Migration	$250,953.00	$248,170.00	Cost	$12,806.67	$9,062.50	$27,860.00
Labor Budget	$243,453.00		Cost			
Material Budget	$5,000.00		Cost			
Other Costs Budget	$2,500.00		Cost			
Project Kickoff		$0.00	Cost			
Initiation		$5,737.50	Cost			
Planning		$32,200.00	Cost			
Execution		$130,382.50	Cost	$10,506.67	$7,062.50	$13,960.00
Formal Project Kickoff		$9,500.00	Cost			
Development Lifecycle		$119,082.50	Cost	$10,506.67	$7,062.50	$13,960.00
Requirements		$21,200.00	Cost			
Definition		$12,600.00	Cost			
Design		$26,800.00	Cost			
Coding		$22,400.00	Cost	$10,506.67		
Testing		$36,082.50	Cost		$7,062.50	$13,960.00
Test Plan		$9,000.00	Cost			
Test Scripts		$27,082.50	Cost		$7,062.50	$13,960.00
Product Testing		$12,062.50	Cost		$7,062.50	$5,000.00
Test component modules to product specifications		$10,662.50	Cost		$7,062.50	$3,600.00
Matt Stevens		$5,162.50	Cost		$1,562.50	$3,600.00
Training Materials		$1,500.00	Cost		$1,500.00	
Travel and Living		$4,000.00	Cost		$4,000.00	$0.00

Figure 4.75 Project Costs are maintained at Summary and Project levels

To facilitate effective management of both budget and costs during project execution, it is important to set the 'Cost Type' custom field on all project resources. From the 'B – Resource Sheet' view ensure that the cost type field is set appropriately for each resource as this will be used to align the costs to each budget resource.

Resource Name	Type	Max Units	Booking Type	Cost Type
Type: Work	Work	780%		
Mark Grace	Work	100%	Committed	Labor
Cindy Process-Local	Work	80%	Committed	Labor
Dan Wilkinson	Work	100%	Committed	Labor
Michael Westbrook	Work	100%	Committed	Labor
Brad Badger	Work	100%	Committed	Labor
Curt Schilling	Work	100%	Committed	Labor
Matt Stevens	Work	100%	Committed	Labor
Russ Springer	Work	100%	Committed	Labor
Project Manager	Work	0%	Proposed	Labor
Type: Material	Material			
Training Materials	Material		Committed	Labor
Type: Cost	Cost			
Labor Budget	Cost		Committed	Labor
Travel and Living	Cost		Committed	Fees and Permits
Material Budget	Cost		Committed	Hardware
Other Costs Budget	Cost		Committed	Labor
				Software
				Training
				Travel

Figure 4.76 Ensure Cost Type is assigned to all Resources

Using 'C – Cost Type' view, which is grouped on 'Cost Type' the budget and cost elements of the plan can be reviewed and validated.

Resource Name	Budget Cost	Cost	Details	Nov	Dec
Hardware	**$275,000.00**	**$360,000.00**	Budget Cost		
			Act. Cost		
Hardware Budget	$275,000.00		Budget Cost	$22,648.31	$23,780.72
			Act. Cost		
Hardware Expense		$360,000.00	Budget Cost		
			Act. Cost		
Labor	**$243,453.00**		Budget Cost	$23,103.49	$24,258.66
			Act. Cost		
Labor Budget	$243,453.00		Budget Cost	$23,103.49	$24,258.66
			Act. Cost		
Software	**$50,000.00**	**$75,000.00**	Budget Cost		
			Act. Cost		
Software Expense		$75,000.00	Budget Cost		
			Act. Cost		
Software Budget	$50,000.00		Budget Cost	$4,117.87	$4,323.77
			Act. Cost		
Training	**$107,500.00**	**$105,000.00**	Budget Cost		
			Act. Cost		
Training Expense		$105,000.00	Budget Cost		
			Act. Cost		
Training Budget	$100,000.00		Budget Cost	$8,235.75	$8,647.54
			Act. Cost		
Material Budget	$5,000.00		Budget Cost	$474.50	$498.22
			Act. Cost		
Other Costs Budget	$2,500.00		Budget Cost	$237.25	$249.11

Figure 4.77 Review and Validate Cost and Budget components of the Project

EXCEPTION:

If your organization does not already have a custom field defined for cost type, you can create one by right mouse clicking on any column heading to active the 'Context Menu' and selecting 'Custom Fields'. On the 'Custom Fields' dialog, ensure that the 'Resource' button is selected and then select an available text field and rename it 'Cost Type'. We would also recommend setting 'Custom Attribute – Lookup Table' to ensure that the field can contain only the defined budget types. Finally, select the 'Roll Down unless manually entered' radio button in the 'Calculation for assignment rows' section.

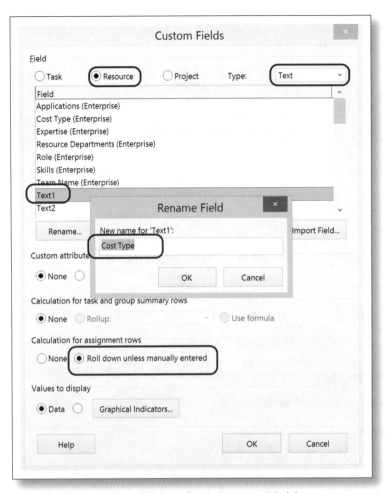

Figure 4.78a Define Custom Field

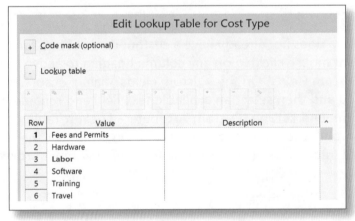

Figure 4.78b Create an Edit Lookup
Table for Cost Type

WORK SESSION #10 – CREATING THE PROJECT BUDGET

OBJECTIVE

The final step to developing the baseline schedule is to ensure that all project costs are included and that the project budget reflects the full project costs. This work session will add Budget Resources to the project to support project budget management.

STEP 1   Add Cost Resources to track non-resource costs

Add a Cost Resource to your plan for Training costs (or use an Enterprise Cost Resource if one exists) and assign this resource to the 'Build Work Breakdown Structure' task with a cost of $5000 to cover initial vendor training.

STEP 2   Add Budget Resources for the Project Budget

Add a 'Budget Resource' for Labor and Training and assign them to the 'Project Summary Task'. These Budget Resources will be used to record the Project Budget for each budget line, Labor and Training.

STEP 3   Set Cost Type

Set the 'Cost Type' for all Work Resources to Labor and set it to Training for the Training Cost.

STEP 4   Create Project Budget

Determine the Project Budget from the total of the Labor Costs and Training costs using View C – Cost Type. Use these values to set the 'Budget Cost' for the 'Budget Resources'.

EXPECTED RESULTS

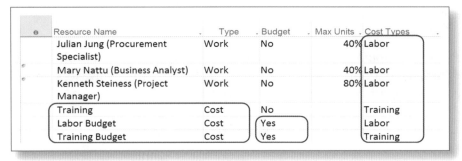

Figure WS.10a – Create Budget/Cost Resources

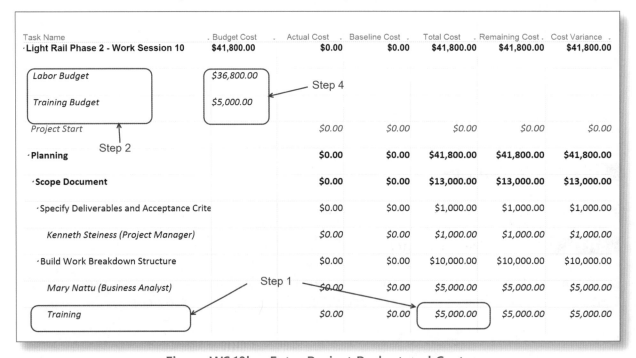

Figure WS.10b – Enter Project Budget and Costs

4.11 Setting the Project Baseline

Once you have the complete WBS built out, assigned resources, entered the effort estimates, built your dependency network, added your deadlines and constraints and created the project budget, it is time to set the project baseline. The baseline reflects the schedule agreed upon at the start of the project as well as any approved changes along the way. It is also a powerful tool to help identify variances since progress on tasks are measured against the baseline to identify 'Finish Variance', 'Work Variance', 'Cost Variance', etc.

Think of the baseline feature in Microsoft Project as an old-fashioned Polaroid camera, where you take a snapshot of a point in time and you instantly have a picture of what things looked like on a certain date. You can then hold that picture up against your current schedule to see if and how things are different. Baselining and variance reporting is also what allows for more visual reporting, such as 'traffic light' indicators.

By following a few simple best practices, the baseline feature can be a tremendous help to any project manager and provide a heads-up on variances where we need to take corrective actions to avoid delays or cost overruns.

4.11.1 Setting the Original Baseline

The original baseline represents the schedule as it was first approved, before project execution starts. Typically, this is the only time we save the baseline for the entire project. After this point, we should avoid re-baselining since that would overwrite the actuals-to-date, but rather add to or maintain the baseline. To set the original baseline, from the 'Project ribbon > Schedule section', select 'Set Baseline' and then 'Set Baseline' to launch the 'Set Baseline' dialog.

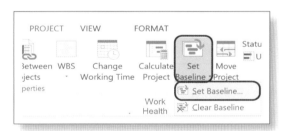

Figure 4.79 Set the Baseline

Select the 'Set Baseline' and 'Entire Project' radio buttons.

Figure 4.80 Set the Baseline
for the Entire Project

You now have the baseline set with a complete copy of the 'Budget Cost', 'Budget Work', 'Cost', 'Deliverable Finish', 'Deliverable Start', 'Duration', 'Finish', 'Start' and 'Work' values. In other words, everything you would want to report against throughout the project. In the screenshot below, you will notice that the 'Work' and 'Finish' values have been copied into their respective baseline fields and the Tracking Gantt shows the baseline underneath the current schedule bars.

Figure 4.81 07 - Baselining View

Note: *If you are doing rolling wave planning, you can use the 'Selected tasks' option to add one phase of the project schedule at a time to the baseline. In this case, you would use the same principle of Maintaining the Baseline as defined in Chapter 6 to add phases after the detailed scope has been defined and scheduled.*

4.11.2 Saving a History of Baselines

Since the baseline can change throughout the project, it is important to save a history each time the baseline is updated. This helps us revert back, if necessary, and allows for comparison between baselines. To save the original baseline, from the 'Project ribbon > Schedule section', select 'Set Baseline' and then 'Set Baseline' to launch the 'Set Baseline' dialog, the same as you just did for setting the original baseline. But this time on the 'Set Baseline' dialog, select the 'Set interim plan' and copy 'Baseline' into 'Baseline10'

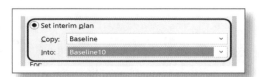

Figure 4.82 Set the Baseline

Having saved a history is like having a backup of your baseline plan. If subsequent changes are made and then rejected, you can always revert back to the original baseline by copying from Baseline10 to Baseline. In addition to Baseline (which always represents the most recent version of the approved schedule), there are 10 baselines that can be used to save copies of baselines (Baseline1 through Baseline10). We always recommend that you use Baseline10 only once to copy the Original baseline and then cycle through Baseline1 through Baseline9 for other approved changes on your project. Each baseline is stamped with a date, but it is also a good idea to keep a log on the side to describe what each baseline represents.

4.12 Save and Publish to Project Server

4.12.1 Publish to Project Server

With the baseline completed, it's now time to publish the approved plan to PWA so that the team (and the rest of the company) can access the plan and to allow work to begin on completing the project tasks.

Select 'File' to open the 'Back Stage' and then select 'Publish'

4.12.2 Change Resource Requirements to Project Plan

With Project Planning now complete, you should also switch to 'Calculate Resource Requirements' from the completed project plan as opposed to the resource plan. From PWA, select and open your project and then from the 'Project ribbon > Navigate section' select 'Resource Plan'.

Figure 4.83 Change PWA Resourcing to use Project Plan

This will launch the 'Resource Plan' view, where from the 'Plan ribbon > Resource Utilization section', select the 'Calculate from' dropdown list and change the setting to 'Project Plan'. This will ensure that the resource allocations from your project plan are included in the enterprise resource management for your organization.

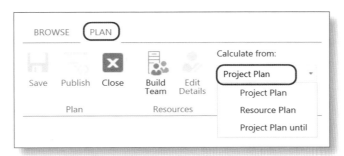

Figure 4.84 Calculate Resource
Requirements from Project Plan

WORK SESSION #11 – SET THE ORIGINAL BASELINE AND PUBLISH THE PLAN

OBJECTIVE

This work session concludes the development of the baseline schedule by saving the original baseline. The baseline will be used during project execution to validation of actual progress against the approved plan.

STEP 1　　　Set Project Baseline

Set the baseline for the entire project

STEP 2　　　Preserve Original Baseline

Copy the 'Baseline' into 'Baseline10' to preserve a copy of the original baseline for future reporting and comparisons.

STEP 3　　　Publish Project Plan

Publish the completed plan to PWA (Microsoft Project only users can skip this step)

STEP 4　　　Set Resource Utilization

Change resource utilization from the resource plan to the project plan (Microsoft Project only users can skip this step)

EXPECTED RESULTS

ⓘ	Task Mode	Task Name	Work Health	Baseline Work	Work	Work Variance	Schedule Health	Baseline Finish	Finish	Finish Variance
		Light Rail Phase 2 - Work Session 11		**320 hrs**	**320 hrs**	**0 hrs**		**Mar 16**	**Mar 16**	**0 days**
		Project Start		*0 hrs*	*0 hrs*	*0 hrs*		*Jan 6*	*Jan 6*	*0 days*
		Planning		**320 hrs**	**320 hrs**	**0 hrs**		**Mar 16**	**Mar 16**	**0 days**
		Scope Document		**64 hrs**	**64 hrs**	**0 hrs**		**Jan 26**	**Jan 26**	**0 days**
		Specify Deliverables and Acceptance Crite		8 hrs	8 hrs	0 hrs		Jan 8	Jan 8	0 days
		Build Work Breakdown Structure		40 hrs	40 hrs	0 hrs		Jan 26	Jan 26	0 days
		Document Project Assumptions		16 hrs	16 hrs	0 hrs		Jan 15	Jan 15	0 days
		Scope Document complete		*0 hrs*	*0 hrs*	*0 hrs*		*Jan 26*	*Jan 26*	*0 days*
		Procurement Plan		**216 hrs**	**216 hrs**	**0 hrs**		**Mar 16**	**Mar 16**	**0 days**
		Determine Procurement Requirements		8 hrs	8 hrs	0 hrs		Jan 29	Jan 29	0 days
		Define & Publish Subcontractor Scope		16 hrs	16 hrs	0 hrs		Feb 5	Feb 5	0 days
		Identify Potential Subcontractors		128 hrs	128 hrs	0 hrs		Mar 16	Mar 16	0 days
		Identify Subcontract Type		32 hrs	32 hrs	0 hrs		Feb 19	Feb 19	0 days
		Document Subcontractor Management P		32 hrs	32 hrs	0 hrs		Mar 5	Mar 5	0 days
		Procurement Plan complete		*0 hrs*	*0 hrs*	*0 hrs*		*Mar 16*	*Mar 16*	*0 days*
		Risk Management Plan		**40 hrs**	**40 hrs**	**0 hrs**		**Jan 22**	**Jan 22**	**0 days**
		Identify Project Risks		20 hrs	20 hrs	0 hrs		Jan 14	Jan 14	0 days
		Analyze Project Risks		10 hrs	10 hrs	0 hrs		Jan 19	Jan 19	0 days
		Document Risk Management Plan		10 hrs	10 hrs	0 hrs		Jan 22	Jan 22	0 days
		Risk Management Plan complete		*0 hrs*	*0 hrs*	*0 hrs*		*Jan 22*	*Jan 22*	*0 days*
		Planning Phase complete		*0 hrs*	*0 hrs*	*0 hrs*		*Mar 16*	*Mar 16*	*0 days*
		Light Rail Phase 2 complete		*0 hrs*	*0 hrs*	*0 hrs*		*Mar 16*	*Mar 16*	*0 days*

Figure WS.11 – Project Baseline

5

CHAPTER 5:

Collaborating and Tracking Progress

In this chapter, we change our approach significantly and focus on the role that the team member has in Proactive Project Portfolio Management (PPM). Up to this point in the book, our focus has been on developing an effective project plan, but from this chapter forward, we change from planning an effective project to now focus on delivery and managing our proactive project plan. And the team members are a vital participant in this, as they are the ones with the facts (time worked, effort remaining and project status) that we need to track progress against the plan. Therefore, we now change hats from project manager to team member and focus on capturing the appropriate information to track progress against the plan, and more importantly to evaluate whether the progress to date is on track or whether our project is ahead or behind schedule. We do that with key input from our team, primarily in the form of timesheets and status reports. But, effective project execution, while heavily based on tracking progress against the plan, requires collaboration from the team to ensure that risks, issues, and action items are effectively managed and that shared workspaces are available to support the team's completion of all project deliverables.

5.1 The SharePoint Project Site

Each project published to PWA has an associated project site which is accessible to the project manager and all team members. The project site is intended to be a single place to go for project information and is the place where project team members can collaborate on issues, risks, documents, and other project-related items. The project site, which is actually delivered through SharePoint, provides a focal point for the additional project support needed for Proactive PPM.

The project site is a collaboration space which contains project announcements, overall status, issues, risks, documents, project deliverables, key performance indicators, key contact information and relevant project links.

The Project Site is accessed from Project Web App (PWA).

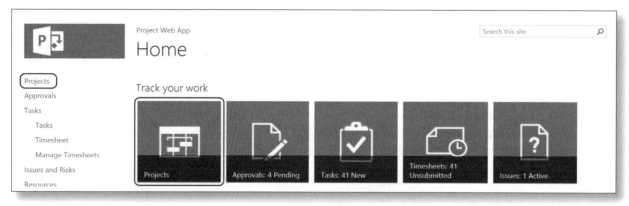

Figure 5.1 PWA Home Page

From the PWA main page, select 'Projects' in the Quick Launch, then select the 'Projects ribbon', and from the 'Data section' select the 'My Projects and Proposals' view to only show the projects that you are assigned to, own or where you are the status manager. Then click on the name of the project that you are going to work on at this time (as you may be assigned to multiple projects) to go to the 'Project Drill-Down' for that project.

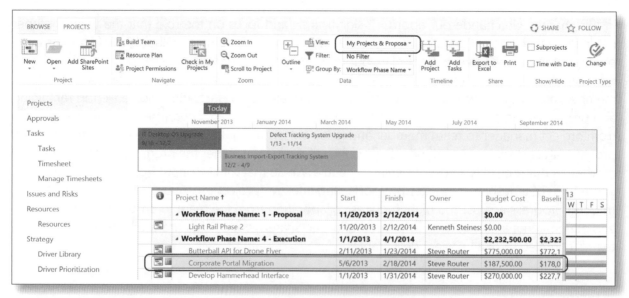

Figure 5.2 PWA Project Center

Select 'Project Site' from the drill-down on the left to launch the project site.

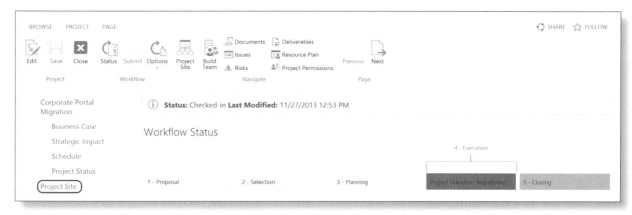

Figure 5.3 Project Home Page/Work Flow - Select Project Site

The project site has been designed to easily and effectively present all the information that you need to understand the current state of the project at a glance. The project summary section of the screen provides a rotating view of the 'Project Timeline' and the 'Project Highlights'. The 'Project Timeline' displays the timeline previously created in Microsoft Project and the 'Project Summary' highlights the 'The Next Project Deliverable Due, Late Tasks and Upcoming Tasks' – a mini-project dashboard.

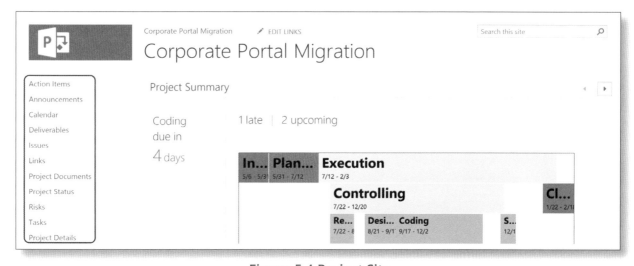

Figure 5.4 Project Site

In Sensei's version of the project site, we also include the following on the 'Home Page':

- Latest announcements
- Project status
- Top 5 active issues
- Key contacts
- Links
- Top 5 active risks
- Your personal action items
- Your personal active tasks
- Recently changed documents
- Top 5 deliverables

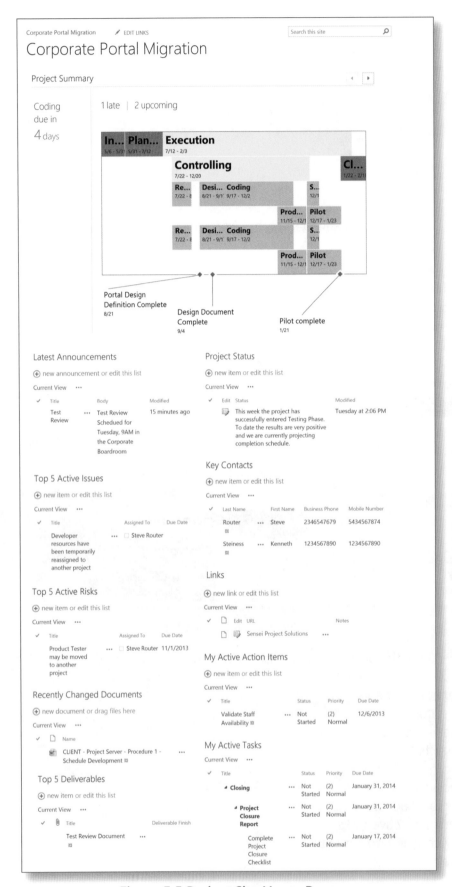

Figure 5.5 Project Site Home Page

As previously stated, our purpose is Proactive PPM, so we will simply draw your attention to these features and how valuable they are to Proactive PPM, but will not be going into details on how to setup or maintain these SharePoint features as there are many excellent reference books on SharePoint if you need assistance in this area.

5.1.1 Working with Risks and Issues

While risks and issues are delivered using SharePoint we feel that it is important to spend a little time explaining the importance of risk and issue management, as we can't be a proactive project manager without stringent risk and issue control on your projects. For those of you unfamiliar with the terms, a risk is 'an uncertain event or condition that, if it occurs, has a positive or negative effect on a project objective'. Risks are any type of problem or concern that MAY occur during the life of the project which should be communicated to the project team and stakeholders. An issue is any type of problem or concern during the life of the project that HAS ALREADY occurred which should be communicated to the project team and stakeholders and needs active management to resolve.

While the top five risks and issues are shown on the project site home page discussed above, on a typical project there are often more than five risks/issues that need to be managed. To view the complete list of risk and issues, select the appropriate link from the Quick Launch. As with any SharePoint list, you can sort and filter the lists to aid in management.

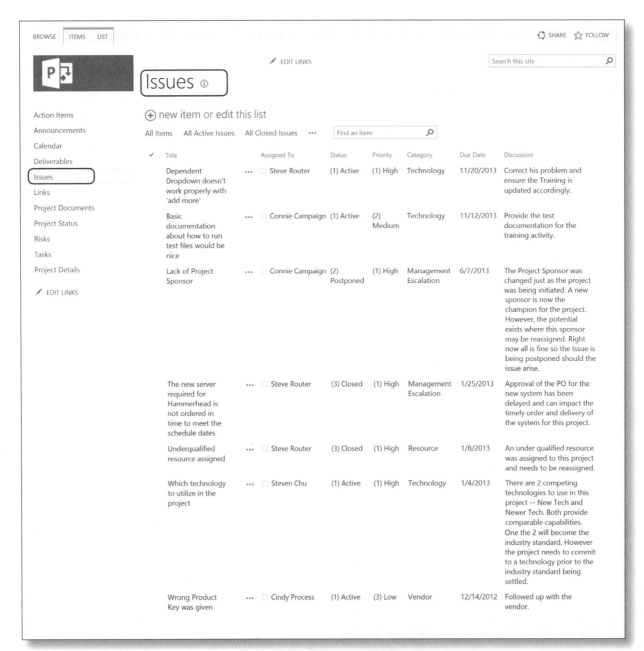

Figure 5.6 Complete Issues List

Figure 5.7 Complete Risks List

All open issues and risks should be very closely managed as the possibility of negative impacts to the project is very real. For any that cannot be resolved immediately, we recommend maintaining a complete history recording the actions taken to resolve the issue/risk.

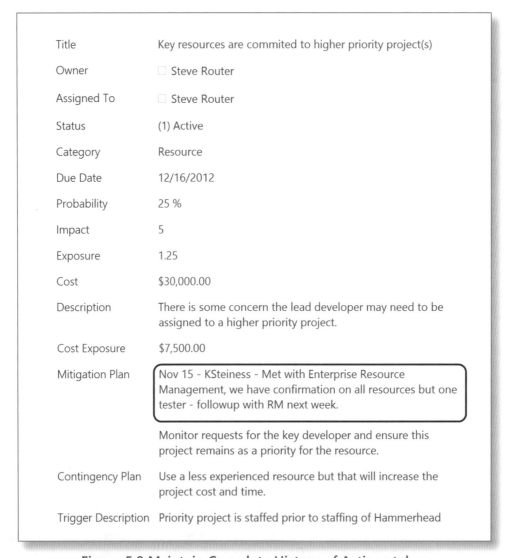

Title	Key resources are commited to higher priority project(s)
Owner	☐ Steve Router
Assigned To	☐ Steve Router
Status	(1) Active
Category	Resource
Due Date	12/16/2012
Probability	25 %
Impact	5
Exposure	1.25
Cost	$30,000.00
Description	There is some concern the lead developer may need to be assigned to a higher priority project.
Cost Exposure	$7,500.00
Mitigation Plan	Nov 15 - KSteiness - Met with Enterprise Resource Management, we have confirmation on all resources but one tester - followup with RM next week.
	Monitor requests for the key developer and ensure this project remains as a priority for the resource.
Contingency Plan	Use a less experienced resource but that will increase the project cost and time.
Trigger Description	Priority project is staffed prior to staffing of Hammerhead

Figure 5.8 Maintain Complete History of Actions taken

Similar actions should be taken for any risk which has a due or trigger date in the near future to ensure that the appropriate mitigation actions are taken to prevent the risk event from occurring. Once the trigger or due date has passed, the risk should be closed or moved to the Issue list to ensure proactive management to closure.

5.1.2 Working with Project Documents

Another Project Site feature that supports proactive project management is maintaining a complete and easily accessible library of every document (formal deliverables and working papers) that the project produces. Formal project documents generally consist of deliverables, project artifacts and reference material. The project document library provides a location for project team members and stakeholders to store, view, and edit them.

We recommend developing a standard set of folders for every project to allow for consistency across projects allowing team members to move from project to project and always know that the management folder contains project status reports and that the team folder contains team meeting minutes, for example.

The document library is opened using the 'Project Documents' link from the Quick Launch. This presents the root of the project library which can be navigated using standard Windows Explorer functionality.

SharePoint provides very robust functionality for managing the project library through the 'Files and Library ribbons'.

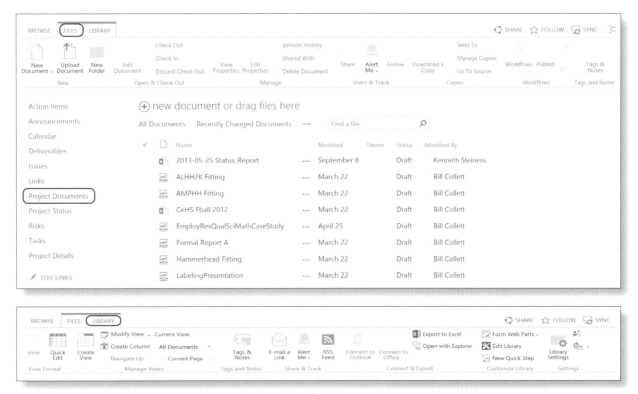

Figure 5.9 and Figure 5.10 File and Library Ribbons support Project Document Management

We encourage you to explore this SharePoint functionality and become very familiar with using the document library as it is critical that all project documents are stored in this repository to ensure currency and availability of all project documents. Three key features that we draw your attention to are:

- All documents managed within the repository have full version control with check-in/out functionality to ensure everyone is using the most current document and that no changes are lost due poor version management.
- All documents have properties (or meta-data) attached to the document which can be used for searching, filtering and creating views.
- Alerts can be created for libraries and/or specific documents, a feature that I use to be automatically notified whenever a change is made to an approved document, which then lets me know that either someone is changing something that they shouldn't or that a new version of an approved document needs to be started to track the changes through to the next approval stage.

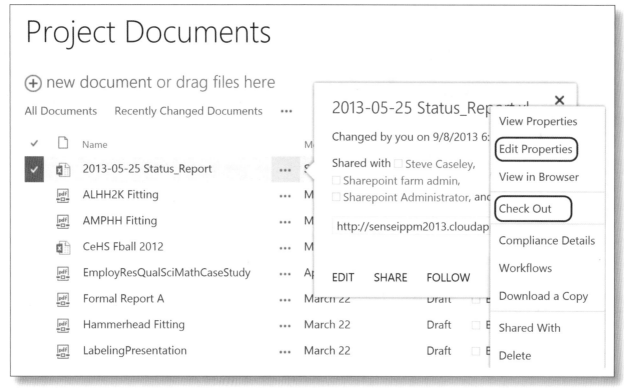

Figure 5.11 Project Documents Library

The other thing that a proactive project manager can do in the document library is to periodically validate with the team that documents currently checked out by them are in fact under active maintenance as opposed to simply checked out and forgotten.

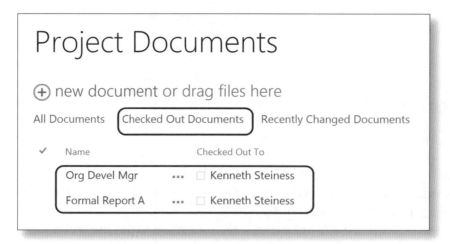

Figure 5.12 List of Documents Checked Out

5.1.3 Working with Action Items

Effectively managing project action items is critical to being a proactive project manager. Action items are another SharePoint list available in your project site. The key facet of effective action item management is capturing them in PWA, assigning responsibility for resolving each individual action item to a team member and then tracking each action item until it is completed.

One of the most critical activities that project managers can do during their projects is tracking action items to completion. It's amazing how this one form of activity can provide mini-successes to projects and can quickly provide measurable benefits to team members, stakeholders and an entire organization. And more personally, managing action items successfully can influence the organization's perception of you as a project manager.

Action items are a way of tracking WHO does WHAT by WHEN during a project. Action items are activities that usually take less than 1hr of effort to complete so they aren't usually tracked in a project schedule. Often times they're identified during weekly team meetings, during Rolling Wave planning sessions, while decomposing the project deliverables and most often as a result of dealing with daily emails.

TIPS & HINTS:
Some of my mentors use action items religiously during meetings and have suggested to associate WWW as an acronym to easily remember WHO does WHAT by WHEN. If you attend a lot of meetings you can use this acronym for quick reference and as you begin to hone your skills as commander of action items you'll have improved success in your career and your projects.

Action items provide the following benefits to the project:

- Improve the collaboration on your team
- Improve the communication across the team
- Improve productivity across your team and projects
- Improve the visibility to leadership
- Reduce errors and issues
- Reduce the length of status meetings.

While time spent working on action items is part of the project, action items are very different than project tasks in that typically the amount of time spent on an action item is relatively small, a few hours, and that the results of an action item typically answers a question, clarifies an unclear point or helps make a project decision as opposed to tasks which are typically days in length and always focused on preparing a formal project deliverable.

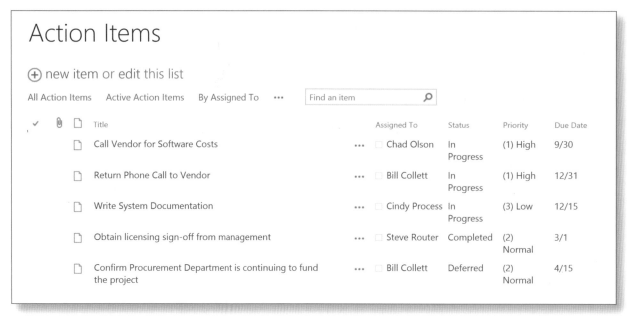

Figure 5.13 Action Items List

Action Items are accessed from the Quick Launch and are maintained in the Action Item list where the key pieces of information managed include the status, priority and due date. A proactive project manager reviews, maintains and adds to the action item list constantly and should explicitly review it with the team in weekly team meetings.

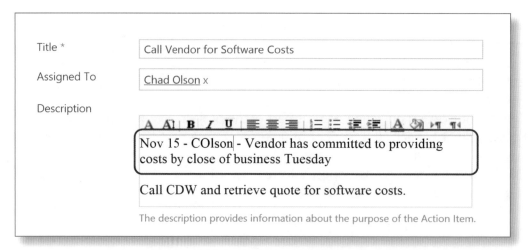

Figure 5.14 Action Item Edit Screen

5.1.4 Viewing Project Tasks

In order to ensure that team members get the big picture of a specific project, they can view the project plan using the 'Tasks' link from the 'Quick Launch' within a project site. This provides a view of the project plan that the team member can review to develop a better understanding of the complete project and/or put their tasks into context of the overall project.

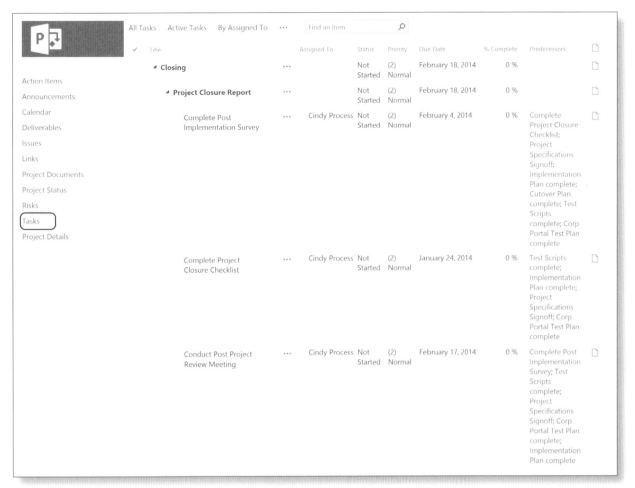

Figure 5.15 View Project Tasks - Viewing project tasks
ensures team members always see the "big picture"

The team member has no ability to change the project with this list and therefore all the commands on the 'Tasks ribbon' are grayed out, with the exception of the 'Alert' button. The 'List ribbon' is active and available to the team member to manipulate the information being displayed, specifically using the 'Manage Views section' the team member can select different views, such as 'My Active Tasks', 'Late Tasks' or 'Upcoming' to see a specific segment of the schedule of interest to them.

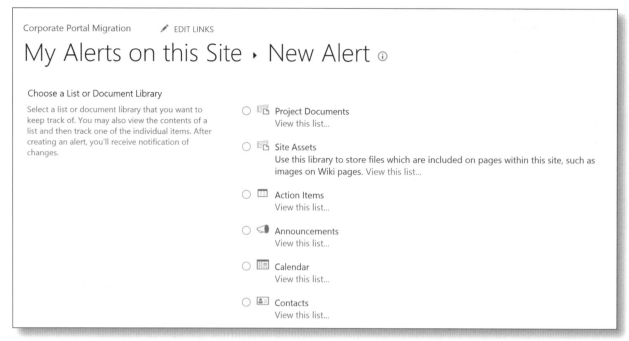

Figure 5.16 Manage Alerts to keep up to date on project changes

5.2 My Tasks and Timesheet

While the task view discussed above allows a team member to view all tasks for a project, most times the team member will want to focus on just the tasks they are responsible for (assigned to). As a team member will often be assigned to multiple projects, My Tasks and Timesheets are accessed from the PWA main page. A team member may quickly view his or her assigned project tasks by selecting either Tasks or Timesheets from the PWA Quick Launch. Tasks differs from the Timesheet in that only project task assignments are visible from Tasks while administrative categories, such as vacation, sick, etc. are also displayed on the Timesheet. The other key distinction is that the Timesheet provides a 1 week view of project assignments while the Tasks view shows all assignments.

**Figure 5.17
Tasks and
Timesheets
in PWA**

5.2.1 Viewing all Task assignments
The 'Tasks' view provides a complete list of all task assignments across all projects categorized into Planning Windows for 'In Progress for Current Period', 'Near Future – Next 2 Periods', 'Distant Future' and 'Completed'. These planning windows makes the viewing and management of project tasks easier as you can directly access the timeframe of interest. This view is used by the team member to understand

all the work that is assigned to them. The Timesheet, which is discussed below, is used to update actual hours spent on tasks and to update the remaining work.

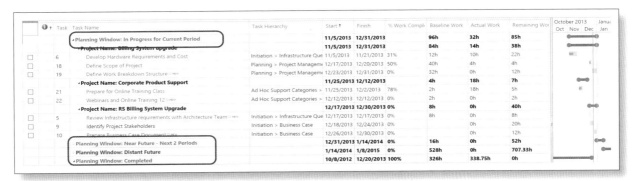

	Task	Task Name	Task Hierarchy	Start ↑	Finish	% Work Compl.	Baseline Work	Actual Work	Remaining Wo	October 2013 Oct Nov Dec	Janua Jan
		▲Planning Window: In Progress for Current Period		11/5/2013	12/31/2013		96h	32h	85h		
		▲Project Name: Billing System upgrade		11/5/2013	12/31/2013		84h	14h	38h		
☐	6	Develop Hardware Requirements and Cost	Initiation > Infrastructure Que	11/5/2013	11/21/2013	31%	12h	10h	22h		
☐	18	Define Scope of Project	Planning > Project Managem	12/17/2013	12/20/2013	50%	40h	4h	4h		
☐	19	Define Work Breakdown Structure	Planning > Project Managem	12/23/2013	12/31/2013	0%	32h	0h	12h		
		▲Project Name: Corporate Product Support		11/25/2013	12/12/2013		4h	18h	7h		
☐	21	Prepare for Online Training Class	Ad Hoc Support Categories >	11/25/2013	12/2/2013	78%	2h	18h	5h		
☐	22	Webinars and Online Training 12	Ad Hoc Support Categories >	12/12/2013	12/12/2013	0%	2h	0h	2h		
		▲Project Name: RS Billing System Upgrade		12/17/2013	12/30/2013	0%	8h	0h	40h		
☐	5	Review Infrastructure requirements with Architecture Team	Initiation > Infrastructure Que	12/17/2013	12/17/2013	0%	8h	0h	8h		
☐	9	Identify Project Stakeholders	Initiation > Business Case	12/18/2013	12/24/2013	0%		0h	20h		
☐	10	Prepare Business Case Document	Initiation > Business Case	12/26/2013	12/30/2013	0%		0h	12h		
		Planning Window: Near Future - Next 2 Periods		12/31/2013	1/14/2014	0%	16h	0h	52h		
		Planning Window: Distant Future		1/14/2014	1/8/2015	0%	528h	0h	707.33h		
		▲Planning Window: Completed		10/8/2012	12/20/2013	100%	326h	338.75h	0h		

Figure 5.18 My Tasks View

EXCEPTION:

If your view does not show the Gantt Chart on the right, from the 'Tasks ribbon > Display section' select 'Layout' and select Gantt Chart from the dropdown list.

5.2.2 Completing the Timesheet

Before we get into the details of using PWA for completing timesheets, we need to step back and examine two strategies for how team members will be expected to track and record time. This discussion is based on the assumption that most team members will not be resourced full time to projects and therefore also needs to be able to track time for non-project (support and administrative) activities, in addition to the time spent on the project.

The first of these strategies is based having team members assigned to both project and specific support tasks with timesheet line(s) for recording all time spent on both. In this scenario, the team member explicitly tracks the time spent on all assigned project and support tasks and allows for more detailed management of the support work. The total time worked on project tasks plus support tasks would be the same as the total hours worked in the week. All other time would be considered non-working time, such as Sick, Vacation, etc.

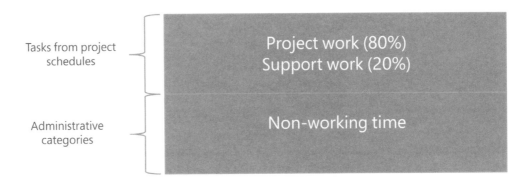

Max Units = 100%

Figure 5.19 Resource Availability - Max Units 100%

The second strategy is based on the timesheet containing only the planned project tasks and all remaining work, including support work would be recorded against general administrative tasks. This strategy simplifies time tracking for the team member as they do not have to explicitly track time spent on support tasks as the administrative tasks simply becomes the difference between total time worked and project specific work. Detailed timesheet lines would still exist for each assigned project task. When using this method, it is critical that at an organizational level, the resource max units are reduced to ensure that adequate time is available for team members to work on support tasks.

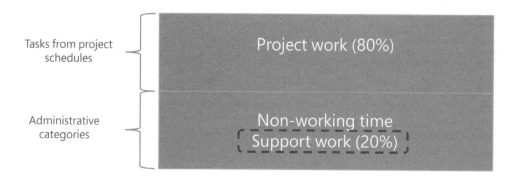

Max Units = 80%

Figure 5.20 Resource Availability - Max Units 80%

As shown in the diagrams above, the project time (80%) remains constant. As this book is focused on Proactive PPM we will not be going into details of one strategy or the other and are very content that we will be receiving detailed timesheet details at the project task level. Either strategy allows for detailed project time tracking and even supports resources working on multiple projects, where Johnny's 80% availability for project work is shared equally between Project X and Project Y. As discussed in Chapter 4, enterprise resource management is responsible for ensuring that Johnny's total project allocation does not exceed the available 80% and the individual project managers are responsible for ensuring that their project 'Max Units' does not exceed the approved amount, resulting in a weekly timesheet that won't exceed Johnny's standard work week.

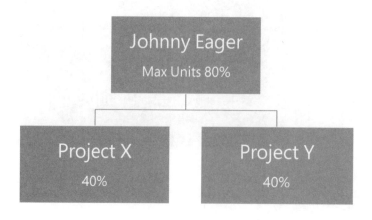

5.21 – Resource Sharing Across Projects

At the end of each week, all project resources must fill in a timesheet with project time and non-project time for the past reporting period. This is the primary mechanism for reporting the progress and remaining effort on all active projects across, so it is vitally important that the data is accurate.

To enter time details, on a weekly basis each team member, including ourselves as the project managers, select 'Timesheet' from the 'Task section' of the PWA Quick Launch.

Assuming you are completing your timesheet for the current week, this will take you directly to the appropriate timesheet, but you should always validate the timesheet date. We will discuss selecting a different time period below when we discuss personal time off (PTO) later in this Chapter.

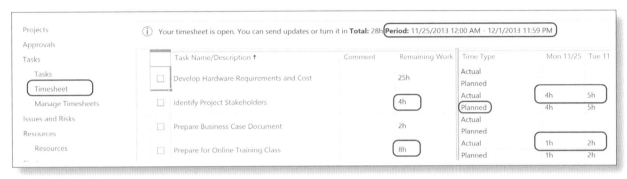

5.22 - PWA Timesheet

We recommend ensuring that the 'Planned' hours are visible to help each team member plan and track their time on a weekly basis. If 'Planned' is not showing on your current view, select the 'Options' tab to reactivate the ribbon and then ensure that the 'Planned' checkbox is selected in the 'Show/Hide section'.

Each team member will be required to enter three key pieces of information into the timesheet

1. Actual time worked per day on each task
2. Estimated effort to complete the task (realistic estimate, not just the subtraction of actual from original plan)
3. Any non-project (Administrative) time

5.23 - Non-Project Time Capture on Timesheet

On a daily (worst case weekly) basis, each team member will be expected to record hours by task by entering the actual hours worked on each task directly into the timesheet cells. Once all the detailed time is entered, the 'Save' button from the 'Timesheet ribbon > Submit section' should be selected as it not only saves the time entered, it also reduces the 'Remaining Work' column by the time worked during the week.

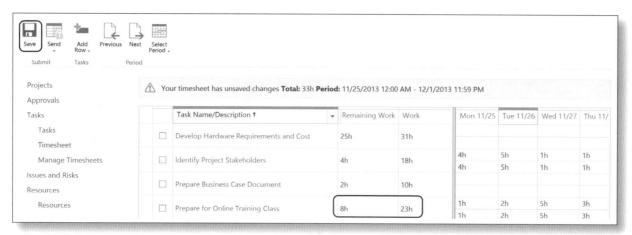

Figure 5.24 - Click Save to update Work and Remaining Work columns

Prior to submission, each team member is expected to review and update the 'Remaining Work' column to accurately reflect their current expectation on how much work remains to fully complete the task. We recommend paying particular attention to any tasks where the 'Save' reduced the 'Remaining Work' to zero to ensure that the task is really done as opposed to just running out of time. It is strongly encouraged that comments are added to any tasks where there is a significant change (up or down) in the remaining work to help explain the change. We, as the project manager, can then use these comments to better understand the reasons for the change and possible work directly with the team member to clarify the expectations of the task to avoid doing extra or out-of-scope work.

Tasks that are completed should always have the 'Remaining Work' set to zero to indicate that the task is complete.

	Task Name/Description ↑	Comment	Remaining Work
☐	Develop Hardware Requirements ar		25h
☐	Identify Project Stakeholders	4 hours added as an additional Stakeholder was identified	4h
☐	Prepare Business Case Document		0h

Figure 5.25 Provide Comments and Validate Zero Remaining Work Tasks

At any time during timesheet entry, a team member can select a task name to bring up the 'Task Details' window showing the tasks progress to date, start and finish dates and history of current changes to the task. Scrolling this window provides information related to risks, issues and documents associated with the task, details of resource assignment, and the tasks predecessors and successors.

If a team member works on a task that doesn't appear on the current timesheet, they can add a new row to the timesheet using the 'Timesheet ribbon > Tasks section >Add Row'. This command provides the following options for adding a task:

- **Select From Existing Assignments** – this would be used if the team member starts work on a task that is assigned to them, but not scheduled for the current time period. While working on a future task can be considered a good thing as it might indicate that the team member is ahead of schedule, it also may indicate that the team member is simply ignoring the project schedule and finding the fun stuff to work on, in which case we need to manage this carefully as the tasks skipped to get to the fun stuff could be critical tasks with predecessors holding up other tasks for other team members
- **Add a New Task** - this would be used when the team member takes on a new task that isn't in the project plan. As a project manager, we need to manage this closely as this is often un-authorized work and that a change request may be required to bring the work into scope for the project.
- **Add Yourself to a Task** - this would be used when the team member is taking over (or assisting on) a task from an existing team member. Assuming that this team member has skills and expertise for this new task, this can often be considered a good thing, but we should validate whether the work estimates for the original team member are appropriate. As a proactive project manager, we prefer that task assignments are negotiated with us in advance to ensure appropriate resource utilization and therefore should discourage our team members from doing this dynamically without prior review and approval.
- **Add Team Tasks** – this would be used when a team member takes on a task that had previously assigned to a team resource. As above, this is not a recommended approach, as all task resource assignments should be done in advance through the project manager.
- **Add Non-Project Line** – this would be used when the team member needs to add a new administrative task that isn't available on the standard list provided by the organization, for example jury duty where it isn't already populated on the existing list of administrative tasks.
- **Add Personal Line** - this would be used when the team member needs to add a new task for work that would be considered personal time and would typically be classified as unpaid time off. In many organizations this feature will be disabled.

Figure 5.26 Adding Rows
to a Timesheet

Adding rows to the timesheet will invoke a selection window where the team member can navigate to the appropriate project, deliverable and task that they want to add to their timesheet.

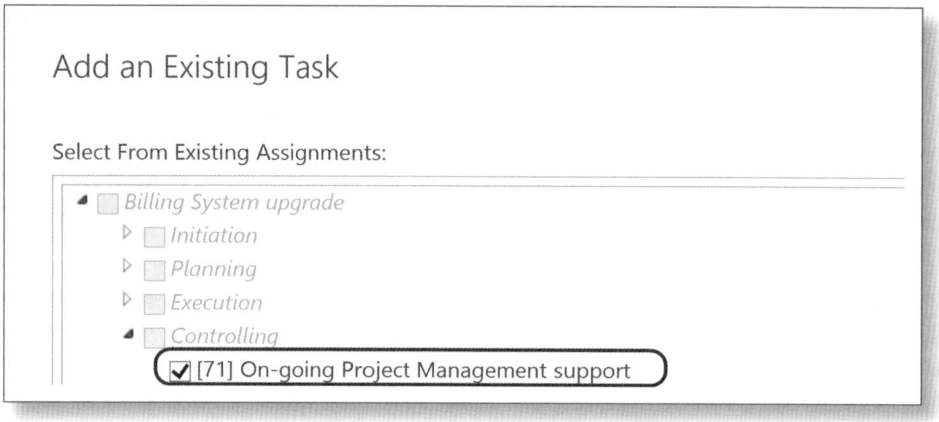

Add an Existing Task

Select From Existing Assignments:

- ◢ ☐ *Billing System upgrade*
  - ▷ ☐ *Initiation*
  - ▷ ☐ *Planning*
  - ▷ ☐ *Execution*
  - ◢ ☐ *Controlling*
    - ☑ [71] On-going Project Management support

Figure 5.27 Add an Existing Task

Finally, the team member would enter any non-project time into the administrative section of the timesheet. We have included rows for administrative, sick, support and vacation but each organization is likely to have their own categories for non-project time tracking. The total of all time worked each week should never be less than the standard work hours for your organization.

Administrative	Actual		1h			
	Planned					
Sick	Actual	2h				
	Planned					
Support	Actual	1h				
	Planned					
Vacation	Actual					
	Planned					
	Actual	8h	8h	9h	8h	8h
	Planned	5h	7h	9h	8h	8h

Figure 5.28 Ensure Timesheet equals standard work hours

Typically at the end of each week, each team member would use the 'Timesheet ribbon > Submit section' to 'Send' their timesheet selecting 'Turn in Final Timesheet' from the dropdown list. As you can see from the screenshot, there are options to submit incremental progress that will be discussed in a later section in this chapter.

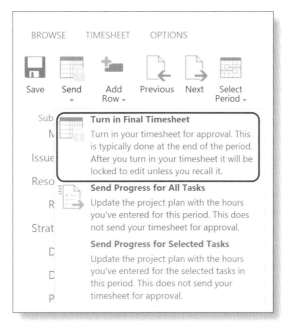

Figure 5.29 Submit Final Timesheet
at end of week

Assuming that the 'Turn in Final Timesheet' option was selected, the timesheet is then locked against future edits by the team member. PWA will then route the individual project status updates to the appropriate project managers for review and approval (prior to updating the project plans). The process for a project manager approving timesheets will be discussed in Chapter 6 – Processing Updates and Taking Corrective Actions.

Depending on your option settings, you may be prompted to enter additional comments when you submit your timesheet.

5.2.3 Planning PTO in the Future

In order to ensure that project work is not scheduled during PTO, resources should enter planned vacation days in their timesheets as soon as possible, even if the original recording of vacation time is only a placeholder to reserve a week in the future. This ensures that the project schedule reflects a period of unavailability, even if the actual dates may change by a week or two as the vacation plans finalize.

To enter a future PTO, you select 'Manage Timesheets' from the 'Task section' of the of the PWA Quick Launch. This will provide a list of all your timesheets, past, present and future. You can control the number of timesheets shown using the views available from 'Timesheet ribbon > Views section'. Select the appropriate timesheet based on planned vacation dates and select 'Click to Create' to open the timesheet for that future period.

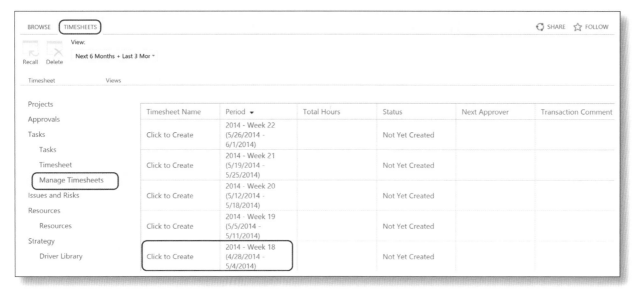

Figure 5.30 Submit PTO for a Future Period

With the timesheet open, you then enter the number of hours per day of your scheduled PTO into either the planned or actual fields. If the PTO is for a full week and the dates are firm and not subject to change, it is recommended that the time is entered into the actual field and then the timesheet can be finalized by 'Turn in Final Timesheet'. This ensures that the timesheet is recorded and available for processing should the team member forget to submit their timesheet when they are actually leaving for their vacation.

Figure 5.31 Enter Vacation Time into either Planned or Actual depending on how firm plans are

If, however, the PTO is either not for a full week, or the dates are tentative, the vacation time would typically be entered into the planned fields and the timesheet would be saved, rather than submitted. This is done from the 'Timesheet ribbon > Submit section > Save button'. This will ensure that the PTO time is recorded to reduce the hours available for project work. Later, when the actual week of PTO comes, the team member would open the week's timesheet and record both the actual hours worked and taken as vacation and then 'Turn in Final Timesheet'.

5.2.4 Recalling a Timesheet

If you accidentally submit a timesheet or discover a mistake after it is sent, you have the option of recalling a timesheet. To recall a timesheet you follow a very similar process as entering PTO, you select 'Manage Timesheets' from the 'Task section' of the PWA Quick Launch. This will provide a list of all your timesheets, past, present and future. Select the timesheet you wish to recall by selecting the appropriate 'Timesheet Period' from the 'Period Column' to select that row on the screen (Selecting the timesheet from the 'Timesheet Name' column simply opens the timesheet). With the row selected, from the 'Timesheet ribbon > Timesheet section' buttons select the 'Recall' button.

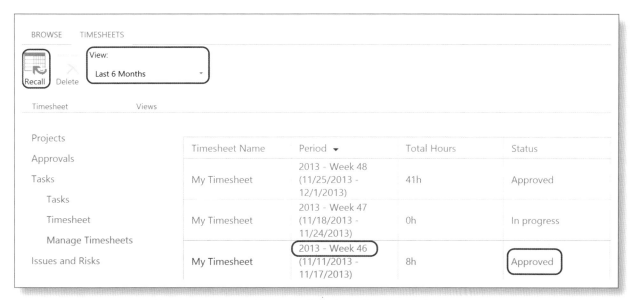

Figure 5.32 Recall a previously submitted timesheet

This will change the status of the timesheet back to 'In Progress' and allows you to make additional changes to the timesheet. Now, if you select the timesheet from the 'Timesheet Name' column, the timesheet details is opened where you can make the required changes.

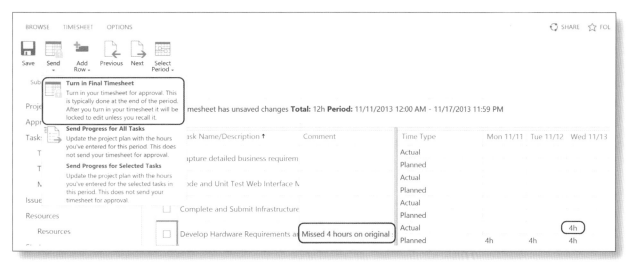

Figure 5.33 Resubmitting a recalled timesheet

Once the changes are completed, the timesheet would be submitted for re-approval as described above.

EXCEPTION:
A timesheet cannot be recalled from a closed time reporting period.

5.2.5 Reporting Status to the Project Manager

When an interim, mid-week status is required, for example to prepare for a major Steering Committee meeting or to perform very granular tracking during a very time critical portion of the project, as a project manager we would request that the team complete their timesheet actuals and remaining work as per the procedure described above, but instead of 'Turn in Final Timesheet' from the 'Timesheet ribbon > Submit section' we would request that the team members select 'Send Progress for All Tasks' or 'Send Progress for Selected Tasks'.

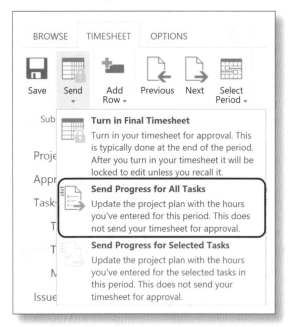

Figure 5.34 Mid-week Status Reporting

This will update the project plan with the current status to allow us to review and validate the project status without submitting the timesheet for approval. Later, at week end, the team members would complete tracking time and updating remaining work for the rest of the week and then submit the timesheet for approval. This will update the project plan with any changes to previous time tracked plus add in the additional time worked.

WORK SESSION #12 – SUBMITTING A TIMESHEET

OBJECTIVE

To provide task status through the PWA Timesheet.

STEP 1   Create Timesheet

Provide task status through the PWA Timesheet. (If you do not have PWA, enter the same timesheet information directly into Microsoft Project)

Complete the timesheet for the first week (January 05, 2015 – January 09, 2015) of the project:

Monday: 4 hours on 'Specify Deliverables and Acceptance Criteria'

Tuesday: 4 hours on 'Specify Deliverables and Acceptance Criteria'

Wednesday: 2 hours on 'Specify Deliverables and Acceptance Criteria'

Increase 'Remaining Work' to 20 hours on 'Specify Deliverables and Acceptance Criteria' and enter a comment to reflect the reason why the time was increased – '5 new deliverables identified which will require 20 more hours'.

STEP 2   Submit Timesheet

Submit the timesheet for approval

EXPECTED RESULTS

Figure WS.12a – PWA Timesheet

Figure WS.12b – Microsoft Project Resource Usage

6

CHAPTER 6:

Processing Updates and Taking Corrective Action

The project plan has been created and baselined (Chapter 4) and we've received updates on actual work performed from our team (Chapter 5). In this chapter we're going to process the status updates and review the impact this has on our project plan and take the appropriate actions to adjust the plan to keep it on schedule. This chapter reviews the critical WEEKLY activities that we, as project managers, must take to monitor and control our schedules.

6.1 Weekly Schedule Updates

It is vitally important that schedules are updated each week so that reporting is accurate, and that the appropriate corrective actions are performed. Without timely and accurate project information the data quality becomes suspect, and the project governance process breaks down. Everyone must participate to ensure the effectiveness of the system. This includes charging time to the correct projects, applying submitted hours to the project schedule, rescheduling incomplete work, and properly closing completed projects (Chapter 8).

Project Web App (PWA) reduces the time required to update and maintain accurate project schedules by enabling the project team members to submit progress updates to the project manager (Chapter 5). It is our responsibility as the project manager to ensure that we have received all team member updates, and that the updates are reviewed and processed properly. Status inputs submitted by team members will not be reflected in the schedule until the project manager has reviewed, accepted, and published the input. This provides the opportunity to review the updates and correct any mistakes before the project is rescheduled from this data. Once the updates have been completed and published the updated information is available to the project team in PWA.

PWA allows you to create rules which can be used to automate as much of this process as you would like. The rules can be defined to be applied to specific projects, tasks and/or resources to help improve the weekly status update process.

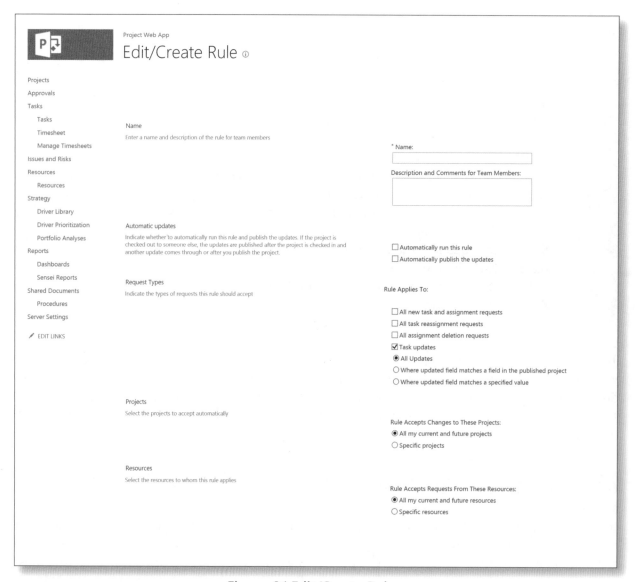

Figure 6.1 Edit/Create Rules

On the first day of each status report period (typically Monday), the project manager must perform the actions described in this chapter to ensure the project properly reflects the new reality of another week's work on the project. During this week, new work may have been identified, tasks estimates may have been changed as a result of increased understanding of the task, team changes due to resignations or reassignments, and so on. Depending on the size and complexity of your project, we recommend blocking your calendar for 1-3 hours on the first day of each reporting period to ensure that you have the time to complete this critical proactive project management activity.

6.1.1 Review for Submitted Timesheets

Before we can begin to process the weekly status updates, the first step is to check to see if all team members have submitted updates. The recommended method for doing this is to run a report to validate that all team members have in fact submitted their timesheets. In PWA, from Quick Launch select 'Sensei Reports'. From 'Report Area 5 – Project Status and Portfolio Reporting section', select the 'Timesheet Compliance by Project Manager' report (your organization may have different reports in place, but you should have a method available for checking timesheet compliance).

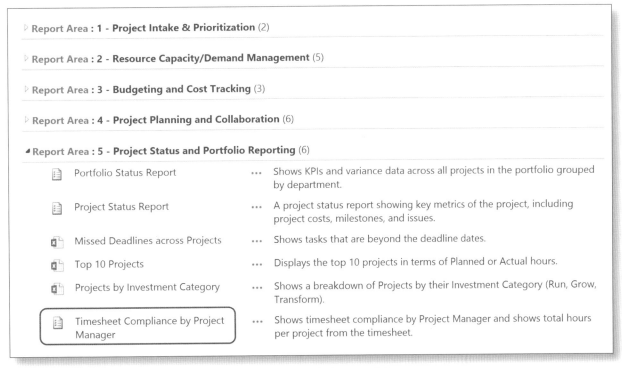

Figure 6.2 Sensei Report Menu

This will launch a screen where you will enter the timesheet period (it defaults to the previous timesheet period) and select the project manager you are running the report for (most likely yourself, but you have the ability to run this for your team leads or other project managers you may be assisting).

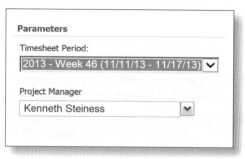

Figure 6.3 Timesheet
Compliance by Project Manager
Report Parameters

Review the report to validate that your project is Green, i.e. all timesheets have been submitted. Green means the timesheet has been submitted, Yellow means it is still in progress and Red means it hasn't been started yet.

Once your project shows 100% and green for all team members, you're ready to proceed to the next step. However, as is often the case, and one or more team members haven't submitted their timesheets, you will need to start walking around and requesting timesheets are submitted immediately.

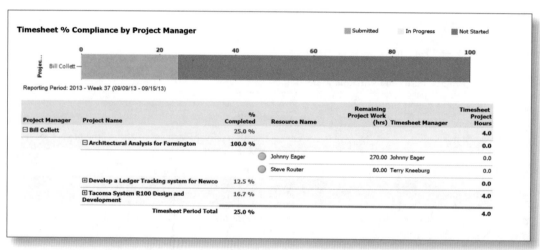

Figure 6.4 Timesheet Compliance by Project Manager Report

EXCEPTION:

It's my experience that with organizations newly implementing Proactive PPM, adherence to timesheet policies is the most difficult thing to implement – team members are resistant to tracking time, forget to submit timesheets on time and then are mysteriously away from their desks on Monday mornings. Stringent policies to help enforce timesheet policies may be required to ensure that ALL timesheets are submitted on time.

I've worked in organizations where email send capabilities are disabled when timesheets are not entered and even in an organization where annual performance reviews reflect the number of occurrences of late timesheet submission. While I don't recommend such severe enforcement in the early days, it is critical to ensure that team members understand the importance of submitting timesheets on time.

This process of running the timesheet compliance report and chasing team members needs to be repeated until all timesheets for your project have been submitted. There may still be many organizational resources who haven't submitted timesheets, but at this time, we are only concerned about ensuring that all the timesheets for our project have been submitted.

6.1.2 Approve Status Updates

Once all timesheets have been submitted, we are ready to move on to the next step in the weekly process; approving the status updates and updating the project schedule. (As an aside, we are only approving the portions of the timesheets (status updates) related to our project(s). Other project managers and resource managers will be approving other project and administrative time recorded).

From the PWA Quick Launch, select 'Approvals'. This will open the 'Approvals Center' with a view of all status updates from the projects you manage. The left side of the screen provides the summary of the changes made as it relates to start and finish dates and remaining work. Any changes made by the team member are highlighted in Red. The right side of the screen provides the day by day details of the status updates.

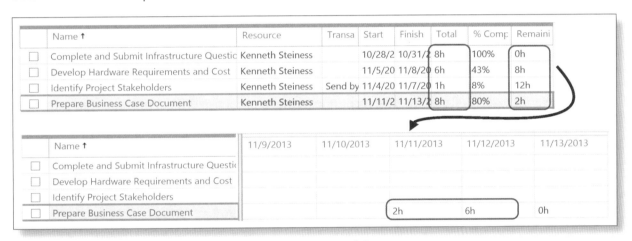

	Name ↑	Resource	Transa	Start	Finish	Total	% Comp	Remaini
☐	Complete and Submit Infrastructure Questic	Kenneth Steiness		10/28/2	10/31/2	8h	100%	0h
☐	Develop Hardware Requirements and Cost	Kenneth Steiness		11/5/20	11/8/20	6h	43%	8h
☐	Identify Project Stakeholders	Kenneth Steiness	Send by	11/4/20	11/7/20	1h	8%	12h
☐	Prepare Business Case Document	Kenneth Steiness		11/11/2	11/13/2	8h	80%	2h

	Name ↑	11/9/2013	11/10/2013	11/11/2013	11/12/2013	11/13/2013
☐	Complete and Submit Infrastructure Questic					
☐	Develop Hardware Requirements and Cost					
☐	Identify Project Stakeholders					
☐	Prepare Business Case Document			2h	6h	0h

Figure 6.5 Approval Center

Clicking on the task name in this view will provide more details on updates provided by the team member if you need to dig deeper into the updates prior to approving them. This detail screen provides a history of all status updates from the start of the task, including all changes in remaining work. This will allow you to better understand any task variances and will help determine if this is a one-time variance or an ongoing and worsening issue.

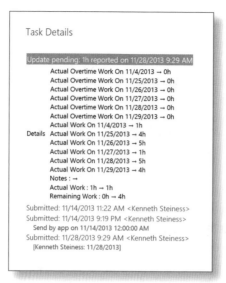

**Figure 6.6 Task Details Window
- Provides History of
Status Updates**

Of specific interest are any changes to the Remaining Work as this indicates an estimate change that most likely warrants additional discussions with the team member to validate that the additional time is required. It's my experience that in many instances, team members will inadvertently augment a task's scope unnecessarily. Therefore, we recommend that a proactive project manager pay particular attention to any significant changes to a task's estimate.

To better understand the impact that these actuals or modified remaining work will have on the overall project plan, you can select the checkbox(s) to the left of the task(s) of interest and then from the 'Approvals ribbon > Actions section' select the 'Preview Updates' button.

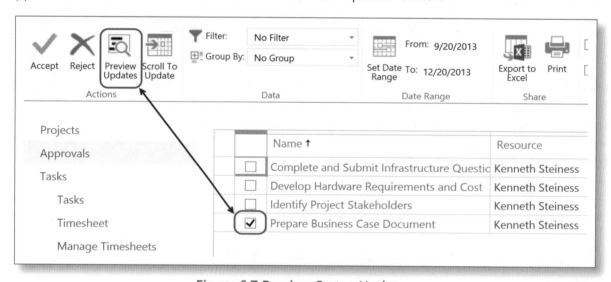

Figure 6.7 Preview Status Updates

This will display a version of the project schedule with yellow highlighting for all changes that results from the status updates. As well, the task(s) which were the source of the change are shown in blue to aid in better understanding these impacts. The 'Gantt Area' of this view also provides a graphical representation of the changes by showing the baseline in gray and the current schedule in blue/dark blue for actual work completed and light blue for remaining work. This screen provides a view of exactly what the impact of accepting the status updates will have on the overall project.

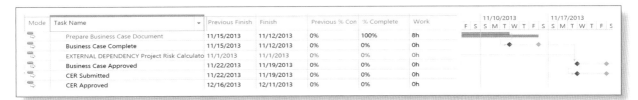

Mode	Task Name	Previous Finish	Finish	Previous % Con	% Complete	Work	
	Prepare Business Case Document	11/15/2013	11/12/2013	0%	100%	8h	
	Business Case Complete	11/15/2013	11/12/2013	0%	0%	0h	
	EXTERNAL DEPENDENCY Project Risk Calculato	11/1/2013	11/1/2013	0%	0%	0h	
	Business Case Approved	11/22/2013	11/19/2013	0%	0%	0h	
	CER Submitted	11/22/2013	11/19/2013	0%	0%	0h	
	CER Approved	12/16/2013	12/11/2013	0%	0%	0h	

Figure 6.8 Full impact of each status update preview

Once you have reviewed the impact of the status updates and discussed any concerns with the team member(s), you may decide to reject one or more status updates. You do this from the 'Approvals ribbon > Actions section' using the 'Reject' button. You should never reject a status update without adequate comments and/or previous discussion with the team member as it is critical that they understand the reason their update has been rejected; so that they can make the appropriate changes and resubmit. Once you have completed your review of all the status updates (including updated and resubmitted ones) you select all the updates and apply all the actuals to the project plan using the 'Approvals ribbon > Actions section > Accept button' to apply all the status updates to the schedule.

BEST PRACTICE:
> **Best practice is to update one project at a time as this makes the review and approval simpler.**

6.1.3 Set the Status Date
The project plan should now be opened in Microsoft Project, as the next set of activities for processing updates and taking proactive actions are done here.

TIPS & HINTS:
> If you had the project plan open in Microsoft Project while you were approving status updates in PWA, these are not automatically applied to the open plan. You must first close the plan and then reopen it to have the changes applied. Therefore, we recommend you always save and check-in your project plans as soon as you are finished making changes to avoid having this happen.

Once you open the plan in Microsoft Project, the first thing you need to do is set the Status Date (PMI calls it the Data Date). The Status Date represents the end of the previous reporting period and the date as of which your status information is current.

From the 'Project ribbon > Status section', select the 'Calendar' icon to open the 'Status Date' dialog. The status date should be set to the date that the current timesheet period ended on, not the current date. The status date would typically be the prior Saturday or Sunday, depending on your organizational timesheet policies.

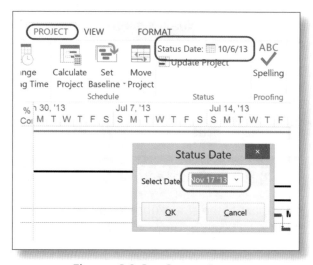

Figure 6.9 Set Status Date

6.1.4 Track Time for Local Resources

If you have any local resources (these were discussed in chapter 2) allocated to your plan you will have to track time for them in Microsoft Project as local resources do not have the timesheet functionality in PWA available to them. As a quick reminder, local resources are often used for business unit subject matter experts or external consultants; specifically any project resources not being managed by the Project Management Office (PMO). Based on actual hours worked and revised remaining work obtained from these local resources, using the 'A – Resource Usage View' you would directly enter this information by resource and task based on hours worked per day. The 'Remaining Work' column should also be updated to reflect the updated estimate to complete from the resource.

TIPS & HINTS:

  You may need to add the 'Actual Work' field to 'Time-Phased' view. To do this, Right Mouse click anywhere in the area and select the 'Actual Work' field

---

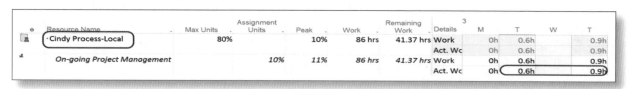

Figure 6.10 Tracking Time Manually for Local Resources

Tracking time for local resources directly in Microsoft Project maintains the same data that PWA does when timesheet status is applied from PWA. Once the local resource's time is tracked, the project plan should be current for the current status period.

6.1.5 Update Milestone Status

The next step is to update any project milestones that were completed in this status period. Milestones are not updated by team members as they do not appear on a timesheet. We recommend using the '10 – Project Status' view for updating the status of milestones completed. Review the project milestones to determine if any were completed in the status period. To complete a milestone, select it and then from the 'Task ribbon > Schedule section' select the 100% complete icon. If the 'Actual Finish' was different from what was scheduled, you can now update that date also.

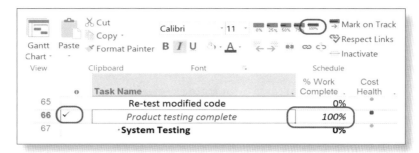

Figure 6.11 Update Milestone Status

6.1.6 Update Project Costs

To date, our actions in this chapter have been focused on the tracking and managing the project schedule. As discussed in Chapter 4, typically a significant amount of the project costs are automatically maintained as a result of tracking and processing the work completed by the project's resources, there are other costs which require separate attention for tracking and management.

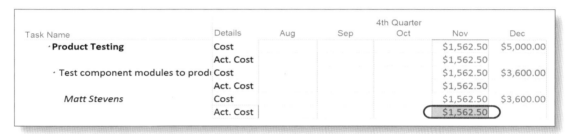

Figure 6.12 09 - Cost Tracking View -
Actual Costs calculated from Actual Hours entered on Timesheets

Material resource usage must be tracked manually using a similar technique defined above for 'Track Time for Local Resources'. Using the 'A – Resource Usage' view, enter the material resources consumed in this time period in the 'Actual Work' area and update any remaining material requirements in the 'Remaining Work' column.

Figure 6.13a Material Costs - Record actual consumption as Units Used

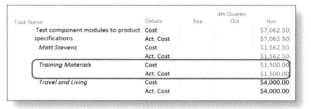

Figure 6.13b Material Costs - Costs are calculated (in this instance 12 units @ $125)

Using the '09 – Cost Tracking' view, non-resource costs can be recorded directly against the appropriate tasks and cost resources for which a cost was incurred. You enter this actual costs directly into the appropriate dates in the calendar area of the view. The 'Remaining Cost' column would also be updated to reflect the updated remaining cost for the task.

Task Name	Actual Cost	Baseline Cost	Total Cost	Remaining Cost	Details	Nov	Dec
· Product Testing	**$7,062.50**	**$6,200.00**	**$12,062.50**	**$5,000.0(**	Cost	$7,062.50	$5,000.00
					Act. Cost	$7,062.50	
· Test component modules to product specifications	$7,062.50	$4,800.00	$10,662.50	$3,600.0(	Cost	$7,062.50	$3,600.00
					Act. Cost	$7,062.50	
Matt Stevens	$1,562.50	$4,800.00	$5,162.50	$3,600.0(	Cost	$1,562.50	$3,600.00
					Act. Cost	$1,562.50	
Training Materials	$1,500.00	$0.00	$1,500.00	$0.0(	Cost	$1,500.00	
					Act. Cost	$1,500.00	
Travel and Living	$4,000.00	$0.00	$4,000.00	$0.0(	Cost	$4,000.00	$0.00
					Act. Cost	$4,000.00	

**Figure 6.14 Other Costs - Other costs are recorded
as incurred directly into the Actual Cost Field**

With all costs recorded against the plan (work, material and cost), it is important to review overall actual cost performance against the Project Budget. To do this, we compare actual costs against the budget resources.

Using the 'C – Cost Type' view, which groups your resources using the 'Cost Type' field, to compare the values in the 'Budget Cost' and 'Cost' columns, determines your project's financial performance against the project budget. If the project's cost performance requires attention, meet with senior management to review overall budget performance to determine the appropriate management corrective actions.

Resource Name	Budget Cost	Baseline Cost	Cost	Actual Cost	Remaining Cost	Cost Variance
· Hardware	**$275,000.00**	**$275,000.00**	**$360,000.00**	**$0.00**	**$360,000.00**	**$85,000.00**
· Hardware Budget	$275,000.00					
Butterball API for Drone Flye	$275,000.00					
· Hardware Expense		$275,000.00	$360,000.00	$0.00	$360,000.00	$85,000.00
Complete and Submit Infrast		$275,000.00	$360,000.00	$0.00	$360,000.00	$85,000.00
· Software	**$50,000.00**	**$50,000.00**	**$75,000.00**	**$0.00**	**$75,000.00**	**$25,000.00**
· Software Expense		$50,000.00	$75,000.00	$0.00	$75,000.00	$25,000.00
Complete and Submit Infrast		$50,000.00	$75,000.00	$0.00	$75,000.00	$25,000.00
· Software Budget	$50,000.00					
Butterball API for Drone Flye	$50,000.00					

**Figure 6.15 C - Cost Type View - Groups Resources by Cost Type
to facilitate comparisons of Costs Actuals to Budget**

The Budget is presented at the top of the view based on the Budget Resources associated with the Project Summary Task. The Planned costs are presented lower on the view based on the costs associated with each task in the plan. Compare the Budget values contained in the Budget Cost column to the Actual Cost and Remaining Cost columns to determine overall budget performance.

WORK SESSION #13 – UPDATE PROJECT COSTS

OBJECTIVE

Update Cost Resources for the current period and review the overall financial performance of the project

STEP 1   Record Actuals Costs

Record $3,000 actual costs for training on the 'Develop Work Breakdown Structure' task. Leave the remaining $2,000 costs for a future time period.

STEP 2   Review Budget performance

Validate the financial performance of the project by reviewing current costs against the budget costs.

EXPECTED RESULTS

	Task Name	Actual Cost	Baseline Cost	Total Cost	Remaining Cost	Details	1/5	1/12	1/19
	· Build Work Breakdown Structure	$3,000.00	$10,000.00	$9,000.00	$6,000.00	Cost	$3,000.00	$1,200.00	$4,800.00
						Act. Cost	$3,000.00	$0.00	$0.00
	Mary Nattu (Business Analyst)	$0.00	$5,000.00	$2,500.00	$2,500.00	Cost		$750.00	$1,750.00
						Act. Cost			
	Training	$3,000.00	$5,000.00	$5,000.00	$2,000.00	Cost	$3,000.00	$0.00	$2,000.00
						Act. Cost	$3,000.00	$0.00	$0.00

Figure WS.13a – Enter Non-Resource Actual Costs

	Resource Name	Budget Cost	Baseline Cost	Cost	Actual Cost	Remaining Cost	Cost Variance
	No Value		$0.00	$1,500.00	$0.00	$1,500.00	$1,500.00
	· Labor	$36,800.00	$36,800.00	$37,050.00	$1,250.00	$35,800.00	$250.00
	Julian Jung (Procurement Specialist)		$4,800.00	$4,800.00	$0.00	$4,800.00	$0.00
	Mary Nattu (Business Analyst)		$5,000.00	$3,750.00	$0.00	$3,750.00	($1,250.00)
	Kenneth Steiness (Project Manager)		$27,000.00	$28,500.00	$1,250.00	$27,250.00	$1,500.00
	· Labor Budget	$36,800.00					
	· Training	$5,000.00	$5,000.00	$5,000.00	$3,000.00	$2,000.00	$0.00
	· Training		$5,000.00	$5,000.00	$3,000.00	$2,000.00	$0.00
	Build Work Breakdown Struc		$5,000.00	$5,000.00	$3,000.00	$2,000.00	$0.00
	· Training Budget	$5,000.00					
	Light Rail Phase 2 - Work Session 13	$5,000.00					

Figure WS.13b – Review Budget Performance

6.1.7 Update Project Key Performance Indicators

We have added a number of custom fields to the project information dialog to allow for maintaining key performance indicators (KPIs) for cost, project, schedule and work. The cost, schedule and work KPIs are determined by comparing the current status against the baseline and are automatically calculated for you. You will need to update the 'Project KPI' yourself as it gives you the opportunity to reflect on the actual project status based on more than the numerical facts for cost, schedule and work and allows you to reflect overall project health in this KPI.

Project KPIs are accessed from the 'Project ribbon > Properties section > Project Information button'. This opens the 'Project Information' dialog. While you cannot change the cost, schedule or work KPIs, we encourage you to view these as they should aid in setting the project KPI. To change the Project KPI, select the dropdown list and rate the project as 'On Track, On Watch or Troubled'.

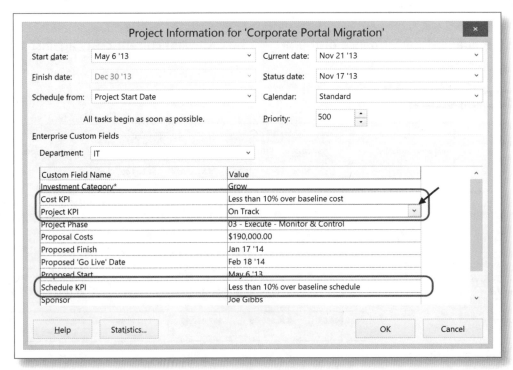

Figure 6.16 Update Project KPIs –
Cost and Schedule are calculated, Project KPI set manually

6.1.8 Reschedule Incomplete Work from the Past

In a perfect project delivery situation, where every team member completes every task on schedule, there should never be unfinished work scheduled in the past, i.e. before the project status date. In reality, very few weeks go by without at least one task not getting completed on schedule and therefore is late. Having a late task in the plan, while obviously not ideal, does not necessarily mean that the project is red, it simply means that the work scheduled for that task did not happen on schedule.

The assigned resource can no longer complete the work on those tasks on the originally planned date. Therefore we need to move this work forward and rescheduled it to a date when it can be completed (as this work still needs to get done).

The first step is moving the scheduled dates for all incomplete work forward of the status date (which represents the last day of the reporting period), as this is the earliest possible date on which the work can get completed. Next, review the plan to potentially reschedule it further, depending on resource availability and task dependencies as bringing the rescheduled work forward has potentially over-allocated some resources.

This is accomplished from the 'Project ribbon > Status section' select 'Update Project' to launch the 'Update Project' dialog.

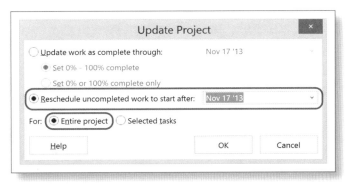

Figure 6.17 Reschedule Uncompleted Work

On this dialog, select the second option 'Reschedule uncompleted work to start after' and ensure that the date field is set to the current status date. Then ensure that the 'Entire project' radio button is selected and press 'OK'. Project will then move all tasks with uncompleted work forward to start (or continue if some actual work had been recorded) after the current status date. Change highlighting will provide full details of the changes made to the overall project as this will not only move the uncompleted tasks forward, but also move forward any predecessor tasks and could even create resource over-allocations as this work is rescheduled (we will discuss how to resolve these resource over-allocations in the next section).

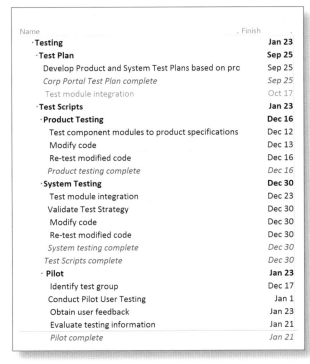

Figure 6.18a Before Rescheduling of Uncompleted Work

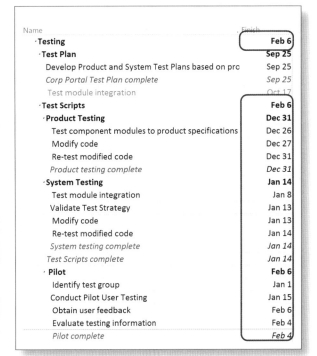

Figure 6.18b After Rescheduling of Uncompleted Work

CAUTION:

Do not select the first option from the 'Update Project' dialog – 'Update work as complete through'. This option assumes that all work has completed based on the original plan as of the status date and updates the completion percentage accordingly. A proactive project manager would not want the project status updated automatically without detailed status and timesheets from the team members.

6.1.9 Resolve Resource Over-allocations

The results of the actions taken to process the weekly status updates may result in resource over-allocations as show by the burning man icon in the 'Indicator Column'.

It isn't necessary to level resources on a weekly basis as an hour or 2 over-allocation as a result of tracking actuals/revising remaining work to be higher one week may well be cleared next week as a result of the same resource completing another task under estimate the following week.

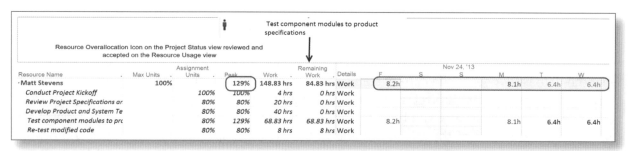

Figure 6.19 Review and Validate Resource Overallocations resulting from processing status Updates

Therefore, while you should always review and be aware of any resource over-allocations, we believe you can still be a proactive project manager allowing some resources to be slightly over-allocated for a week or two. However, if there is a weekly trend of exceeding estimates and or an escalating level of over-allocation, corrective actions are needed to resolve the over-allocations on one or more resources. Resolving resource over-allocations as part of weekly status updates will follow the same process defined in Chapter 4 – Level Resource Workload.

TIPS & HINTS:

During project execution, resource leveling can be performed with the option of 'Level only within available slack' set, which will level the resource workload as best as possible without moving dates on the critical path. This is often a good option to resolve the most serious over-allocations.

6.2 Identify Variances and Take Corrective Action

The project baseline reflects the approved project at the beginning of the project as well as any approved changes along the way and is used to measure project progress. Actuals from the status updates are compared to the baseline and variance is calculated for start date, finish date, work, duration and cost, etc.

The '07 – Baselining' view summarizes the key variance fields and show the traffic light (red, yellow, green) key performance indicators.

On a weekly basis, a proactive project manager reviews all variances, paying particular attention to variances on critical tasks. The reason is that variance on critical tasks have a direct impact on the project finish date.

Many times, the project KPIs are adversely affected by updates from team members which include slipping tasks, delays in tasks and schedule. Slipping tasks and project delays can also cause over-allocation of the project resources. When these situations occur, the project manager needs to proactively take action to level the workload for existing resources, assign additional resources, and negotiate increases to resource availability to work on the project.

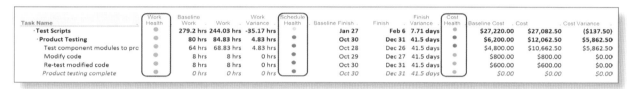

Task Name	Work Health	Baseline Work	Work	Work Variance	Schedule Health	Baseline Finish	Finish	Finish Variance	Cost Health	Baseline Cost	Cost	Cost Variance
Test Scripts	●	279.2 hrs	244.03 hrs	-35.17 hrs	●	Jan 27	Feb 6	7.71 days	●	$27,220.00	$27,082.50	($137.50)
Product Testing	●	80 hrs	84.83 hrs	4.83 hrs	●	Oct 30	Dec 31	41.5 days	●	$6,200.00	$12,062.50	$5,862.50
Test component modules to pro	●	64 hrs	68.83 hrs	4.83 hrs	●	Oct 28	Dec 26	41.5 days	●	$4,800.00	$10,662.50	$5,862.50
Modify code	●	8 hrs	8 hrs	0 hrs	●	Oct 29	Dec 27	41.5 days	●	$800.00	$800.00	$0.00
Re-test modified code	●	8 hrs	8 hrs	0 hrs	●	Oct 30	Dec 31	41.5 days	●	$600.00	$600.00	$0.00
Product testing complete	●	0 hrs	0 hrs	0 hrs	●	Oct 30	Dec 31	41.5 days	●	$0.00	$0.00	$0.00

Figure 6.20 Review Project Variances - '07 - Baselining View'

Once variances are analyzed, changes to the project plan may be required to reduce or control these variances. You can change any aspect of the project such as changing resourcing, modifying dependencies and even changing estimates to deal with identified variances. Each project variance will require a different action based on the specific circumstance that caused the variance. Following the principles of developing a proactive project plan in Chapter 4, the project plan can be updated to deal with identified variances.

6.2.1 Taking Corrective Action on the Critical Path

One of the key variances that is likely to occur through processing weekly status updates is schedule slippage. As such, it is important to be able to quickly identify where to take effective corrective action. Delays on the critical path push the project completion date, so any corrective action on these tasks will have the biggest impact on getting the project back on track. Below is a technique to help identify the longest tasks on the critical path, which is where project managers should look to take action when they experience schedule slippage.

1. Filter for tasks on the Critical Path
2. Hide all Summary Tasks
3. Sort the critical tasks based on duration
4. Review and make changes to the longest critical tasks

We recommend using the '10 – Project Status' view for this technique.

STEP 1

Filter for tasks on the Critical Path – As the tasks on the critical path determine the end date for the project, in all likelihood these are the tasks that we need to focus on. (In fact, shortening non-critical path tasks will have no impact on the project's end date and therefore are typically not the focus of the weekly status update procedure). To highlight the critical path, from the 'Format ribbon > Bar

Styles section' select the 'Critical Path' checkbox. This will change the color of all critical path tasks in the Gantt area of the view. You should also filter the view to show only the critical tasks. To do this, select the filter arrow from the 'Critical Path' column heading and select only the tasks where this flag is set to 'Yes'. We like to do both since tasks can become non-critical when you take corrective action and will turn blue on the Gantt chart.

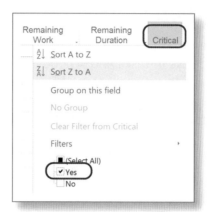

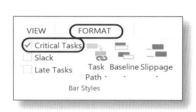

Figure 6.21a Step 1
Display Critical Tasks

Figure 6.21b Step 1 -
Autofilter on Critical
column

STEP 2

Hide all Summary Tasks – Without hiding summary tasks, the sort on duration will only sort within each deliverable. We hide the summary tasks to view the critical path across phases and deliverables.

From the 'Format ribbon > Show/Hide section' deselect the 'Summary Tasks' checkbox.

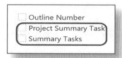

Figure 6.22
Step 2 Deselect
Summary Tasks

STEP 3

Sort the critical tasks based on duration – As our focus is on reducing the overall schedule variance for the project, sorting the tasks based on 'Duration' allows for a focus on the longer duration tasks (or at least the tasks where a change is likely to have the largest impact to the overall project duration). From the 'View ribbon > Data section' select the 'Sort' button to bring up the 'Sort' dialog. Then sort by 'Duration' in descending order. (This sort works even if the 'Duration' column is not visible, but we find showing it during these technique actually helps as it provides instant feedback in how effective the changes are)

Figure 6.23a Step 3
– Sort by Duration

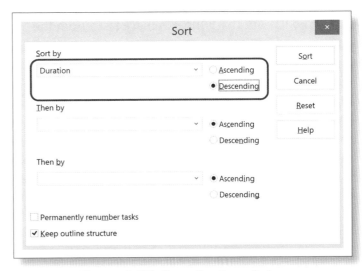

Figure 6.23b Step 3 – Sort dialog

STEP 4

Review and make changes to the longest critical tasks – Starting at the top of the sorted list, examine the task and determine if it is feasible to make any changes to reduce the duration.

Task Name	Duration
Obtain user feedback	16 days
Test component modules to product specifications	10 days
Portal Design Implementationr testing (primary debugging)	7.5 days
Test module integration	5 days
Validate Test Strategy	3.13 days
Evaluate testing information	2.5 days
Prepare Cutover Plan	2.5 days
Modify code	1.25 days
Re-test modified code	1.25 days
Conduct Pilot User Testing	1.25 days
Summarize activities required to move product into production	1.25 days

Figure 6.24 Step 4 – Review the Critical Tasks
with the Longest Duration

Make any changes to the task that you consider feasible to shorten the duration. As discussed in the section above, you can change resourcing, dependencies, estimates, etc., following the principles defined in Chapter 4.

Once you make a change that results in an improvement in the task duration, take a deep breath and review the change to ensure that you are not compromising the overall integrity of the project to deal with a schedule overrun. It is always better to negotiate a schedule change than to compromise the overall project and have a sub-standard, unacceptable on-time delivery.

Continue making changes to the longest critical tasks until you have achieved the desired schedule changes.

Once you have finished this technique, you will need to undo Steps 1-3. To do this, press F3 on your keyboard to clear all filters. Then, from the 'View ribbon > Data section' select the 'Sort' button and select 'Sort by ID'. Add back the summary tasks from the 'Format ribbon > Show/Hide section' and select 'Summary Tasks'.

**Figure 6.25a
Restore
Project Settings –
Sort by ID**

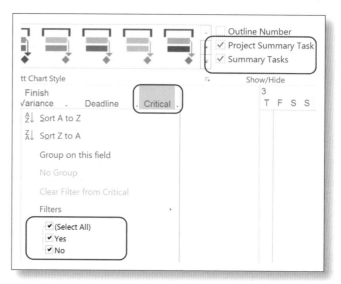

**Figure 6.25b
Restore Project Settings – Display Summary
Tasks and Remove Critical Path Filter**

6.3 Dealing with Changes on the Project

Occasionally there will be other changes to the project that require a more substantial change to the project than tweaking the plan to adjust for a few days schedule slippage.

6.3.1 Slipping Tasks

You may encounter tasks that are slipping due to a number of reasons (poor estimates, resource unavailability, uncontrollable risk events occurring, etc.). Bottom line, you have tasks slipping that no matter how many changes you make using the technique described above, a critical deadline cannot be met. In this situation, you may have no choice but to change the 'Remaining Duration' for the task.

Figure 6.26a Dealing with Slipping Tasks - Before Change

Figure 6.26b Dealing with Slipping Tasks - After Change - Note Resource Overallocation

Alternatively, you may have to do a significant resource reallocation to free up additional resources to work on the current critical tasks by delaying or rescheduling other tasks.

In both these instances, these are last measure efforts and should only be taken as a case of last resort as both alternatives are not ideal – forced overtime or robbing from other tasks to deal with a current emergency (which will likely result in another future emergency when the other task is late and missing a deadline)

6.3.2 Changes in task duration

Changes in the project environment demand that tasks on the project must be done more quickly. To do this, change the 'Remaining Duration' for the task to shorten the length of the task. In a perfect world, the assigned resources will still have adequate capacity to complete the task and all is good. In a more likely scenario, the assigned resources will be over-allocated as a result of this change and you would need to follow the technique above for taking corrective action on the critical path.

6.3.3 Delay in Schedule

Something comes up and your project must be delayed for a period of time (emergency maintenance request, corporate reshuffle, natural disaster). When your project encounters a delay or stall and you need to stop work on current tasks and reschedule all remaining work to a future date, from the 'Project ribbon > Status section' select 'Update Project'. This will launch the 'Update Project' dialog, from which you select the 'Reschedule uncompleted work to start after:' and then from the calendar select the anticipated restart date.

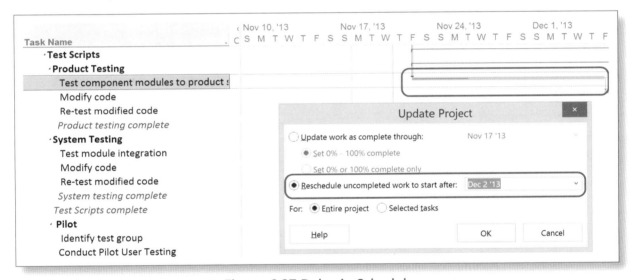

Figure 6.27 Delay in Schedule

This will do 2 things: First it will create a split in any in-progress tasks to ensure that actuals recorded remain in the appropriate timeframe and moves all future work forward to the restart date. Second, it will create a 'Start no earlier than' constraint on any other tasks that didn't automatically reschedule due to dependencies on the in-progress tasks. While, in general we do not recommend task constraints, in this case, the constraint is acceptable as it reflects the reality that these tasks cannot start until after the constraint date.

Figure 6.28 Delay in Schedule Results - Split Task and Rescheduled Tasks

WORK SESSION #14 – PROCESS STATUS UPDATES

OBJECTIVE

Process the team member's status updates and review the impact that these have on the overall project schedule. Remedial actions will be required to maintain the project schedule as a result of a significant task overrun from one team member.

STEP 1   **Confirm all timesheets have been entered**

Validate all timesheets have been entered by running the 'Timesheet Compliance by Project Manager' report and validate that there are no exceptions for this timesheet period (January 05, 2015 – January 09, 2015). (If you do not have PWA, this step (and the next 3) are not necessary as you entered the timesheets directly in Microsoft Project through the previous exercise and therefore would be aware of any missing timesheets.)

STEP 2   **Review status update changes**

Review the schedule changes resulting from the status updates using the 'Approval' process in PWA

STEP 3   **Accept Status Updates**

Accept the status updates in PWA.

STEP 4   **Update Status Date**

Open the plan in Microsoft Project and set the status date January 11, 2015 (the Sunday at the end of the timesheet period – this is based on our timesheets period running from Monday thru Sunday – your organization may have a different weekly timesheet period).

STEP 5   **Mark Milestones as complete**

Update the 'Project Start' milestone to complete to reflect the fact that the project has started.

STEP 6   **Update KPIs**

Review and update the Project KPI to be on-track.

STEP 7   **Reschedule uncompleted work**

Reschedule all uncompleted work forward the current status date – January 11, 2015

| STEP 8 | Address schedule slippage |

As a result of processing the status updates and rescheduling the uncompleted work, the project is now late and we are not forecasting to meet the project deadline. Following the technique described above to 'Taking Corrective Action on the Critical Path', take appropriate actions to try to bring the project back on schedule.

EXPECTED RESULTS

Task Name	% Work Complete	Cost Health	Work Health	Schedule Health	Duration	Finish	Finish Variance	Deadline	Critical
Light Rail Phase 2 - Work Session 14	3%				48.88 days	Mar 12	-1.63 days	NA	Yes
Project Start	100%				0 days	Jan 6	0 days	NA	No
Planning	3%				48.88 days	Mar 12	-1.63 days	NA	Yes
Scope Document	12%				14.38 days	Jan 23	-1.63 days	NA	Yes
Specify Deliverables and Acceptance Crite	33%				6.13 days	Jan 15	4.63 days	NA	Yes
Build Work Breakdown Structure	0%				6.25 days	Jan 23	-1.63 days	NA	Yes
Document Project Assumptions	0%				5 days	Jan 22	4.63 days	NA	Yes
Scope Document complete	0%				0 days	Jan 23	-1.63 days	NA	Yes
Procurement Plan	0%				34.5 days	Mar 12	-1.63 days	NA	Yes
Determine Procurement Requirements	0%				2.5 days	Jan 27	-1.63 days	NA	Yes
Define & Publish Subcontractor Scope	0%				5 days	Feb 3	-1.63 days	NA	Yes
Identify Potential Subcontractors	0%				1 mon	Mar 12	-1.63 days	NA	Yes
Identify Subcontract Type	0%				10 days	Feb 17	-1.63 days	NA	Yes
Document Subcontractor Management P	0%				10 days	Feb 19	-9.63 days	NA	Yes
Procurement Plan complete	0%				0 days	Mar 12	-1.63 days	NA	Yes
Risk Management Plan	0%				12.5 days	Feb 3	7.56 days	NA	No
Identify Project Risks	0%				6.25 days	Jan 23	7.56 days	NA	No
Analyze Project Risks	0%				3.13 days	Jan 28	7.56 days	NA	No
Document Risk Management Plan	0%				3.13 days	Feb 3	7.56 days	NA	No
Risk Management Plan complete	0%				0 days	Feb 3	7.56 days	NA	No
Planning Phase complete	0%				0 days	Mar 12	-1.63 days	NA	Yes
Light Rail Phase 2 complete	0%				0 days	Mar 12	-1.63 days	Feb 13	Yes

Figure WS.14 – Results of Process Status Updates

6.4 Maintain the Baseline for Scope Changes

For approved project scope changes, new tasks need to be added to the schedule and selectively baselined, saved and published. The baseline should only be updated if there are valid reasons to do so.

It goes without saying that baselines should only be updated with proper authorization.

We typically see baseline changes for these reasons:

1. Formal Change Requests
   Any formal request for new scope on the project is a valid reason for updating the baseline.

2. Customer directed reschedule
   When a customer delays the schedule for any reason, I typically use the 'Update Project' feature to push all remaining work out and show the customer the new schedule that resulted from their delay. I then add all affected tasks to the baseline. While the customer may not formally have 'approved' change to the project, they did so indirectly by forcing the schedule change. We can still track target dates through the deadline date.

3. Reporting on new variance
   If a project falls far enough behind that all remaining work shows up with red indicators, it may be time to ask the sponsor for approval to update the baseline to allow the team to track the new variance. By this point, we have bigger problems than baseline perfection and it may be valuable to see where we are hitting additional delays on the remaining work. You will still have a backup of the other baselines to revert back to for final reporting.

6.4.1 Maintaining the Baseline

As major changes occur on the project, it is important to add any new, approved scope to the schedule and update the baseline to reflect the new approved work while preserving the current status of the project's performance to date against the original baseline.

In addition to adding the new scope of work to the baseline, we can also add any tasks that are affected by the added scope. Imagine your sponsor asks to add a task to 'Validate Test Strategy' (20 hours of work), which will impact your subsequent tasks and the project completion date. In that case, you would need to include not only the 'Validate Test Strategy' task, but also the impacted tasks to reflect the new agreed upon schedule. This approach helps to ensure that we keep the history of actuals-to-date and captures the changes for upcoming work.

To maintain the baseline on the project that is now in execution, follow these steps:

STEP 1

Add the task (or tasks) that represent the new scope of work, then add the effort estimate, assign resources and include the tasks in the dependency network.

Task Name	Work Health	Baseline Work	Work	Work Variance	Schedule Health	Baseline Finish	Finish	Finish Variance	Dec 22, '13 S S M T W T F S S M T W	Dec 29, '13
·System Testing	●	88 hrs	63.2 hrs	-24.8 hrs	●	Nov 20 '13	Dec 30 '13	26.42 days		0%
Test module integration	●	72 hrs	32 hrs	-40 hrs	●	Nov 14 '13	Dec 23 '13	26.04 days	0%	0%
Validate Test Strategy		0 hrs	20 hrs	20 hrs		NA	Dec 30 '13	0 days		0%
Modify code	●	8 hrs	3.2 hrs	-4.8 hrs	●	Nov 18 '13	Dec 30 '13	28.42 days		0%
Re-test modified code	●	8 hrs	8 hrs	0 hrs	●	Nov 19 '13	Dec 30 '13	27.42 days		0%
System testing complete	●	0 hrs	0 hrs	0 hrs	●	Nov 20 '13	Dec 30 '13	26.42 days		12/30
Test Scripts complete	●	0 hrs	0 hrs	0 hrs	●	Nov 20 '13	Dec 30 '13	26.42 days		12/30

Figure 6.29 Add Additional Task - Task Details, Effort Estimate, Resources and Dependencies

STEP 2

Select all the new tasks at the same time and from the 'Task ribbon' select 'Tasks > Inactivate', which will act much the same as 'Track Changes' in Word, where it deletes the changes, but let's you see what you deleted. This way, we are viewing the current schedule, but with the new scope of work ready to be activated.

Task Name	Work Health	Baseline Work	Work	Work Variance	Schedule Health	Baseline Finish	Finish	Finish Variance	Dec 22, '13 S S M T W T F S S M T W	Dec 29, '13
·System Testing	●	88 hrs	43.2 hrs	-44.8 hrs	●	Nov 20 '13	Dec 24 '13	23.29 days		0%
Test module integration	●	72 hrs	32 hrs	-40 hrs	●	Nov 14 '13	Dec 24 '13	26.04 days	0%	0%
Validate Test Strategy		0 hrs	20 hrs	20 hrs		NA	Dec 30 '13	0 days		
Modify code	●	8 hrs	3.2 hrs	-4.8 hrs	●	Nov 18 '13	Dec 24 '13	25.29 days		0%
Re-test modified code	●	8 hrs	8 hrs	0 hrs	●	Nov 19 '13	Dec 24 '13	24.29 days		0%
System testing complete	●	0 hrs	0 hrs	0 hrs	●	Nov 20 '13	Dec 24 '13	23.29 days		12/24
Test Scripts complete	●	0 hrs	0 hrs	0 hrs	●	Nov 20 '13	Dec 24 '13	23.29 days		12/24

Figure 6.30 Inactivate Task - Note Strikeout

STEP 3

With the new tasks still selected, press 'Tasks > Inactivate' again to activate the tasks that represent the new scope of work. Now, change highlighting will indicate which detailed tasks are affected by the new scope of work.

    a. In the example, the new task has change highlighting as well as the downstream task finish dates. As a result, all tasks with change highlighting can be added to the updated baseline.

    b. Using the 'Background Color' from the 'Task ribbon > Font section' set the 'Background Color' of all lines in the project plan where Change Highlighting is set to aid in communicating the impact of the changes to the Sponsor

    c. We can now tell the sponsor the impact of proposed change

Task Name	Work Health	Baseline Work	Work	Work Variance	Schedule Health	Baseline Finish	Finish	Finish Variance	Dec 22, '13 S S M T W T F S S M T W	Dec 29, '13
·System Testing	●	88 hrs	63.2 hrs	-24.8 hrs	●	Nov 20 '13	Dec 30 '13	26.42 days		0%
Test module integration	●	72 hrs	32 hrs	-40 hrs	●	Nov 14 '13	Dec 23 '13	26.04 days	0%	0%
Validate Test Strategy		0 hrs	20 hrs	20 hrs		NA	Dec 30 '13	0 days		0%
Modify code	●	8 hrs	3.2 hrs	-4.8 hrs	●	Nov 18 '13	Dec 30 '13	28.42 days		0%
Re-test modified code	●	8 hrs	8 hrs	0 hrs	●	Nov 19 '13	Dec 30 '13	27.42 days		0%
System testing complete	●	0 hrs	0 hrs	0 hrs	●	Nov 20 '13	Dec 30 '13	26.42 days		12/30
Test Scripts complete	●	0 hrs	0 hrs	0 hrs	●	Nov 20 '13	Dec 30 '13	26.42 days		12/30

Figure 6.31 Change Impact Highlighted for Approval -
Blue Background new tasks and Green Background impacted tasks

STEP 4

Select the tasks that are highlighted. From the 'Project ribbon > Baseline section' select 'Set Baseline', choose the 'Selected Tasks' checkbox and choose to 'Roll up baselines' and 'To all summary tasks'.

Figure 6.32 Set Baseline Dialog

The baseline now represents the original schedule as well as the approved change from the sponsor. You will notice that we didn't overwrite the variance on task two, where we went over the baseline work estimate and ran late. With this method, we preserve overages that have already occurred, but incorporate approved dates for new and existing tasks.

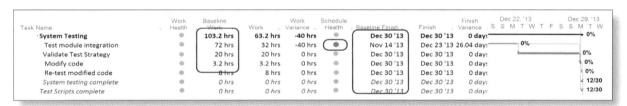

Figure 6.33 Updated Project Baseline - Original baseline
preserved while baseline is reset for approved changes

In our scenario, we have completed the task 'Test module integration' where we went over the baseline work estimate by 40 hours. As a result, the schedule health indicator has turned red and since this task was not included in the change impacts, the performance against baseline is preserved.

At this point, you will want to repeat the steps in 'Saving a History of Baselines' above, but choose Baseline9 (or Baseline1 if you prefer) this time as we want to always preserve Baseline10.

If the sponsor changes her mind on this new scope of work, we can simply delete the added tasks and copy Baseline10 into Baseline to return the schedule to the previous state.

WORK SESSION #15 – PROCESS PROJECT CHANGE REQUEST

OBJECTIVE

Process an approved project change request and update the project baseline to include the approved changes

STEP 1   Add tasks to the schedule

Management has notified you that based on recommendations from the vendor, they approve you adding an additional task to your plan to review the project risks with the vendor to ensure adequate risk mitigation plans are in place. You negotiate with management that 16 hours will be required to complete this task. Insert this task into the plan prior to the 'Documentation of the Risk Management Plan', assign it to yourself and make the appropriate changes to the existing dependencies.

STEP 2   Obtain formal approval of schedule changes

Review and validate the impact this change has on the overall project plan and obtain final management approval of the changes.

STEP 3   Update Baseline

With Management approval of the change, add the new and changed tasks to the Project Baseline

EXPECTED RESULTS

	Task Mode	Task Name	Work Health	Baseline Work	Work	Work Variance	Schedule Health	Baseline Finish	Finish	Finish Variance
		Light Rail Phase 2 - Work Session 15		**325.6 hrs**	**358 hrs**	**32.4 hrs**		**Mar 16**	**Mar 12**	**-1.63 days**
✓		*Project Start*		*0 hrs*	*0 hrs*	*0 hrs*		*Jan 6*	*Jan 6*	*0 days*
		Planning		**325.6 hrs**	**358 hrs**	**32.4 hrs**		**Mar 16**	**Mar 12**	**-1.63 days**
		Scope Document		**64 hrs**	**86 hrs**	**22 hrs**		**Jan 26**	**Jan 23**	**-1.63 days**
		Specify Deliverables and Acceptance Crite		8 hrs	30 hrs	22 hrs		Jan 8	Jan 15	4.63 days
		Build Work Breakdown Structure		40 hrs	40 hrs	0 hrs		Jan 26	Jan 26	-0.63 days
		Document Project Assumptions		16 hrs	16 hrs	0 hrs		Jan 15	Jan 22	4.63 days
		Scope Document complete		*0 hrs*	*0 hrs*	*0 hrs*		*Jan 26*	*Jan 23*	*-1.63 days*
		Procurement Plan		**216 hrs**	**216 hrs**	**0 hrs**		**Mar 16**	**Mar 12**	**-1.63 days**
		Determine Procurement Requirements		8 hrs	8 hrs	0 hrs		Jan 29	Jan 27	-1.63 days
		Define & Publish Subcontractor Scope		16 hrs	16 hrs	0 hrs		Feb 5	Feb 3	-1.63 days
		Identify Potential Subcontractors		128 hrs	128 hrs	0 hrs		Mar 16	Mar 12	-1.63 days
		Identify Subcontract Type		32 hrs	32 hrs	0 hrs		Feb 19	Feb 17	-1.63 days
		Document Subcontractor Management P		32 hrs	32 hrs	0 hrs		Mar 5	Mar 3	-1.63 days
		Procurement Plan complete		*0 hrs*	*0 hrs*	*0 hrs*		*Mar 16*	*Mar 12*	*-1.63 days*
		Risk Management Plan		**56 hrs**	**56 hrs**	**0 hrs**		**Feb 3**	**Feb 3**	**0 days**
		Identify Project Risks		20 hrs	20 hrs	0 hrs		Jan 14	Jan 21	5.56 days
		Analyze Project Risks		10 hrs	10 hrs	0 hrs		Jan 19	Jan 26	5.56 days
		Review Risks with SAS Vendor		16 hrs	16 hrs	0 hrs		Jan 29	Jan 29	0 days
		Document Risk Management Plan		10 hrs	10 hrs	0 hrs		Feb 3	Feb 3	0 days
		Risk Management Plan complete		*0 hrs*	*0 hrs*	*0 hrs*		*Feb 3*	*Feb 3*	*0 days*
		Planning Phase complete		*0 hrs*	*0 hrs*	*0 hrs*		*Mar 16*	*Mar 12*	*-1.63 days*
		Light Rail Phase 2 complete		*0 hrs*	*0 hrs*	*0 hrs*		*Mar 16*	*Mar 12*	*-1.63 days*

Figure WS.15 Change Request Processed

7

CHAPTER 7:

Preparing Status Reports

At this point, we have accepted all the status updates from our team members into the project and scheduled, leveled and adjusted our project to accommodate the changes from our team and, hopefully, been able to successfully keep the project on track. Next, we need to prepare the project status reports as communication is a key part being an effective project manager. This chapter will review how Microsoft Project and Project Web App (PWA) support effective communication.

7.1 Prepare the Project Timeline

If you are not already familiar with the 'Project Timeline' feature in Microsoft Project, we encourage you to explore it and begin to use it. If you are already familiar, I expect you're nodding your head in agreement that is it a tremendous tool to help us effectively communicate project status.

From the 'View ribbon > Split View section' ensure that the 'Timeline' checkbox is selected. As you will note, you can have only one split screen at a time, so you can either have the screen split to show the timeline on the top or the detailed screen on the bottom.

Figure 7.1 Add the Timeline to the view

If you select the Timeline window, and then go to the 'Format ribbon', the commands on the ribbon change to be specific to creating and formatting the timeline.

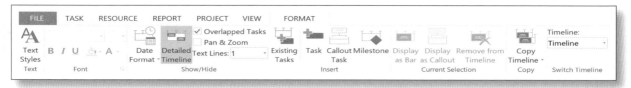

Figure 7.2 Timeline Format ribbon

Now, select the elements of the project plan you would like to display on the Timeline. You can include Summary Tasks, Detailed Tasks or Milestones. Tasks can be added to the Timeline in three ways:

- select the appropriate line from the plan and use the 'Shortcut Menu' to 'Add to Timeline'
- from the 'Task ribbon > Properties section', select 'Add to Timeline' or
- from the 'Format ribbon > Insert section > Existing Tasks' launch the 'Add Tasks to Timeline' dialog. This dialog presents the project plan structure allowing you to select which elements you wish to add to the 'Timeline'.

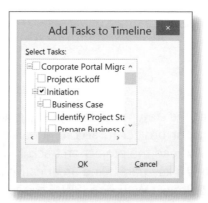

Figure 7.3 Add Task to Timeline Dialog

As a starting point, we recommend collapsing your schedule to show only outline level 1 elements and include all these on your timeline. That means we're starting with the Project Summary task as well as all the phases and project-level milestones to ensure the high level structure of the project is included on the Timeline.

**Figure 7.4 Select Plan Elements for
display on the timeline**

Next, we recommend filtering your view to display only milestone tasks and selecting all major milestones for including on the Timeline.

Finally, expand the view again to include all project tasks and select any other key project components critical for display on the Timeline, recognizing that the Timeline is intended to be a project summary only.

With these elements on the timeline, you can then begin to manipulate the format of the timeline to improve the presentation and readability.

For example, using 'Overlapped' checkbox from the 'Format ribbon > Show/Hide section' you can select whether tasks would overlap or display in separate lines. Similarly, from the same area you can control the thickness of the bars by controlling the number of 'Text Lines'. You can change the color of a bar by selecting it and then changing the fill color from the 'Font section' of the ribbon.

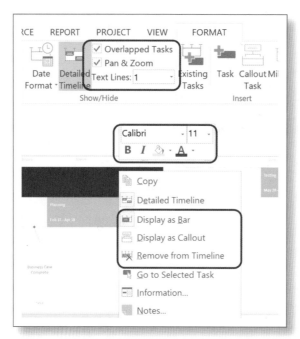

Figure 7.5 Timeline View Customizations

We like to use the 'Display as Callout' option for the Project Summary Task and then adjust the font style and size to ensure it is very visible. Similarly, consider using different fonts/colors for key project milestones so that they standout on the Timeline. Use a lighter background color so that key activities can be easily reviewed.

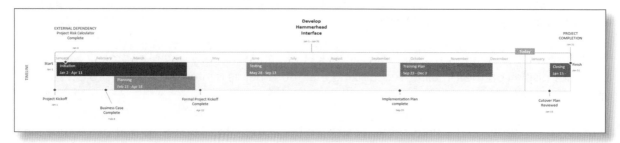

Figure 7.6 Timeline in Microsoft Project

With this quick review of formatting options completed, we then suggest you expand your 'Project Outline' and review the project plan to select other key elements of the project that your stakeholders would be interested in seeing.

We leave it to you to explore these various formatting methods to develop an effective timeline to provide a valuable graphic representing the current status of the key elements of your project plan.

Once you publish your plan, the timeline will automatically display on the Project Site home page.

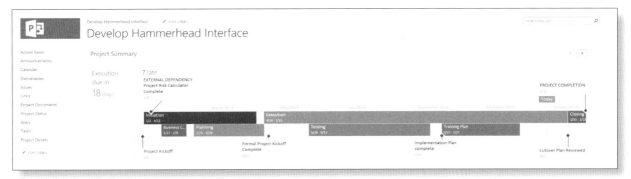

Figure 7.7 Timeline on Project Site Home Page

You also have the option of copying the timeline and using it in PowerPoint as an Office Object. From the 'Format ribbon > Copy section' select the 'Copy Timeline' pull down menu and select 'Full Size' and paste it into another Microsoft Office product, such as PowerPoint and Word. You are welcome to experiment with the other two copy options 'For Email and For Presentation', but we're found we get the best results from 'Full Size' and then managing the picture size in the destination tool. If the timeline comes across wider than the document you are pasting into, consider resizing the Microsoft Project window before copying as that will resize nicely rather than trying to do it manually afterwards.

Figure 7.8 Copy Timeline for use outside
Microsoft Project

7.2 Update SharePoint Project Status

Each week, you should provide a narrative where you can provide additional insight into the successes, problems and specific relevant information about the current project activities.

In PWA, from the 'Project Site Home Page' go to the 'Project Status' area and select '+ New Item' to enter a summary narrative of the weekly project status. Selecting 'Save' moves the previous status entry to the historical status list and replaces it with the current status entry just created.

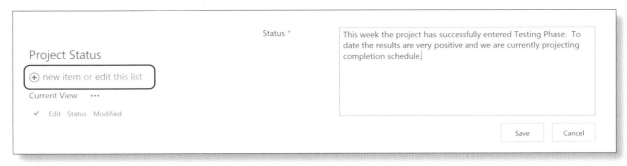

Figure 7.9 PWA Project Status - Add weekly status update

You can view the full list of weekly status entries by selecting the 'Project Status' link from the 'Quick Launch' on the left.

Figure 7.10 PWA Project Status area

7.3 Access Reports in the Business Intelligence Center

The Business Intelligence Center has a number of reports that use the information maintained in PWA to create status reports and project dashboards.

You access these reports from PWA's Quick Launch 'Reports > Sensei Reports'. Report Area 5 has a number of valuable reports for effective status communication with your project stakeholders.

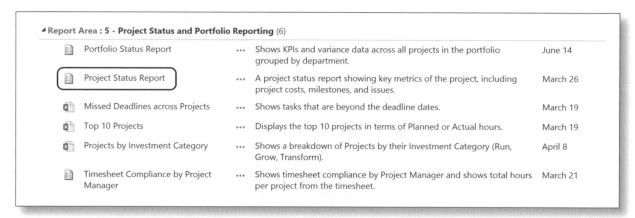

Figure 7.11 Business Intelligence Center - Project Status Reports

We call your attention specifically to the Project Status Report. Click on this report and then select your project from the 'Parameter' section on the right and then click 'Apply' to display the project's status report. This report summarizes your schedule and project site data and can be exported to PDF or Microsoft Word format.

Project Status Report

Corporate Portal Migration

Status Date: 11/17/2013

Project Summary

Project Health	Schedule Health	Work Health	Cost Health
●	●	●	●
Start	**Baseline Finish**	**Finish**	**Finish Variance**
5/6/2013	2/7/2014	2/7/2014	0 days
Project Phase	**Project Manager**	**Sponsor**	**Department**
03 - Execute - Monitor & Control	Steve Router	Joe Gibbs	IT

Project Description

Create a new Corporate Portal which reflects the new business groups and products based on merger between the Barcelona Company and the Venice Corporation. The new company name will be Barcelona but will have business groups and product offerings from both companies.

% Complete

Project Status

11/26/2013 - This week the project has successfully entered Testing Phase. To date the results are very positive and we are currently projecting completion schedule.

Current Project Milestones

Milestone	Baseline Finish	Finish	Variance
Portal Design Implementation Code/Developer Testing Complete	10/11/2013	12/2/2013	36 days
Product testing complete	10/30/2013	12/16/2013	32 days
System testing complete	12/30/2013	12/30/2013	0 days
Test Scripts complete	12/30/2013	12/30/2013	0 days
Pilot complete	1/27/2014	1/27/2014	0 days
Implementation Plan complete	12/19/2013	1/28/2014	26 days
Cutover Plan complete	12/23/2013	1/31/2014	26 days
Project Closure Report complete	12/31/2013	2/7/2014	26 days
Corp Portal PROJECT COMPLETE	2/7/2014	2/7/2014	0 days

Figure 7.12a Project Status Report Page 1

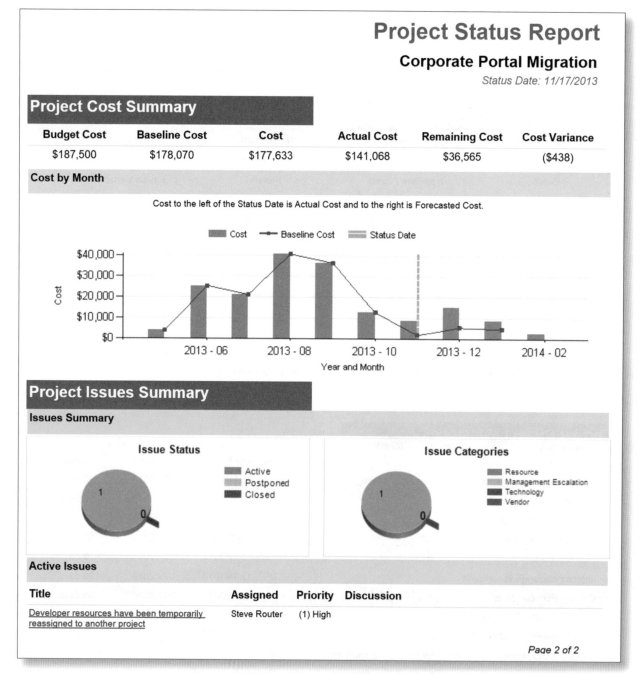

Project Status Report
Corporate Portal Migration
Status Date: 11/17/2013

Project Cost Summary

Budget Cost	Baseline Cost	Cost	Actual Cost	Remaining Cost	Cost Variance
$187,500	$178,070	$177,633	$141,068	$36,565	($438)

Cost by Month

Cost to the left of the Status Date is Actual Cost and to the right is Forecasted Cost.

Project Issues Summary

Issues Summary

Issue Status
- Active
- Postponed
- Closed

Issue Categories
- Resource
- Management Escalation
- Technology
- Vendor

Active Issues

Title	Assigned	Priority	Discussion
Developer resources have been temporarily reassigned to another project	Steve Router	(1) High	

Page 2 of 2

Figure 7.12b Project Status Report Page 2

Another key project status document available in the Business Intelligence Center is the 'Portfolio Status Report' which provides a summary of the Key Performance Indicators for all projects.

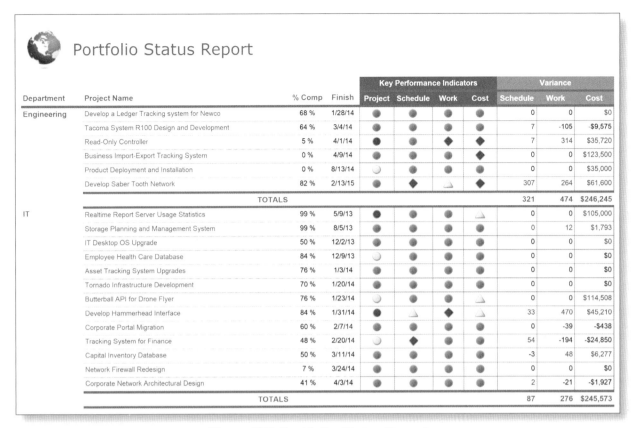

Department	Project Name	% Comp	Finish	Key Performance Indicators				Variance		
				Project	Schedule	Work	Cost	Schedule	Work	Cost
Engineering	Develop a Ledger Tracking system for Newco	68 %	1/28/14	●	●	●	●	0	0	$0
	Tacoma System R100 Design and Development	64 %	3/4/14	●	●	●	●	7	-105	-$9,575
	Read-Only Controller	5 %	4/1/14	●	●	◆	◆	7	314	$35,720
	Business Import-Export Tracking System	0 %	4/9/14	●	●	●	◆	0	0	$123,500
	Product Deployment and Installation	0 %	8/13/14	○	●	●	●	0	0	$35,000
	Develop Saber Tooth Network	82 %	2/13/15	●	◆	△	◆	307	264	$61,600
	TOTALS							321	474	$246,245
IT	Realtime Report Server Usage Statistics	99 %	5/9/13	●	●	●	△	0	0	$105,000
	Storage Planning and Management System	99 %	8/5/13	●	●	●	●	0	12	$1,793
	IT Desktop OS Upgrade	50 %	12/2/13	●	●	●	●	0	0	$0
	Employee Health Care Database	84 %	12/9/13	○	●	●	●	0	0	$0
	Asset Tracking System Upgrades	76 %	1/3/14	●	●	●	●	0	0	$0
	Tornado Infrastructure Development	70 %	1/20/14	●	●	●	●	0	0	$0
	Butterball API for Drone Flyer	76 %	1/23/14	○	●	●	△	0	0	$114,508
	Develop Hammerhead Interface	84 %	1/31/14	●	△	◆	△	33	470	$45,210
	Corporate Portal Migration	60 %	2/7/14	●	●	●	●	0	-39	-$438
	Tracking System for Finance	48 %	2/20/14	○	◆	●	●	54	-194	-$24,850
	Capital Inventory Database	50 %	3/11/14	●	●	●	●	-3	48	$6,277
	Network Firewall Redesign	7 %	3/24/14	●	●	●	●	0	0	$0
	Corporate Network Architectural Design	41 %	4/3/14	●	●	●	●	2	-21	-$1,927
	TOTALS							87	276	$245,573

Figure 7.13 Portfolio Status Report

WORK SESSION #16 – PROJECT STATUS REPORTING

OBJECTIVE

Provide an accurate status of the project to project stakeholders.

STEP 1   **Develop Project Timeline**

Develop a project timeline suitable for submitting to management as part of a project status report.

(The remaining 3 steps are all performed in PWA – therefore if you are using Microsoft Project standalone, while we would expect that you would perform these three remaining steps, you would complete them as appropriate for the tools being used in your organization).

STEP 2   **Review and Update Issues, Risks and Action items**

Review and update all action items, issues and risks in preparation for reporting current project status

STEP 3   **Update Project Home page**

Review the Project Home page to validate currency and accuracy for status reporting

STEP 4   **Distribute Project Status report**

Produce Project Status report and distribute to project stakeholders.

EXPECTED RESULTS

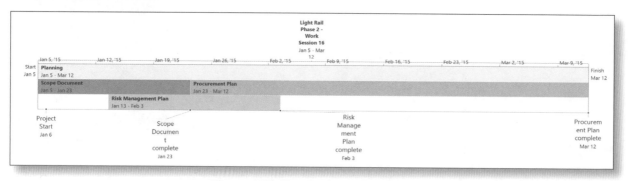

Figure WS.16 – Project Timeline

8

CHAPTER 8:

Closing out the Project

CHAPTER AT A GLANCE

The hard work on our project is now done, the project has been delivered successfully and the team has moved on to work on other projects. But our work isn't quite done yet, as we need to do a little housekeeping to close out the project in Project Web App (PWA).

Frequently, we encounter clients who say that their team members complain about cluttered task lists and timesheets because many tasks from completed projects are still visible, even though the projects are complete. Similarly, resource managers may feel that the Resource Center is unusable due to the volume of old tasks left behind. By following the processes described in this chapter, this will no longer be the case in your organization.

Closing tasks and the entire project is vitally important. We all know that resources don't like to fill out timesheets and this is made worse when there are old tasks cluttering it. Anything we can do to improve the timesheet experience will probably result in a higher percentage of resources complying with the timesheet policy, thus providing a more accurate picture of work taking place. We also want to improve the effectiveness of resource managers by providing resource assignment views that contain only tasks that still apply. All of this is closely related to a proper governance process for closing projects. In this chapter, we will review some best practices on this topic.

We will review how to ensure that tasks that are part of completed or cancelled projects do not appear in My Tasks, Timesheet, and Resource Assignments views while ensuring that any actual work on these tasks is still be correctly rendered in Resource Availability views and in the reports that include actuals. Finally, we will define the appropriate steps to close out the project schedule.

8.1 Close Tasks to Updates

Throughout the project as key deliverables and phases are completed, you can lock the detailed tasks to further updates to make sure that team members don't reopen a completed task and track more time against it. This would skew your project status and communicate new finish dates on tasks that you previously reported as complete.

Open the project in PWA, and from the 'Project Drill-down' on the left, select 'Schedule'. Choose 'Edit in Browser' from the 'Task ribbon > Project section' to ensure that the project is checked out to our PWA session.

CAUTION:

> **Ensure that you do NOT have the schedule open in Microsoft Project at this time, as we will be making changes to the schedule in PWA and need to be able to open the project for edit.**

From the 'Task ribbon > Data section' select the 'Close Tasks to Update' view.

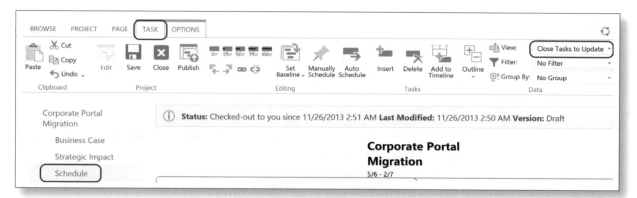

Figure 8.1 Lock Tasks in PWA

This view includes the column 'Locked' which we will change to 'Yes' for any tasks we want to lock for future task updates. You may choose to 'Lock' completed tasks from previous phases on an ongoing basis to prevent accidental time from being tracked against completed tasks and reduce the number of tasks appearing on the team's timesheets.

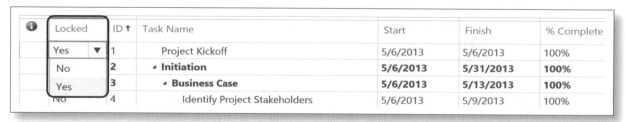

Locked	ID ↑	Task Name	Start	Finish	% Complete
Yes ▼	1	Project Kickoff	5/6/2013	5/6/2013	100%
No	2	◢ Initiation	5/6/2013	5/31/2013	100%
Yes	3	◢ Business Case	5/6/2013	5/13/2013	100%
No	4	Identify Project Stakeholders	5/6/2013	5/9/2013	100%

Figure 8.2 Close Tasks to Update View - Select YES

As a project is closed, all tasks should be locked as it has the following effects for resources:

- The tasks are no longer visible in My Tasks
- The tasks remain in any existing timesheets
- The tasks are not available in new timesheets
- The tasks remain in the Resource Assignment view

CAUTION:
Ensure that all hours have been submitted, approved, and published before closing the task to updates. The project manager should also set the Remaining Work to 0 for any task that will be closed.

8.2 Close Out a Project Schedule

Now that we understand the best way to clean up old tasks from team member timesheets, we turn our attention to the project closure process. A Proactive PPM system includes proper governance to ensure the accuracy and integrity of the data. An essential element of this governance is addressing projects that are completed or cancelled, and to perform several actions on them. We want to ensure that all work effort has been captured, that resources have no remaining work on the project, and that PWA views of active projects and tasks no longer include these completed and cancelled tasks.

When a project is completed, we need to take the appropriate steps to close out the project schedule. This work is done in Microsoft Project. Once all project progress has been recorded, do the following:

STEP 1

Process all updates from team members
It probably goes without saying that we want to capture the total work effort for each project. Since some of the next steps will impact the ability of team members to report their actual work, the first order of business is to inform the project team that you will be closing the project and that they need to submit all hours worked. Once all hours have been submitted, and any discrepancies have been addressed, approve and publish all the task updates. See Chapter 5 for details on processing team member status updates.

STEP 2

Update the Project Status Date
The project status date is the mechanism by which the project manager communicates how up to date the project progress is. This date should reflect the end of the reporting period for which task updates were received. Set this date in the' Project Information' dialog as described in Chapter 5 for Setting Project Status Date.

STEP 3

Update project milestones
Project milestones are not automatically updated by the process of accepting team member progress updates, so the project manager must mark them complete. See Chapter 5 for details on updating project milestones.

STEP 4

Remove any remaining work

If there is any remaining work on a project it will impact resource utilization and availability. To ensure that this data is accurate it is vital to remove any remaining work on completed and cancelled projects. In Microsoft Project, using the '11 Project Closure' view set 'Remaining Work' and 'Remaining Duration' to 0 for all tasks in the project that are not already 0.

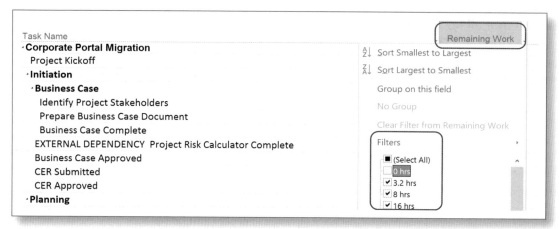

Figure 8.3 Remove Remaining Work – Filter Non-zero Remaining Work

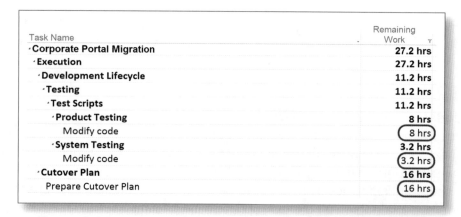

Figure 8.4 Remove Remaining Work – Zero Remaining Work

STEP 5

Remove project tasks from My Tasks, Timesheets, and Resource Assignments views.

The 'Publish' field may be utilized to manage the tasks that are pushed to team members for execution. To remove tasks from these views, set the 'Publish' field to NO using the '11 Project Closure' view. If the project manager changes Publish to No for a task that was previously published, the following changes occur.

- The tasks are no longer visible in My Tasks
- The tasks are no longer visible in any existing timesheets
- The tasks are not available in new timesheets
- The tasks are no longer visible in the Resource Assignment view

Figure 8.5 Remove Tasks from My Tasks

STEP 6

Update the project status to reflect that the project is no longer active
Most likely your organization uses a project-level custom field to distinguish the state of a project, e.g. Active, Closed, Cancelled, etc. This field is typically used to filter non-active projects from PWA views. For example, the Sensei 'Active Project Summary' view only includes projects where the project state is 'Active'. To remove the completed or cancelled project from the active project views, from the 'Project ribbon > Properties section, and select 'Project Information' to open the 'Project Information' dialog and set the project state field used by your organization. If your organization uses a workflow to manage project phases then this project status may be updated automatically.

Figure 8.6 Project Workflow - 5 - Closing

STEP 7

Publish the project
After completing steps 1-6, your project is now ready to be officially closed. From the File menu; Save the project and then Publish it.

STEP 8

Close out Issues and Risks
The final step is to close out any remaining action items, risks and issues in the Project Site. See Chapter 5 for details on managing these items in the Project Site.

APPENDIX A:

Connect to Project Web App

This procedure provides the detailed steps to 1) Connect Internet Explorer to Project Web App (PWA) and 2) Connect Microsoft Project Professional to PWA

Access Project Web App

Follow these instructions to access PWA from a web browser

1. Launch 'Internet Explorer'.
2. Enter **http://'Your Company'/pwa** (where you would replace **'Your Company'** with the address of PWA provided by your Administrator) in the address field.
3. Enter your User name and password, if requested.
4. If the link is correct and you have permissions to the site then the Project Web App home page will be displayed.

Figure A.1 PWA Home Page

5. Save the PWA URL to 'Favorites' for quick access in the future.

**Figure A.2 Add PWA to
your Favorites List**

Figure A.3 Favorites Dialog

Connect Microsoft Project to PWA

Follow these instructions to connect to PWA from Microsoft Project

1. Launch Microsoft Project Professional
2. Select the 'Computer' profile in the Login dialog.

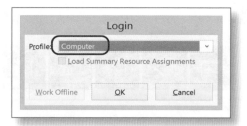

**Figure A.4 Microsoft Project
Login Screen**

3. From the 'File Ribbon', go to the 'Backstage' and select 'Info' from the menu in the left

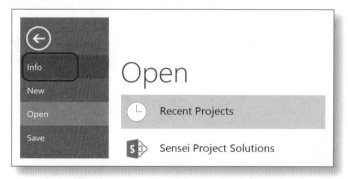

Figure A.5 Backstage - Select Info

4. Select 'Manage Accounts'

Figure A.6 Backstage Info – Manage Accounts

5. This will launch the 'Project Web App Accounts' window.
    a. At the bottom of the screen, we recommend selecting the 'Choose an Account' when starting as this allows you to move between PWA accounts and/or standalone Microsoft Project use.
    b. Select 'Add' to define the PWA account you will be connecting to.

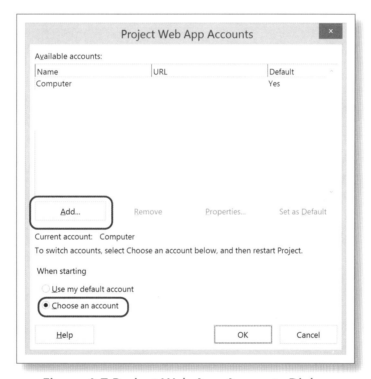

Figure A.7 Project Web App Accounts Dialog

6. This will launch the 'Account Properties' dialog
    a. Provide a meaningful name in the 'Account Name:' recognizing that you may be using more than one PWA system (Production and Training for example)
    b. Enter http://'Your Company'/pwa (where you would replace 'Your Company' with the address of PWA provided by your Administrator) in the Project Server URL field.

c.   Select the 'Set as Default' checkbox if this is the account you will be using most often

Figure A.8 Accounts Properties

d.   In order for the changes to PWA Accounts to take effect close Microsoft Project and re-launch the application.
7.   In the Login dialog
   a.   Select the 'Profile' just created above
   b.   Uncheck "Load Summary Resource Assignments".
8.   You are now able to open schedules from PWA.

**Figure A.9 Microsoft Project
Login Screen**

B

APPENDIX B:
Sensei Custom Views

Throughout this book we have provided references to specific views which we created to facilitate Effective Project and Portfolio Management. In this Appendix we will review each view and provide the details on its expected usage and contents.

Table Name	Intended Use
01 – Detailed Scope – WBS	This view is intended to be used for the initial development of the Work Breakdown Structure (WBS).
02 – Budgeting and Cost Planning	This view is intended to be used to enter budget and costs details for the project.
03 – Dependencies	This view is intended to be used to validate and maintain task dependencies.
04 – Deadlines and Constraints	This view is intended to be used to validate and maintain Deadlines and Constraints.
05 – Planning Gantt	This view is intended to be used in support all the planning activities associated with assigning resources and estimates to the plan and developing the final project schedule.
06 – Leveling Gantt	This view is intended to be used in support of leveling the project to ensure resources are not over-allocated.
07 – Baselining	This view is used to review the project's progress as compared to the original plan based on work, costs and finish date variances.
08 – Tracking Gantt	This view is typically used during the weekly status update process to review the impacts of any updates/changes from the timesheet status updates on the project schedule.
09 – Cost Tracking	This view is typically used during the weekly status update process to review the impacts of any updates/changes to project costs against the overall project budget.
10 – Project Status	This view is used to review the project's status on a weekly basis
11 – Project Closure	This view is used to review the project's readiness for being closed.

Table Name	Intended Use
A – Resource Usage	This view has two purposes. First it is used in the planning and leveling processes to review and validate resource allocation to tasks and secondly, it is used during the weekly timesheet status update process to track actual use of local and material resources.
B – Resource Sheet	This view is used to view resource details for enterprise resources and enter/maintain resource details for local, material and budget resources.
C – Cost Type	This view is used in the manage project budget process to group resources by cost type to allow for ease of comparisons to budget resources.

01 – Detailed Scope – WBS

This view is intended to be used for the initial development of the Work Breakdown Structure (WBS).

	0	Task Mode	Task Name	Duration
0			Corporate Portal Migration	210.75 days?
1	✓		Project Kickoff	0 days
2			Initiation	18.21 days
3			Business Case	6.85 days
4	✓		Identify Project Stakeholders	3.33 days
5			Prepare Business Case Document	3.52 days
6	✓		Business Case Complete	0 days
7	✓		EXTERNAL DEPENDENCY Project Risk Calculator Complete	0 days
8	✓		Business Case Approved	0 days
9	✓		CER Submitted	0 days
10	✓		CER Approved	0 days

Figure B.1 '01 - Detailed Scope - WBS'

As a result it has only minimal information showing to allow the user to focus on creating an effective WBS without the distraction of other fields. 'Duration' is only used to create milestones.

Table Area Data

Field	Intended Use
Indicator	The Indicator field is used to display special characteristics of the task. All indicators should be reviewed and validated to ensure the WBS is being developed appropriately
Task Mode	This field indicates whether the field is 'Manually Scheduled' or 'Auto Scheduled'. The expectation is that most, if not all tasks are 'Auto Scheduled'. Any occurrences of 'Manually Scheduled' should be reviewed and corrected as appropriate.

Field	Intended Use
Task Name	Task Names should be created following the WBS Naming Conventions – Noun Phrases for Summary tasks, Verb Phrases for Detailed Tasks and "Deliverable Name completed" for Milestones
Duration	Duration is used to change tasks to be milestones (Duration = 0)

Time-Phased Data

The traditional Gantt display has been moved to the far right to eliminate it from view, as this information is not relevant during WBS creation.

02 – Budgeting and Cost Planning

This view is intended to be used to enter budget and costs details for the project.

	Task Name	Budget Cost	Cost	Notes	Details	Qtr 2 May	Jun	Jul
0	Corporate Portal Migration	$7,500.00	$248,170.00		Budget Cost	$676.16	$711.74	$782.92
					Cost	$6,497.50	$27,653.33	$20,986.67
	Material Budget	$5,000.00			Budget Cost	$450.77	$474.50	$521.95
					Cost			
	Other Costs Budget	$2,500.00			Budget Cost	$225.39	$237.25	$260.97
					Cost			
1	Project Kickoff		$0.00		Budget Cost			
					Cost			
2	Initiation		$5,737.50		Budget Cost			
					Cost	$5,737.50		
3	Business Case		$5,737.50		Budget Cost			
					Cost	$5,737.50		
4	Identify Project Stakeholders		$1,800.00		Budget Cost			
					Cost	$1,800.00		
	Kenneth Steiness		$1,800.00		Budget Cost			
					Cost	$1,800.00		
5	Prepare Business Case Document		$3,937.50		Budget Cost			
					Cost	$3,937.50		
	Michael Westbrook		$1,687.50		Budget Cost			
					Cost	$1,687.50		
	Curt Schilling		$2,250.00		Budget Cost			
					Cost	$2,250.00		
6	Business Case Complete		$0.00		Budget Cost			
					Cost			

Figure B.2 '02 – Budgeting and Cost Planning'

While this view presents the cost details for all project resources, the intended use of this view is to enter the budget/cost details for 'Cost Resources' and 'Budget Resources'.

Table Area Data

Field	Intended Use
Task Name	In this view, the task name field contains both the task name (regular font) as well as the resource name(s) (italic font and indented) assigned to the task. The task name column is used to validate that the budget is being applied to the appropriate task/resource.

Field	Intended Use
Budget Cost	While the 'Budget Cost' is shown as a cell for all tasks in the plan, only 'Budget Resources' assigned to the 'Project Summary Task' can be changed. Project level budget costs should be entered into each of these budget lines on the 'Project Summary Task'.
Cost	The 'Cost' field is automatically calculated for all 'Work and Material Resources' on the project. Use this column to enter the costs for the 'Cost Resources' assigned to the project tasks.
Notes	Use the 'Notes' column to fully document any assumptions made and/or details required to determine the project costs

Time-Phased Data

A detailed breakdown of the project budget and costs are provided to allow for fine-tuning how the budget and costs are allocated over time. By default, costs are evenly distributed over the task duration, but you can adjust this by directly entering the values into the cells – 'Budget Costs' for 'Budget Resources' and 'Costs' for 'Cost Resources'.

03 – Dependencies

This view is intended to be used to validate and maintain task dependencies.

Figure B.3 '03 – Dependencies'

This view provides the information in both the Table and Time Phases presentations to allow viewing and updating the project's dependencies (predecessor and successor)

Table Area Data

Field	Intended Use
Indicator	The Indicator field is used to display special characteristics of the task. All indicators should be reviewed and validated to ensure the dependencies are being developed appropriately
Task Name	The task name is used to validate that the dependencies are being maintained for the correct task.

Field	Intended Use
Predecessors	The predecessor column shows the 'Line ID' of any tasks that are predecessors to this task. As well, this column displays the type of predecessor (Finish-Start (FS), Start-Start (SS), Finish-Finish (FF), and Start-Finish (SF) as well as any lag associated with the dependency (+5 days). When the dependency and lag are not shown the default of FS with 0 lag is applied to the dependency.
Successors	The successor column shows the 'Line ID of any tasks that are successors to this task. The same display characteristics described above for Predecessor apply to this column.

Time-Phased Data

A standard GANTT view is provided with dependency lines visible to allow for viewing the dependencies in graphical format.

04 – Deadlines and Constraints

This view is intended to be used to validate and maintain Deadlines and Constraints.

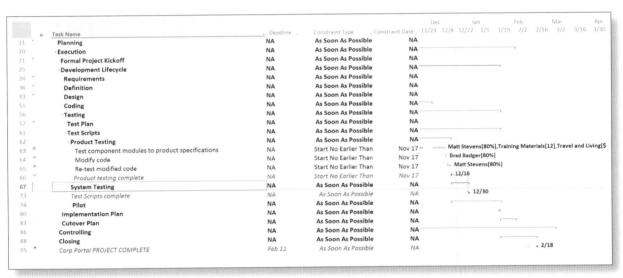

Figure B.4 '04 – Deadlines and Constraints'

While this view supports both methods of defining schedule restrictions, it is our recommendation to use deadlines instead of constraints as deadlines provide more flexibility for the scheduling engine while achieving similar results to using constraints.

Table Area Data

Field	Intended Use
Indicator	The indicator field is used to display special characteristics of the task. An indicator appears when a constraint is set for a task. A different indicator appears when the current schedule will not meet a deadline.

Field	Intended Use
Task Name	The task name is used to validate that the deadlines and constraints are being maintained for the correct task.
Deadline	Use this column to set 'Deadline' dates for any line in the plan. Deadlines can be set on Summary Tasks, Detailed Tasks and/or Milestones. To set a 'Deadline', either type the date directly in the column or select the down-arrow to activate the calendar display.
Constraint Type	The type of 'Constraint' is set in this column. Using the dropdown select the type of constraint required – 'As Late As Possible, Must Start On, Must Finish On, Start No Later Than, Start No Earlier Than, Finish No Later Than, Finish No Earlier Than and the default As Soon As Possible'.
Constraint Date	Use this column to set 'Constraint' dates for any line in the plan. To set a 'Constraint' date, either type the date directly in the column or select the down-arrow to activate the calendar display.

Time-Phased Data

A standard GANTT view is provided specifically for viewing the 'Deadline' date as it is visible on the Gantt display.

05 – Planning Gantt

This view is intended to be used in support all the planning activities associated with assigning resources and estimates to the plan and developing the final project schedule.

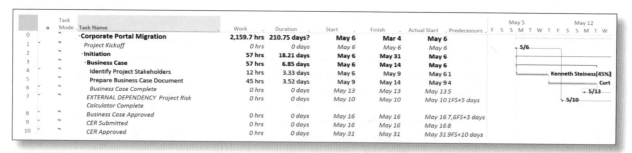

Figure B.5 '05 – Planning Gantt'

This view will be used extensively in plan development to support the planning activities associated with developing the baseline schedule and would include assigning resources and estimating work to complete tasks.

Table Area Data

Field	Intended Use
Indicator	The indicator field is used to display special characteristics of the task. Of particular interest during planning is the "Over Allocated" and "Constraint" indicators which are often created as a result of the planning process.

Field	Intended Use
Task Mode	This field indicates whether the field is 'Manually Scheduled' or 'Auto Scheduled'. The expectation is that most tasks are 'Auto Scheduled'. Any occurrences of 'Manually Scheduled' should be reviewed and corrected as appropriate.
Task Name	The task name is used to validate that the planning activities are being applied to the correct task.
Work	This column is used to provide the work based estimate for each task. Most tasks should be of 'Fixed Work, Effort Based' and therefore are estimated by recording the amount of work required for task completion in this column.
Duration	For all but 'Fixed Duration' tasks, which should be used rarely, if ever, in a proactive project plan, this column is for information only and is calculated based on resource availability and work estimates.
Start	This field is for information only and is automatically maintained as tasks are scheduled based on estimates, resource availability and task dependencies. If the Start date is not consistent with your expectations, change one of the drivers listed above as opposed to directly changing the date in this column.
Finish	This field is for information only and is automatically maintained based on the Start date, work estimates and resource availability. Finish date should never be set manually.
Actual Start	Reflects the date on which work was started on each task. This column is for information only and is used when replanning to recognize variances between planned start and actual start dates.
Predecessor	The predecessor column shows the 'Line ID' of any tasks that are predecessors to this task. As well, this column displays the type of predecessor (Finish – Start (FS), Start-Start (SS), Finish-Finish (FF), and Start-Finish (SF) as well as any lag associated with the dependency (+5 days). When the dependency and lag are not shown the default of FS with 0 lag is applied to the dependency. This is used to make dependency changes as part of a larger planning exercise to make the changing of dependencies efficient without having to change to the '03 – Dependency' view

Time-Phased Data

A standard Gantt view is provided specifically for viewing all aspects of the schedule during the planning activities.

06 – Leveling Gantt

This view is intended to be used in support leveling the project to ensure resources are not over allocated.

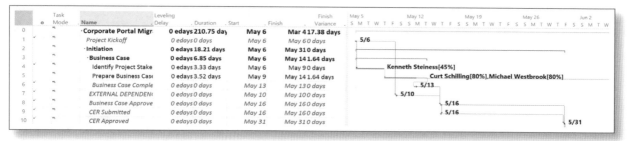

Figure B.6 '06 – Leveling Gantt'

This view introduces a new field, 'Leveling Delay' which is typically used exclusively in the leveling process. This field defines the amount of time that the task can be delayed without impacting the project end date. Tasks with a non-zero leveling delay are not on the project's critical path and can be delayed by the amount of the 'Leveling Delay' days without impacting the end date, while hopefully improving any resource over-allocations.

Table Area Data

Field	Intended Use
Indicator	The indicator field is used to display special characteristics of the task. Of particular interest during leveling is the "Over Allocated" indicator, as these are the tasks requiring resource leveling.
Task Mode	This field indicates whether the field is 'Manually Scheduled' or 'Auto Scheduled'. The expectation is that most tasks are 'Auto Scheduled'. Any occurrences of 'Manually Scheduled' should be reviewed and corrected as appropriate.
Task Name	The task name is used to validate that the leveling activities are being applied to the correct task.
Leveling Delay	This column indicates the number of days that each task can be delayed without impacting the project end date.
Duration	This field is often used on this view to sort the tasks to display the longest duration tasks first, as the longer the duration, typically the greater the opportunity to make changes improve the resource over allocations.
Start	This field is for information only and is automatically maintained as tasks are scheduled based on estimates, resource availability and task dependencies. Typically, leveling is focused on tasks with a 'Start Date' in a relatively close proximity to the current date.
Finish	This field is for information only and is automatically maintained based on the start date, work estimates and resource availability. Finish date should never be set manually.
Finish Variance	This field is for information only and is automatically maintained as the difference between the original planned finish date and the current projected finish date.

Field	Intended Use
Predecessor	The predecessor column shows the 'Line ID' of any tasks that are predecessors to this task. As well, this column displays the type of predecessor (Finish – Start (FS), Start-Start (SS), Finish-Finish (FF), and Start-Finish (SF) as well as any lag associated with the dependency (+5 days). When the dependency and lag are not shown the default of FS with 0 lag is applied to the dependency. This is used to make dependency changes as part of a larger planning exercise to make the changing of dependencies efficient without having to change to the '03 – Dependency' view

Time-Phased Data

A GANTT view is provided which highlights tasks with 'Slack' to allow for visual inspection of these tasks in the context of the overall project schedule.

07 - Baselining

This view is used to review the project's progress as compared to the original plan based on work, costs and finish date variances.

	Task Mode	Task Name	Work Health	Baseline Work	Work	Work Variance	Schedule Health	Baseline Finish	Finish	Finish Variance	Cost Health	Baseline Cost	Cost	Cost Variance
0		Corporate Portal Migration		1,749.2 hrs	2,159.7 hrs	410.5 hrs		Feb 7	Mar 4	17.38 days		$178,070.00	$248,170.00	$70,100.00
1		Project Kickoff		0 hrs	0 hrs	0 hrs		May 6	May 6	0 days		$0.00	$0.00	$0.00
2		Initiation		36 hrs	57 hrs	21 hrs		May 31	May 31	0 days		$3,600.00	$5,737.50	$2,137.50
3		Business Case		36 hrs	57 hrs	21 hrs		May 13	May 14	1.64 days		$3,600.00	$5,737.50	$2,137.50
4		Identify Project Stakeholders		12 hrs	12 hrs	0 hrs		May 9	May 9	0 days		$1,500.00	$1,800.00	$300.00
5		Prepare Business Case Document		24 hrs	45 hrs	21 hrs		May 13	May 14	1.64 days		$2,100.00	$3,937.50	$1,837.50
6		Business Case Complete		0 hrs	0 hrs	0 hrs		May 13	May 13	0 days		$0.00	$0.00	$0.00
7		EXTERNAL DEPENDENCY Project Risk Calculator Complete		0 hrs	0 hrs	0 hrs		May 10	May 10	0 days		$0.00	$0.00	$0.00
8		Business Case Approved		0 hrs	0 hrs	0 hrs		May 16	May 16	0 days		$0.00	$0.00	$0.00
9		CER Submitted		0 hrs	0 hrs	0 hrs		May 16	May 16	0 days		$0.00	$0.00	$0.00
10		CER Approved		0 hrs	0 hrs	0 hrs		May 31	May 31	0 days		$0.00	$0.00	$0.00

Figure B.7 '07 - Baselining - Table Area Data'

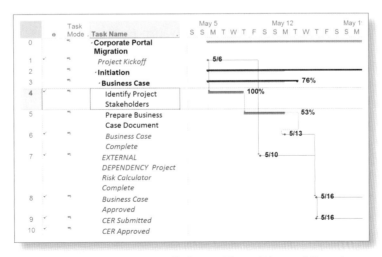

Figure B.8 '07 - Baselining - Time-Phased Data'

This view introduces traffic light health indicators. These traffic Lights are based on comparing the actual project results against the plan and reporting the "health" of the variance as a Green light – within defined tolerance, Yellow light – slightly out of tolerance, and Red light – out of tolerance. While we won't go into details of how these traffic lights are calculated in this section, we encourage you to explore how to create and use traffic lights for other reporting applications you may have.

Table Area Data

Field	Intended Use
Indicator	The indicator field is used to display special characteristics of the task.
Task Mode	This field indicates whether the field is 'Manually Scheduled' or 'Auto Scheduled'. The expectation is that all fields are 'Auto Scheduled'. Any occurrences of 'Manually Scheduled' should be reviewed and corrected as appropriate.
Task Name	The task name is used to validate which tasks have reported variances that require management attention.
Work Health	This column displays Green/Yellow/Red reporting on the variances on 'Work' actual results versus planned estimates. Green = less than 10% variance Yellow = between 10 and 20% variance Red = greater than 20% variance
Baseline Work	'Baseline Work' contains the approved estimate for 'Work' for each task.
Work	'Work' contains the current estimate for the amount of work required to complete the task. It is the sum of 'Actual Work' and 'Remaining Work'. Both these fields are updated weekly through timesheet status updates
Work Variance	This field is calculated as the difference between 'Baseline Work' and 'Work'. This field is the basis of determine the 'Work Health' traffic lights.
Schedule Health	This column displays Green/Yellow/Red reporting on the variances on between planned and forecast task 'Finish' dates Green = less than 10% variance Yellow = between 10 and 20% variance Red = greater than 20% variance
Baseline Finish	'Baseline Finish' contains the approved estimate for the 'Finish' date for each task.
Finish	'Finish' contains the current estimate for 'Finish' date for the task. Finish date is updated weekly as a part of the schedule recalculation resulting from processing timesheet status updates
Finish Variance	This field is calculated as the difference between 'Baseline Finish' and 'Finish'. This field is the basis of determine the 'Schedule Health' traffic lights.

Field	Intended Use
Cost Health	This column displays Green/Yellow/Red reporting on the variances on 'Cost' actual results versus planned estimates. Green = less than 10% variance Yellow = between 10 and 20% variance Red = greater than 20% variance
Baseline Cost	'Baseline Cost' contains the approved estimate for 'Cost' for each task.
Cost	'Cost' contains the current estimate for cost required to complete the task. It is the sum of 'Actual Cost' and 'Remaining Cost'. Both these fields are updated weekly through manage project budget process
Cost Variance	This field is calculated as the difference between 'Baseline Cost' and 'Cost'. This field is the basis of determine the 'Cost Health' traffic lights.

Time-Phased Data

A Gantt view is provided which highlights tasks on the Critical Path as well as displaying the Gantt Bars for both the Baseline and the Current Plan to allow for visual inspection of these tasks in the context of the overall project health.

08 – Tracking Gantt

This view is typically used during the weekly status update process to review the impacts of any updates/changes from the timesheet status updates on the project schedule.

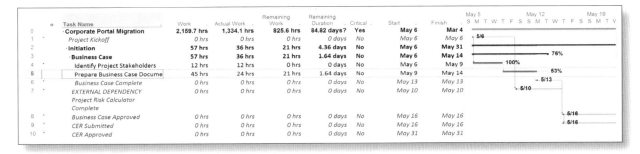

Figure B.9 '08 - Tracking Gantt'

This view is intended for use to review and validate the 'Work' estimates for the project and specifically validate that the 'Remaining Work' as updated by team members during the timesheet status update process is appropriate in light of any potential impacts on the overall project schedule.

Table Area Data

Field	Intended Use
Indicator	The indicator field is used to display special characteristics of the task. Of particular interest during effort tracking is the "Over Allocated" as resources can often get over allocated as a result of expanding task estimates.
Task Name	The task name is used to validate which tasks require management attention as a result of validating work estimates.
Work	'Work' contains the current estimate for the amount of work required to complete the task. It is the sum of 'Actual Work' and 'Remaining Work'. Both these fields are updated weekly through timesheet status updates
Remaining Work	This field is updated on a weekly basis based on information provided by team members on their timesheets. Changes to this field needs to be carefully monitored to ensure that the team fully understands the scope of each task and aren't increasing the estimate to deliver "out of scope" work.
Remaining Duration	The field is automatically maintained and is presented for information only, specifically, because there is limited value in focusing attention on a task that has a very limited amount of time left. This field is included on this view as a potential sort field to focus attention on the tasks with the longer durations.
Critical	This flag indicates whether the task is on the 'Critical Path' and therefore directly impacts the project end date.
Start	This field is for information only and is automatically maintained as tasks are scheduled based on estimates, resource availability and task dependencies. Typically, managing effort is focused on tasks with a 'Start Date' in a relatively close proximity to the current date.
Finish	This field is for information only and is automatically maintained based on the start date, work estimates and resource availability. Finish date should never be set manually.

Time-Phased Data

A Gantt view is provided which highlights tasks on the Critical Path as well as displaying the Gantt Bars for both the Baseline and the Current Plan to allow for visual inspection of the impact of changing 'Work' in the context of the overall project schedule.

09 – Cost Tracking

This view is typically used during the weekly status update process to review the impacts of any updates/changes to project costs on the overall project budget.

Task Name	Actual Cost	Baseline Cost	Total Cost	Remaining Cost	Cost Variance	Details	May	Jun	3rd Quarter Jul
Corporate Portal Migration	$144,667.51	$178,070.00	$248,170.00	$103,502.49	$70,100.00	Cost	$6,497.50	$27,653.33	$20,986.67
						Act. Cost	$4,660.00	$27,653.33	$20,986.67
Material Budget						Cost			
						Act. Cost			
Other Costs Budget						Cost			
						Act. Cost			
Project Kickoff	$0.00	$0.00	$0.00	$0.00	$0.00	Cost			
						Act. Cost			
Initiation	$3,900.00	$3,600.00	$5,737.50	$1,837.50	$2,137.50	Cost	$5,737.50		
						Act. Cost	$3,900.00		
Planning	$32,200.00	$29,500.00	$32,200.00	$0.00	$2,700.00	Cost	$760.00	$27,653.33	$3,786.67
						Act. Cost	$760.00	$27,653.33	$3,786.67
Project Management Plan	$32,200.00	$29,500.00	$32,200.00	$0.00	$2,700.00	Cost	$760.00	$27,653.33	$3,786.67
						Act. Cost	$760.00	$27,653.33	$3,786.67
Define Scope of Project	$9,000.00	$7,500.00	$9,000.00	$0.00	$1,500.00	Cost	$760.00	$8,240.00	
						Act. Cost	$760.00	$8,240.00	
Kenneth Steiness	$9,000.00	$7,500.00	$9,000.00	$0.00	$1,500.00	Cost	$760.00	$8,240.00	
						Act. Cost	$760.00	$8,240.00	
Draft preliminary Portal specifications	$5,600.00	$5,600.00	$5,600.00	$0.00	$0.00	Cost		$5,600.00	
						Act. Cost		$5,600.00	
Michael Westbrook	$2,400.00	$2,400.00	$2,400.00	$0.00	$0.00	Cost		$2,400.00	
						Act. Cost		$2,400.00	
Curt Schilling	$3,200.00	$3,200.00	$3,200.00	$0.00	$0.00	Cost		$3,200.00	
						Act. Cost		$3,200.00	

Figure B.10 '09 – Cost Tracking'

This view is intended for use to review and validate the 'Cost' estimates for the project and specifically validate that the 'Remaining Cost' as updated during the weekly (or monthly) financial updates to the project is accurate.

Table Area Data

Field	Intended Use
Indicator	The indicator field is used to display special characteristics of the task.
Task Name	The task name is used to validate which tasks require management attention as a result of validating cost estimates.
Actual Cost	'Actual Cost' contains actual costs allocated to the task. Costs are allocated to a task based on 'Actual Work' times the resource rate, 'Actual Material' consumed (also recorded on the 'Actual Work' field for 'Material Resources') times the 'Material Costs' as well as any actual costs recorded for 'Cost Resources'
Baseline Cost	This field contains the approved 'Cost' for each task
Remaining Cost	'Remaining Cost' is calculated based on 'Remaining Work' times the resource rate, 'Remaining Material' times the 'Material Costs' as well as any remaining costs recorded for 'Cost Resources'
Cost Variance	This field is calculated as the difference between 'Baseline Cost' and 'Total Cost'
Start	This field is for information only and is automatically maintained as tasks are scheduled based on estimates, resource availability and task dependencies. Typically, managing effort is focused on tasks with a 'Start Date' in a relatively close proximity to the current date.

Field	Intended Use
Finish	This field is for information only and is automatically maintained based on the start date, work estimates and resource availability. Finish date should never be set manually.

Time-Phased Data

A detailed breakdown of the project 'Costs' and 'Actual Costs' are provided to allow for detailed management of when the actual costs have been recorded against the task and when future costs are planned to be incurred.

10 – Project Status

This view is used to review the project's status on a weekly basis

Figure B.11 '10 – Project Status'

This view uses traffic light health Indicators to compare the actual project results against the plan and reporting "health" of the variance as a Green light – within defined tolerance, Yellow light – slightly out of tolerance, and Red light – out of tolerance.

Table Area Data

Field	Intended Use
Indicator	The indicator field is used to display special characteristics of the task. Of particular interest on this view is the indicator for 'Missed Deadline' as this indicates potentially serious schedule slippage.
Task Name	The task name is used to validate which tasks have reported variances that require management attention.
% Complete	This field is a calculated field based on the number of actual hours work versus the planned hours. This field provides a high-level indicator of how close a task is to being complete.

Field	Intended Use
Cost Health	This column displays Green/Yellow/Red reporting on the variances on 'Cost' actual results versus planned estimates. Green = less than 10% variance Yellow = between 10 and 20% variance Red = greater than 20% variance
Work Health	This column displays Green/Yellow/Red reporting on the variances on 'Work' actual results versus planned estimates. Green = less than 10% variance Yellow = between 10 and 20% variance Red = greater than 20% variance
Schedule Health	This column displays Green/Yellow/Red reporting on the variances on between Planned and Forecast task 'Finish' dates Green = less than 10% variance Yellow = between 10 and 20% variance Red = greater than 20% variance
Finish	'Finish' contains the current estimate for the finish date for the task. Finish date is updated weekly as a part of the schedule recalculation resulting from processing Timesheet Status Updates
Finish Variance	This field is calculated as the difference between 'Baseline Finish' and 'Finish'. This field is the basis of determine the 'Schedule Health' traffic lights.
Deadline	This column displays the dates of all deadlines set on the project
Critical	This flag indicated whether the task is on the 'Critical Path' and therefore directly impacts the project end date.

Time-Phased Data

A standard Gantt view is provided for viewing the project schedule.

11 – Project Closure

This view is used to review the project's readiness for being closed.

Figure B.12 '11 – Project Closure'

This view presents the key information that should be validated before the project can be closed, specifically the 'Remaining Work' and 'Remaining Duration' as well as the 'Actual Finish' which should be set.

Table Area Data

Field	Intended Use
Indicator	The indicator field is used to display special characteristics of the task. Of particular interest on this view is the check-mark to indicate that the tasks are complete. Any tasks that do not have a check-mark will require additional attention to ensure the project can be closed.
Task Name	The task name is used to validate which tasks have reported variances that require management attention.
Publish	This field should be set to 'No' for all tasks – ONCE the project has been validated as ready to close. If corrective action is needed to prepare the project for closing, it should be published to PWA one last time before this field is set to 'No'.
Remaining Work	This column should be reviewed for any tasks where the 'Remaining Work' is non-zero. Management actions should be taken to ensure that the tasks can have this field set to zero.
Remaining Duration	This column should be reviewed for any tasks where the 'Remaining Duration' is non-zero. Management actions should be taken to ensure that the tasks can have this field set to zero.
Actual Finish	This column should be reviewed to ensure that an 'Actual Finish' date exists for all tasks. Management actions should be taken to ensure that all tasks have been completed.
Start	This field is for information only and is automatically maintained as tasks are scheduled based on estimates, resource availability and task dependencies.
Finish	This field is for information only and is automatically maintained based on the Start Date, work estimates and resource availability.

Time-Phased Data

A standard Gantt view is provided for viewing the project schedule.

A – Resource Usage

This view has two purposes. First it is used in the Planning and Leveling processes to review and validate resource allocation to tasks and secondly, it is used during the weekly timesheet status update process to maintain actual use of local and material resources.

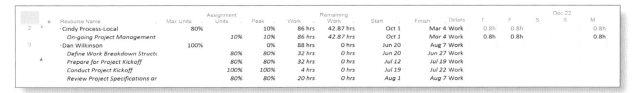

Figure B.13 'A – Resource Usage'

During Planning and Leveling, this view is used to validate resource allocation to tasks to validate that the max units, assignment units and peak are all consistent with the resource's availability to the project.

During the weekly timesheet status update process, the time phase part of this view is used to record actual time and material used by task with material, cost and local resources.

Table Area Data

Field	Intended Use
Indicator	The indicator field is used to display special characteristics of each resource. Of particular interest on this view is the indicator used to identify 'Local Resources'
Resource Name	In this view, the resource name field contains both the resource name (regular font) as well as the task name(s) (italic font and indented) of the tasks they are assigned to. The resource name column is used to validate that the actions are being made to the correct resource/task assignment.
Max Units	This field must be reset every time the plan is reloaded from PWA AND you want to focus on resource leveling. This field is managed in PWA and is typically set to 100% for PMO managed resources. However, your project may only be allocated a portion of each resource, for example 80% for full time resources (to allow time for other routine corporate work) or less, e.g. 40% for resources assigned to other projects. This field needs to be reset each time the project is reloaded to reflect the max units for each resource as allocated to a project. It is specifically important to ensure that max units is set appropriate when you are working on resource leveling.
Assignment Units	This column is used to validate and adjust that individual task assignments do not exceed each resource's max units.
Peak	This column is used to allow a resource's allocation to peak within an assignment to support task specific requirements.
Work	This column reflects the 'Work' allocation for each resource on a task. When multiple resources are assigned to a task, the sum of the resource 'Work' values equals the total work for the task. The 'Work' column is automatically maintained to be the sum of the 'Actual Work' recorded in the Time Phase portion of this view and the 'Remaining Work'.

Field	Intended Use
Remaining Work	This column reflects the 'Remaining Work' allocation for each resource on a task. When multiple resources are assigned to a task, the sum of the resource 'Remaining Work' values equals the total remaining work for the task. The Remaining Work field should be maintained on a weekly basis to reflect the current estimate for the effort for the resource to complete their portion of the task
Start	This field is for information only and is automatically maintained as tasks are scheduled based on estimates, resource availability and task dependencies.
Finish	This field is for information only and is automatically maintained based on the start date, work estimates and resource availability.

Time-Phased Data

A detailed breakdown of the project 'Work' and 'Actual Work' are provided to allow for tracking 'Actual Work' for local and material resources. By default, it is spread over the task duration, but you can adjust this by directly entering the values into the cells for 'Work'

B – Resource Sheet

This view is used to view resource details for enterprise resources and enter/maintain resource details for local, material and budget resources.

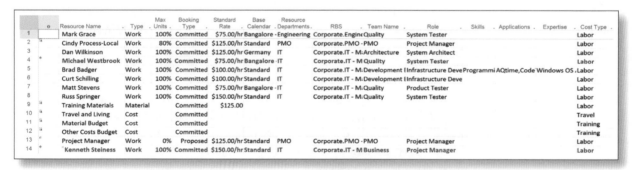

		Resource Name	Type	Max Units	Booking Type	Standard Rate	Base Calendar	Resource Departments	RBS	Team Name	Role	Skills	Applications	Expertise	Cost Type
1		Mark Grace	Work	100%	Committed	$75.00/hr	Bangalore	Engineering	Corporate.Engine	Quality	System Tester				Labor
2		Cindy Process-Local	Work	80%	Committed	$125.00/hr	Standard	PMO	Corporate.PMO - PMO		Project Manager				Labor
3		Dan Wilkinson	Work	100%	Committed	$125.00/hr	Germany	IT	Corporate.IT - M: Architecture		System Architect				Labor
4		Michael Westbrook	Work	100%	Committed	$75.00/hr	Bangalore	IT	Corporate.IT - M Quality		System Tester				Labor
5		Brad Badger	Work	100%	Committed	$100.00/hr	Standard	IT	Corporate.IT - M: Development	Infrastructure Deve	Programmi AQtime, Code	Windows OS	Labor
6		Curt Schilling	Work	100%	Committed	$100.00/hr	Standard	IT	Corporate.IT - M: Development	Infrastructure Deve				Labor
7		Matt Stevens	Work	100%	Committed	$75.00/hr	Bangalore	IT	Corporate.IT - M: Quality		Product Tester				Labor
8		Russ Springer	Work	100%	Committed	$150.00/hr	Standard	IT	Corporate.IT - M: Quality		System Tester				Labor
9		Training Materials	Material		Committed	$125.00									Labor
10		Travel and Living	Cost		Committed										Travel
11		Material Budget	Cost		Committed										Training
12		Other Costs Budget	Cost		Committed										Training
13		Project Manager	Work	0%	Proposed	$125.00/hr	Standard	PMO	Corporate.PMO - PMO		Project Manager				Labor
14		Kenneth Steiness	Work	100%	Committed	$150.00/hr	Standard	IT	Corporate.IT - M Business		Project Manager				Labor

Figure B.14 'B – Resource Sheet'

This view is used primarily to maintain data for all resources which are local to the project.

Table Area Data

Field	Intended Use
Resource Name	The resource name is used to clearly identify each resource to be assigned to the project.
Type	Each resource is assigned a type of work, material or cost.

Field	Intended Use
Max Units	This field must be reset every time the plan is reloaded from PWA AND you want to focus on resource leveling. This field is managed in PWA and is typically set to 100% for PMO managed resources. However, your project may only be allocated a portion of each resource, for example 80% for full time resources (to allow time for other routine corporate work) or less, e.g. 40% for resources assigned to other projects. This field needs to be reset each time the project is reloaded to reflect the max units for each resource as allocated to a project. It is specifically important to ensure that max units is set appropriate when you are working on resource leveling.
Booking Type	This column indicates whether the resource is 'Committed', in which case, management has approved their assignment to the project or 'Proposed', which means the project has been planned based on their availability but risk exists should they not become assigned.
Standard Rate	This column indicates the unit charge for a resource, for work resources is an hourly rate and for material resources is a cost per unit of material used.
Base Calendar	This column indicates the calendar to be used to determine the resource's availability. Only work resources have calendars.
Resource Departments, RBS, Team Name, Role, Skills, Applications and Expertise	These columns display enterprise resource Information and have no impact on project schedule or budget development. They can be used for filtering, sorting and management of resource information.
Cost Type	This custom field is used by the manage project budget process to group resources by 'Cost Type' for to allow for ease of comparisons to budget resources. This field is used in the next view 'C – Cost Type' as part of the manage project budget process.

Time-Phased Data

There is no Time-Phased Data on this Resource View.

C – Cost Type

This view is used in the manage project budget process to group resources by 'Cost Type' to allow for ease of comparisons to budget resources.

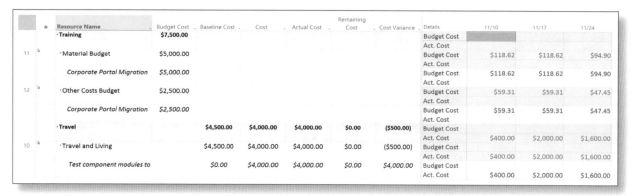

Figure B.15 'C - Cost Type'

This view is used to facilitate effective project budget management. This view is grouped by the custom field 'Cost Type' to group all related projects costs together. In order for this view to work, it is critical that every resource is assigned the appropriate 'Cost Type'.

While data can be changed in this view, due to the way that the data is grouped, it is recommended that this view be used for review and comparisons only and that other views discussed above be used to maintaining this data.

Table Area Data

Field	Intended Use
Resource Name	The resource name is used to clearly identify each resource to be assigned to the project. The resource names are grouped by 'Cost Type'.
Budget Cost	While the budget cost is shown as a cell for all lines in this view, only the budget resources assigned to the project summary task contain values. These values are displayed for comparisons purposes only and should not be changed in this view.
Baseline Cost	Baseline cost contains the approved cost per task/resource assignment in the plan.
Assignment Units	This column is used to validate and adjust that individual task assignments do not exceed each resource's max units.
Cost	This column is calculated as the sum of actual cost and remaining cost.
Actual Cost	'Actual Cost' contains actual costs allocated to the task. Costs are allocated to a task based on actual work times the resource rate, Actual material consumed (also recorded on the actual work field for material resources) times the material costs as well as any actual costs recorded for cost resources.
Remaining Cost	'Remaining Cost' are calculated task based on remaining work times the resource rate, remaining material times the material costs as well as any remaining costs recorded for cost resources.
Cost Variance	This column is calculated as the difference between the baseline cost and cost.

Time-Phased Data

A detailed breakdown of the project budget cost and actual cost are provided to allow for detailed tracking to better understand any variances identified.

APPENDIX C:

Download Area

A download compressed file is available to assist in the completion of all Work Sessions contained in this book. The download file contains:

- PDFs of all Work Sessions and Solutions.
- Microsoft Project MPP files to be used as the Initial File for the Work Sessions and to support the Resource Leveling section of Chapter 4
- Microsoft Project MPP files representing the successful completion of each Work Session.

All Microsoft Project files contained in this download package contain the custom views and filters referenced in this book. Loading any MPP file in this package will provide access to these views and filters as well as the tables and fields used in this book.

Access Download Area

1. Using Internet Explorer connect to **www.senseiprojectsolutions.com/proactiveppm**
2. Follow the directions on the website and complete the form to receive the download package
3. An email will be sent with a compressed file containing all the materials

Contents of Download Package

Initial Files	
Light Rail Phase 2.MPP	This MPP provides the starting point for all Microsoft Project Work Sessions. Instructions for using this file are contained in Work Session #2
Resource Leveling.MPP	This MPP allows you to reproduce and follow along with Chapter 4 section of Resource Leveling Options.

Work Session Material	
Work Session PDF	This printable PDF contains all 16 work sessions. This PDF contains the same material presented as work sessions throughout the book, formatted with each work session beginning on a new page. This will allow you to print each work session as needed. You can use these printouts to make notes while completing each work session.

Work Session Material
Work Session Solutions PDF	This printable PDF is a copy of Appendix E. It is provided as a separate printable PDF to facilitate easier review and validation of the step by step instructions for each work session.

Work Session Solutions
Light Rail Phase 2 Work Session 2 thru 16	This folder contains 15 Microsoft Project MPP files – one for each of Work Session 2 through 16. Each MPP file presents the Light Rail Phase 2 project representing the solution for each completed work session. Use these files to compare your results against expected results and/or to refresh your schedule. If you need to refresh your schedule, follow the instructions defined in Work Session 2 to replace the existing schedule in PWA with the appropriate MPP file from this folder.

APPENDIX D:

Work Sessions

WORK SESSION #1 – SUBMIT A PROJECT PROPOSAL

We will be using the Light Rail Phase 2 project throughout the book, and each work session builds upon the previous one. We have included completed versions of the Microsoft Project plans in the download package representing the end of each session to allow you to compare your results against ours and to ensure you always have an appropriate starting point for each exercise. Sample Project Plans are available for downloading as defined in Appendix C. This is the first of 16 work sessions that develops and then manages the 'Light Rail Phase 2' project. Each Work Session describes the Project Management activities covered and provides screen shots depicting the expected results. Appendix E provides detailed step-by-step solutions for each Work Session.

This short work session aims to submit the project proposal in PWA. We encourage you to work with your PWA administrator to get access to a training area in PWA to allow you to complete these exercises. If this isn't possible and/or you don't have PWA available in your organization, we always provide adjusted Work Session instructions to allow you to complete the segments that are specific to Microsoft Project.

This exercise will be completed exclusively in PWA—if you do not have access to PWA, you can skip this exercise in its entirety.

OBJECTIVE

To initiate a project proposal including the Business Case and Resource Plan.

STEP 1   Initiate a New Project Proposal

In PWA, create a new project proposal and ensure that you select an Enterprise Project Type which is consistent with a software development project (in our environment we would select Software Development).

STEP 2   Complete the Proposal Details

Your project should be named 'ZZ_<Your Name>_Light Rail Phase 2' (Where <Your Name> is your first name just in-case others in your organization are also completing these exercises) and complete the other fields on the Project Initiation screen.

STEP 3   Create the Resource Plan

At this point, consistent with a project proposal, named resources are not known, but the resource roles required for the project are known, therefore you will select the generic resources from the Enterprise Resource Pool that are required for your project.

Assign three generic resources to your project proposal: Project Manager, Business Analyst and Procurement Specialist (or similar roles as defined by your organization).

Create a Resource Plan using January 5, 2015 as your project start date and March 27, 2015 as your end date.

Add the Project Manager to your proposal as a full-time resource for the three-month duration; the Business Analyst as a full-time resource for the first month, and then as a half-time resource for the remaining two months; and the Procurement Specialist as half time resource for the three months of the project.

Submit your Project Proposal for approval.

EXPECTED RESULTS

Project Initiation

Name *	Kenneth Light Rail Phase 2
Description	Sample Project for completing training exercises
Project Departments	IT
Proposed Start Requestor proposed project start date	1/5/2015
Proposed Finish Requester proposed finish date	3/27/2015
Investment Category * Identify the investment category for this project.	Transform
Sponsor Executive Sponsor for this specific project	Joe Gibbs
Owner	Kenneth Steiness Browse...

Figure WS.1a – Project Proposal

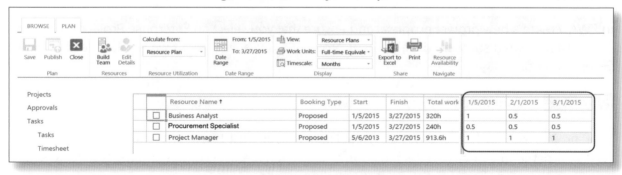

Figure WS.1b – Resource Plan

WORK SESSION #2 – PREPARE THE PROJECT SCHEDULE

OBJECTIVE

This work session kicks off the development of the baseline schedule. It initiates the development of the detailed project schedule in Microsoft Project.

For PWA users, Step 1 is a preliminary step required to pre-load our sample schedule into your Project Server environment.

STEP 1   Connect to Enterprise Environment and Load a Training Schedule

Launch Microsoft Project and log into your Project Server environment. (See Appendix A if you need additional direction on connecting to your Project Server environment).

Open the 'Light Rail Phase 2' plan obtained from the download site (See Appendix C for additional details on how to connect to the download site).

From the File Menu select 'Save As' and save the file to your Enterprise environment. This will save our sample schedule into your environment and make it available for the following Work Sessions.

STEP 2   Complete Project Definition

Set the Project Start Date to January 5, 2015 and validate that the relevant enterprise custom fields project details are set correctly. Any fields with an asterisk are mandatory.

STEP 3   Save and Check in the Plan

Close and Check-in the schedule.

EXPECTED RESULTS

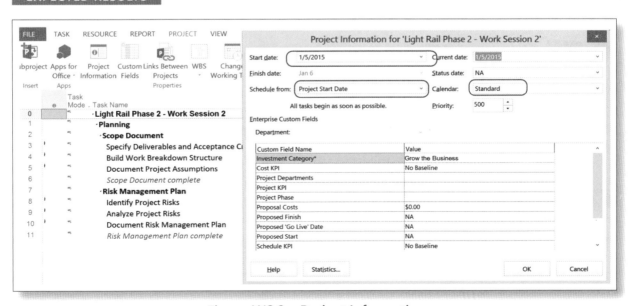

Figure WS.2 – Project Information

WORK SESSION #3 – COMPLETE THE WBS FOR THE PROJECT

OBJECTIVE

This work session is focused on developing the WBS for the project. Over the next several work sessions, you will complete the Work Breakdown Structure for the project, build the team, assign resources, enter effort estimates, establish dependencies and set deadlines and constraints. In this work session, we will complete the development of the WBS loaded in the previous work session.

STEP 1   Add Project Start Milestone

Add a 'Project Start' milestone to the beginning of the project

STEP 2   Add new deliverable

Add the 'Procurement Plan' deliverable with detailed tasks after the scope document deliverable based on the following WBS:

Procurement Plan

Determine Procurement Requirements

Define & Publish Subcontractor Scope

Identify Potential Subcontractors

Identify Subcontract type

Document Subcontractor Management Plan

Procurement Plan complete (Milestone)

STEP 3   Add completion milestones

Add the following additional milestones:

'Planning phase complete' at the end of the Planning phase

'Light Rail Phase 2 complete' milestone at the end of the project.

STEP 4   Add Task Notes

Enter notes for one task.

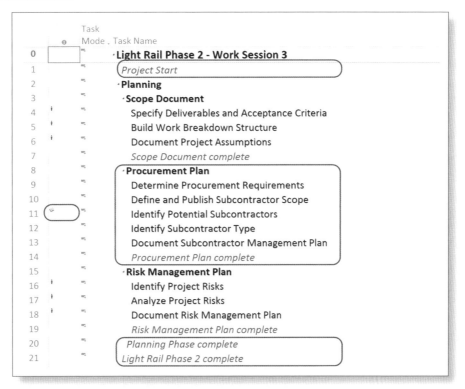

Figure WS.3 – WBS Complete

WORK SESSION #4 – BUILD THE PROJECT TEAM

OBJECTIVE

This work session continues the development of the baseline schedule and is focused on the identification of the named individuals who will be on the project team. This will involve both replacing the generic resources with the named resources as well as adding additional named resources to the team.

If you are not using Enterprise resources you can complete this step in Microsoft Project and create 3 project resources. If you are using Enterprise Resources, use the 'Build Team' dialog (also in Microsoft Project) to add resources to the team.

STEP 1   **Build the team**

Replace the 'Project Manager' with yourself

Replace the 'Procurement Specialist' with an appropriate member of your organization

Replace the 'Business Analyst' with a different appropriate member of your organization

Note: We appended the role to the end of the assigned resource name for the purpose of these work sessions to facilitate ease of knowing which named resource is filling each role – this is not a best practice for actual project delivery.

EXPECTED RESULTS

Figure WS.4 – Build the Team

WORK SESSION #5 – ASSIGN RESOURCES

OBJECTIVE

This work session continues the development of the baseline schedule and involves setting the appropriate project assignment levels for each resource to ensure that they are scheduled for work at the appropriate level.

STEP 1   Assign Resources to Tasks

Assign yourself to all the 'Procurement Plan' detailed tasks at 40%

Assign your colleague to 'Identify Potential Subcontractors' at 40%

EXPECTED RESULTS

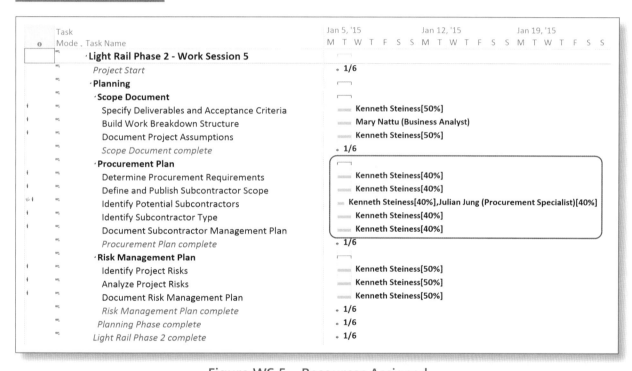

Figure WS.5 – Resources Assigned

WORK SESSION #6 – ESTIMATE EFFORT

OBJECTIVE

In this work session, we add the work estimates to each task in the schedule. These estimates are for the amount of effort required to complete each task. Microsoft Project will calculate the duration for each task based on these estimates and the resource assignments defined in the previous work session.

STEP 1   Add effort estimates to the plan

Enter Work estimates for following tasks

Specify Deliverables and Acceptance Criteria – 8 hours

Build Work Breakdown Structure – 40 hours

Document Project Assumptions – 16 hours

Determine Procurement Requirements – 8 hours

Define and Publish Subcontractor Scope – 16 hours

Identify Subcontractor Type – 32 hours

Document Subcontractor Management Plan – 32 hours

Identify Project Risks – 20 hours

Analyze Project Risks – 10 hours

Document Risk Management Plan – 10 hours

STEP 2   Add duration estimates to the plan

For the 'Identify Potential Subcontractors task', set the task type to 'Fixed Duration' and give it a duration of 1 month.

EXPECTED RESULTS

ℹ	Task Mode	Task Name	Work	Duration
		Light Rail Phase 2 - Work Session 6	**320 hrs**	**20 days**
		Project Start	*0 hrs*	*0 days*
		Planning	**320 hrs**	**20 days**
		Scope Document	**64 hrs**	**5 days**
		Specify Deliverables and Acceptance Criteria	8 hrs	2 days
		Build Work Breakdown Structure	40 hrs	5 days
		Document Project Assumptions	16 hrs	4 days
		Scope Document complete	*0 hrs*	*0 days*
		Procurement Plan	**216 hrs**	**20 days**
		Determine Procurement Requirements	8 hrs	2.5 days
		Define and Publish Subcontractor Scope	16 hrs	5 days
		Identify Potential Subcontractors	128 hrs	1 mon
		Identify Subcontractor Type	32 hrs	10 days
		Document Subcontractor Management Plan	32 hrs	10 days
		Procurement Plan complete	*0 hrs*	*0 days*
		Risk Management Plan	**40 hrs**	**5 days**
		Identify Project Risks	20 hrs	5 days
		Analyze Project Risks	10 hrs	2.5 days
		Document Risk Management Plan	10 hrs	2.5 days
		Risk Management Plan complete	*0 hrs*	*0 days*
		Planning Phase complete	*0 hrs*	*0 days*
		Light Rail Phase 2 complete	*0 hrs*	*0 days*

Figure WS.6 – Task Estimates

WORK SESSION #7 – CREATE DEPENDENCIES

OBJECTIVE

In this work session we will create the task dependencies required to develop the project schedule. Dependencies between project tasks are required to ensure the tasks are executed in the correct order.

STEP 1   Add task dependencies

Add the following dependencies to plan:

Make the first task in the scope deliverable dependent on the project start milestone

For the Scope Document deliverable:

Both the 'Build Work Breakdown Structure' and 'Document Project Assumptions' are Finish-Start dependent on 'Specify Delivery and Acceptance Criteria'.

The deliverable completion milestone is Finish-Start dependent on both the 'Build Work Breakdown Structure' and 'Document Project Assumptions'.

For the Procurement deliverable:

The first task on the Procurement deliverable should be dependent on the completion of the Scope deliverable

The first two tasks, 'Determine Procurement Requirements' and 'Define and Publish Subcontractor Scope' have a Finish-Start dependency.

The third task, 'Identify Potential Subcontractors', has a Finish-Start dependency on 'Publish Subcontractor Scope', but there is 7 day lag before it can start.

Create a Finish-Start dependency between 'Define and Publish Subcontractors Scope' and 'Identify Subcontractor Scope'.

Create a Start-Start dependency between the last 2 tasks, 'Identify Subcontractor Type' and 'Document Subcontractor Management Plan' with a lag of 2 days.

Create a Finish-Start dependency between 'Identify Subcontractor Scope', 'Identify Subcontractor Type' and 'Document Subcontractor Management Plan' and the deliverable completion milestone.

For the Risk Management Plan deliverable:

Create a serial Finish-Start dependency relationship where each task is dependent on the one immediately above it in the plan.

Create a Finish-Start dependency between the 'Project Start' milestone and the first task in the Risk Management Plan

STEP 2   Add milestone dependencies

Make the completion of the three deliverables all predecessors of the 'Planning Phase Complete' milestone

Make the 'Planning Complete' milestone a predecessor of the 'Project Complete' milestone

STEP 3   Validate dependencies

Validate that the dependency diagram is complete by running the following filters:

- '2a – Dependencies on summary tasks',
- '2b – No Predecessors on Detailed Tasks/Milestone' and
- '2c – No Successors on Detailed Tasks/Milestones'.

EXPECTED RESULTS

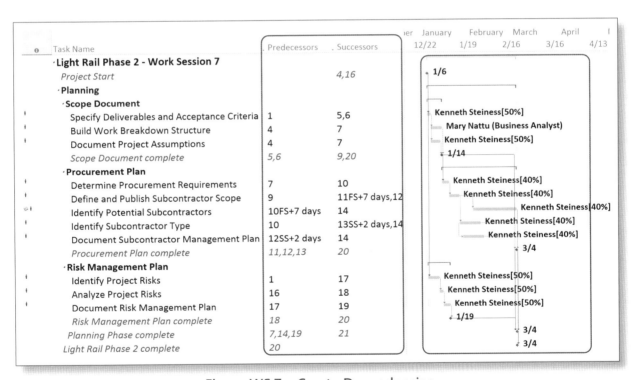

Figure WS.7 – Create Dependencies

WORK SESSION #8 – SET DEADLINES AND CONSTRAINTS

OBJECTIVE

This work session concludes the development of the baseline schedule and consists of setting the required deadline and constraints on the project to satisfy the stated business and organizational milestones.

STEP 1   Add deadlines

Add deadline to 'Light Rail Phase 2 complete' milestone and set it to Friday, 6 weeks after the project start date (Feb 13, 2015)

STEP 2   Add Constraint

Add Start No Earlier Than constraint to 'Identify Potential Subcontractors' task and set it to Tuesday, 3 weeks after the project start date (January 20, 2015).

EXPECTED RESULTS

ⓘ	Task Name	Deadline	Constraint Type	Constraint Date
	Light Rail Phase 2 - Work Session 8	**NA**	**As Soon As Possible**	**NA**
	Project Start	*NA*	*As Soon As Possible*	*NA*
	Planning	**NA**	**As Soon As Possible**	**NA**
	Scope Document	**NA**	**As Soon As Possible**	**NA**
	Specify Deliverables and Acceptance Criteria	NA	As Soon As Possible	NA
	Build Work Breakdown Structure	NA	As Soon As Possible	NA
	Document Project Assumptions	NA	As Soon As Possible	NA
	Scope Document complete	*NA*	*As Soon As Possible*	*NA*
	Procurement Plan	**NA**	**As Soon As Possible**	**NA**
	Determine Procurement Requirements	NA	As Soon As Possible	NA
	Define and Publish Subcontractor Scope	NA	As Soon As Possible	NA
	Identify Potential Subcontractors	NA	Start No Earlier Than	Jan 20
	Identify Subcontractor Type	NA	As Soon As Possible	NA
	Document Subcontractor Management Plan	NA	As Soon As Possible	NA
	Procurement Plan complete	*NA*	*As Soon As Possible*	*NA*
	Risk Management Plan	**NA**	**As Soon As Possible**	**NA**
	Identify Project Risks	NA	As Soon As Possible	NA
	Analyze Project Risks	NA	As Soon As Possible	NA
	Document Risk Management Plan	NA	As Soon As Possible	NA
	Risk Management Plan complete	*NA*	*As Soon As Possible*	*NA*
	Planning Phase complete	*NA*	*As Soon As Possible*	*NA*
◆	Light Rail Phase 2 complete	Feb 13	As Soon As Possible	NA

Figure WS.8 Set Deadlines and Constraints

WORK SESSION #9 – RESOURCE WORKLOAD LEVELING

OBJECTIVE

This work session is focused on ensuring that the resources assigned to the project are being effectively utilized up to their assigned levels. The process of developing the schedule in the previous work sessions will often result in resource over and underutilization. This work session will resolve these and develop a project schedule that honors each resource's allocation to the project.

STEP 1   Set Max Units

Set max units for yourself at 80% and set the max units for the person assigned to the 'Procurement Specialist' tasks and the person assigned to the Business Analyst tasks to 40%

STEP 2   Validate Assignment Units

Validate and correct any instances where any resources are assigned to a task where the Assignment Units is greater than that resource's max units (Hint, there should be one instance of this for the assignment to the 'Build Work Breakdown Structure' task)

STEP 3   Validate Peak Assignment

Validate and correct any instances where any resources' peak assignment exceeds their max units (Hint, there are none of these in this example, but completing this step is critical as this may occur on your projects).

STEP 4   Resolve over-allocations

Correct the over-allocation of yourself on all assigned tasks that are being executed in parallel to be 40%. This is needed as a result of changing your project allocation from an unrealistic 100% to a more realistic 80% - as a result individual parallel task assignments need to change from 50 to 40%

STEP 5   Level Resources

Level the project by setting the leveling options to be Day-by Day and unselect all checkboxes in the 'Resolving over allocations' section and validate the results using '06 – Leveling Gantt' and 'A – Resource Usage'. Result - Task 13 'Develop Subcontractor Management Plan' should be moved to resolve the resource over allocations

EXPECTED RESULTS

Figure WS.9a – Set Resource Project Allocation

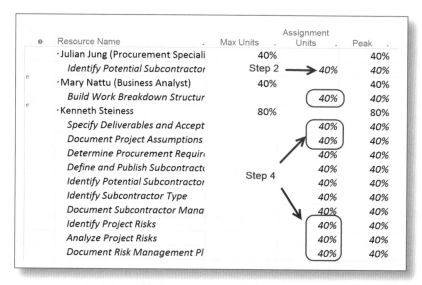

Figure WS.9b – Resource Assignment Units

	Task Mode	Task Name	Work	Duration	Start	Finish
		Light Rail Phase 2 - Work Session 9	**320 hrs**	**49.5 days**	**Jan 6**	**Mar 16**
		Project Start	*0 hrs*	*0 days*	*Jan 6*	*Jan 6*
		Planning	**320 hrs**	**49.5 days**	**Jan 6**	**Mar 16**
		Scope Document	**64 hrs**	**15 days**	**Jan 6**	**Jan 26**
		Specify Deliverables and Acceptance Criteria	8 hrs	2.5 days	Jan 6	Jan 8
		Build Work Breakdown Structure	40 hrs	12.5 days	Jan 8	Jan 26
		Document Project Assumptions	16 hrs	5 days	Jan 8	Jan 15
		Scope Document complete	*0 hrs*	*0 days*	*Jan 26*	*Jan 26*
		Procurement Plan	**216 hrs**	**34.5 days**	**Jan 27**	**Mar 16**
		Determine Procurement Requirements	8 hrs	2.5 days	Jan 27	Jan 29
		Define and Publish Subcontractor Scope	16 hrs	5 days	Jan 29	Feb 5
		Identify Potential Subcontractors	128 hrs	1 mon	Feb 16	Mar 16
		Identify Subcontractor Type	32 hrs	10 days	Feb 5	Feb 19
		Document Subcontractor Management Plan	32 hrs	10 days	Feb 19	Mar 5
		Procurement Plan complete	*0 hrs*	*0 days*	*Mar 16*	*Mar 16*
		Risk Management Plan	**40 hrs**	**12.5 days**	**Jan 6**	**Jan 22**
		Identify Project Risks	20 hrs	6.25 days	Jan 6	Jan 14
		Analyze Project Risks	10 hrs	3.13 days	Jan 14	Jan 19
		Document Risk Management Plan	10 hrs	3.13 days	Jan 19	Jan 22
		Risk Management Plan complete	*0 hrs*	*0 days*	*Jan 22*	*Jan 22*
		Planning Phase complete	*0 hrs*	*0 days*	*Mar 16*	*Mar 16*
		Light Rail Phase 2 complete	*0 hrs*	*0 days*	*Mar 16*	*Mar 16*

Figure WS.9c – Fully Leveled Schedule

WORK SESSION #10 – CREATING THE PROJECT BUDGET

OBJECTIVE

The final step to developing the baseline schedule is to ensure that all project costs are included and that the project budget reflects the full project costs. This work session will add Budget Resources to the project to support project budget management.

STEP 1   Add Cost Resources to track non-resource costs

Add a Cost Resource to your plan for Training costs (or use an Enterprise Cost Resource if one exists) and assign this resource to the 'Build Work Breakdown Structure' task with a cost of $5000 to cover initial vendor training.

STEP 2   Add Budget Resources for the Project Budget

Add a 'Budget Resource' for Labor and Training and assign them to the 'Project Summary Task'. These Budget Resources will be used to record the Project Budget for each budget line, Labor and Training.

STEP 3   Set Cost Type

Set the 'Cost Type' for all Work Resources to Labor and set it to Training for the Training Cost.

STEP 4   Create Project Budget

Determine the Project Budget from the total of the Labor Costs and Training costs using View C – Cost Type. Use these values to set the 'Budget Cost' for the 'Budget Resources'.

EXPECTED RESULTS

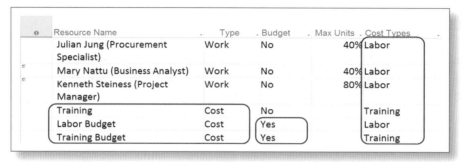

Figure WS.10a – Create Budget/Cost Resources

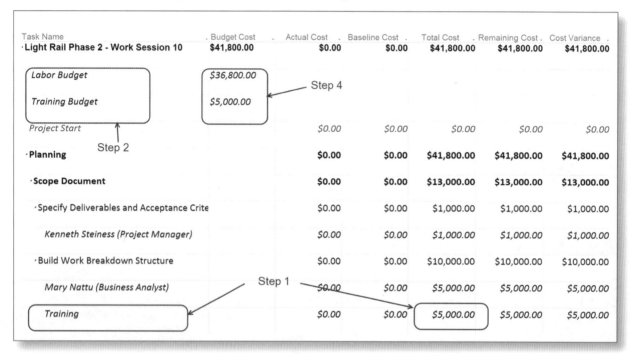

Figure WS.10b – Enter Project Budget and Costs

WORK SESSION #11 – SET THE ORIGINAL BASELINE AND PUBLISH THE PLAN

OBJECTIVE

This work session concludes the development of the baseline schedule by saving the original baseline. The baseline will be used during project execution to validation of actual progress against the approved plan.

STEP 1   Set Project Baseline

Set the baseline for the entire project

STEP 2   Preserve Original Baseline

Copy the 'Baseline' into 'Baseline10' to preserve a copy of the original baseline for future reporting and comparisons.

STEP 3   Publish Project Plan

Publish the completed plan to PWA (Microsoft Project only users can skip this step)

STEP 4   Set Resource Utilization

Change resource utilization from the resource plan to the project plan (Microsoft Project only users can skip this step)

EXPECTED RESULTS

Task Mode	Task Name	Work Health	Baseline Work	Work	Work Variance	Schedule Health	Baseline Finish	Finish	Finish Variance
	Light Rail Phase 2 - Work Session 11		**320 hrs**	**320 hrs**	**0 hrs**		**Mar 16**	**Mar 16**	**0 days**
	Project Start		*0 hrs*	*0 hrs*	*0 hrs*		*Jan 6*	*Jan 6*	*0 days*
	Planning		**320 hrs**	**320 hrs**	**0 hrs**		**Mar 16**	**Mar 16**	**0 days**
	Scope Document		**64 hrs**	**64 hrs**	**0 hrs**		**Jan 26**	**Jan 26**	**0 days**
	Specify Deliverables and Acceptance Crite		8 hrs	8 hrs	0 hrs		Jan 8	Jan 8	0 days
	Build Work Breakdown Structure		40 hrs	40 hrs	0 hrs		Jan 26	Jan 26	0 days
	Document Project Assumptions		16 hrs	16 hrs	0 hrs		Jan 15	Jan 15	0 days
	Scope Document complete		*0 hrs*	*0 hrs*	*0 hrs*		*Jan 26*	*Jan 26*	*0 days*
	Procurement Plan		**216 hrs**	**216 hrs**	**0 hrs**		**Mar 16**	**Mar 16**	**0 days**
	Determine Procurement Requirements		8 hrs	8 hrs	0 hrs		Jan 29	Jan 29	0 days
	Define & Publish Subcontractor Scope		16 hrs	16 hrs	0 hrs		Feb 5	Feb 5	0 days
	Identify Potential Subcontractors		128 hrs	128 hrs	0 hrs		Mar 16	Mar 16	0 days
	Identify Subcontract Type		32 hrs	32 hrs	0 hrs		Feb 19	Feb 19	0 days
	Document Subcontractor Management P		32 hrs	32 hrs	0 hrs		Mar 5	Mar 5	0 days
	Procurement Plan complete		*0 hrs*	*0 hrs*	*0 hrs*		*Mar 16*	*Mar 16*	*0 days*
	Risk Management Plan		**40 hrs**	**40 hrs**	**0 hrs**		**Jan 22**	**Jan 22**	**0 days**
	Identify Project Risks		20 hrs	20 hrs	0 hrs		Jan 14	Jan 14	0 days
	Analyze Project Risks		10 hrs	10 hrs	0 hrs		Jan 19	Jan 19	0 days
	Document Risk Management Plan		10 hrs	10 hrs	0 hrs		Jan 22	Jan 22	0 days
	Risk Management Plan complete		*0 hrs*	*0 hrs*	*0 hrs*		*Jan 22*	*Jan 22*	*0 days*
	Planning Phase complete		*0 hrs*	*0 hrs*	*0 hrs*		*Mar 16*	*Mar 16*	*0 days*
	Light Rail Phase 2 complete		*0 hrs*	*0 hrs*	*0 hrs*		*Mar 16*	*Mar 16*	*0 days*

Figure WS.11 – Project Baseline

WORK SESSION #12 – SUBMITTING A TIMESHEET

OBJECTIVE

To provide task status through the PWA Timesheet.

STEP 1   Create Timesheet

Provide task status through the PWA Timesheet. (If you do not have PWA, enter the same timesheet information directly into Microsoft Project)

Complete the timesheet for the first week (January 05, 2015 – January 09, 2015) of the project:

Monday: 4 hours on 'Specify Deliverables and Acceptance Criteria'

Tuesday: 4 hours on 'Specify Deliverables and Acceptance Criteria'

Wednesday: 2 hours on 'Specify Deliverables and Acceptance Criteria'

Increase 'Remaining Work' to 20 hours on 'Specify Deliverables and Acceptance Criteria' and enter a comment to reflect the reason why the time was increased – '5 new deliverables identified which will require 20 more hours'.

STEP 2   Submit Timesheet

Submit the timesheet for approval

EXPECTED RESULTS

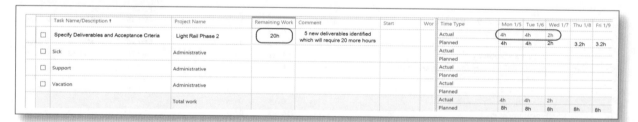

Figure WS.12a – PWA Timesheet

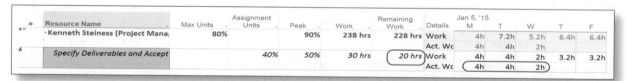

Figure WS.12b – Microsoft Project Resource Usage

WORK SESSION #13 – UPDATE PROJECT COSTS

OBJECTIVE

Update Cost Resources for the current period and review the overall financial performance of the project

STEP 1   Record Actuals Costs

Record $3,000 actual costs for training on the 'Develop Work Breakdown Structure' task. Leave the remaining $2,000 costs for a future time period.

STEP 2   Review Budget performance

Validate the financial performance of the project by reviewing current costs against the budget costs.

EXPECTED RESULTS

	Task Name	Actual Cost	Baseline Cost	Total Cost	Remaining Cost	Details	1/5	1/12	1/19
	Build Work Breakdown Structure	$3,000.00	$10,000.00	$9,000.00	$6,000.00	Cost	$3,000.00	$1,200.00	$4,800.00
						Act. Cost	$3,000.00	$0.00	$0.00
	Mary Nattu (Business Analyst)	$0.00	$5,000.00	$2,500.00	$2,500.00	Cost		$750.00	$1,750.00
						Act. Cost			
	Training	$3,000.00	$5,000.00	$5,000.00	$2,000.00	Cost	$3,000.00	$0.00	$2,000.00
						Act. Cost	$3,000.00	$0.00	$0.00

Figure WS.13a – Enter Non-Resource Actual Costs

	Resource Name	Budget Cost	Baseline Cost	Cost	Actual Cost	Remaining Cost	Cost Variance
	No Value		$0.00	$1,500.00	$0.00	$1,500.00	$1,500.00
	Labor	$36,800.00	$36,800.00	$37,050.00	$1,250.00	$35,800.00	$250.00
	Julian Jung (Procurement Specialist)		$4,800.00	$4,800.00	$0.00	$4,800.00	$0.00
	Mary Nattu (Business Analyst)		$5,000.00	$3,750.00	$0.00	$3,750.00	($1,250.00)
	Kenneth Steiness (Project Manager)		$27,000.00	$28,500.00	$1,250.00	$27,250.00	$1,500.00
	Labor Budget	$36,800.00					
	Training	$5,000.00	$5,000.00	$5,000.00	$3,000.00	$2,000.00	$0.00
	Training		$5,000.00	$5,000.00	$3,000.00	$2,000.00	$0.00
	Build Work Breakdown Struc		$5,000.00	$5,000.00	$3,000.00	$2,000.00	$0.00
	Training Budget	$5,000.00					
	Light Rail Phase 2 - Work Session 13	$5,000.00					

Figure WS.13b – Review Budget Performance

WORK SESSION #14 – PROCESS STATUS UPDATES

OBJECTIVE

Process the team member's status updates and review the impact that these have on the overall project schedule. Remedial actions will be required to maintain the project schedule as a result of a significant task overrun from one team member.

STEP 1   **Confirm all timesheets have been entered**

Validate all timesheets have been entered by running the 'Timesheet Compliance by Project Manager' report and validate that there are no exceptions for this timesheet period (January 05, 2015 – January 09, 2015). (If you do not have PWA, this step (and the next 3) are not necessary as you entered the timesheets directly in Microsoft Project through the previous exercise and therefore would be aware of any missing timesheets.)

STEP 2   **Review status update changes**

Review the schedule changes resulting from the status updates using the 'Approval' process in PWA

STEP 3   **Accept Status Updates**

Accept the status updates in PWA.

STEP 4   **Update Status Date**

Open the plan in Microsoft Project and set the status date January 11, 2015 (the Sunday at the end of the timesheet period – this is based on our timesheets period running from Monday thru Sunday – your organization may have a different weekly timesheet period).

STEP 5   **Mark Milestones as complete**

Update the 'Project Start' milestone to complete to reflect the fact that the project has started.

STEP 6   **Update KPIs**

Review and update the Project KPI to be on-track.

STEP 7   **Reschedule uncompleted work**

Reschedule all uncompleted work forward the current status date – January 11, 2015

STEP 8   Address schedule slippage

As a result of processing the status updates and rescheduling the uncompleted work, the project is now late and we are not forecasting to meet the project deadline. Following the technique described above to 'Taking Corrective Action on the Critical Path', take appropriate actions to try to bring the project back on schedule.

EXPECTED RESULTS

o	Task Name	% Work Complete	Cost Health	Work Health	Schedule Health	Duration	Finish	Finish Variance	Deadline	Critical
	·Light Rail Phase 2 - Work Session 14	**3%**				**48.88 days**	**Mar 12**	**-1.63 days**	**NA**	**Yes**
	Project Start	*100%*				*0 days*	*Jan 6*	*0 days*	*NA*	*No*
	·Planning	**3%**				**48.88 days**	**Mar 12**	**-1.63 days**	**NA**	**Yes**
	·Scope Document	**12%**				**14.38 days**	**Jan 23**	**-1.63 days**	**NA**	**Yes**
	Specify Deliverables and Acceptance Crite	33%				6.13 days	Jan 15	4.63 days	NA	Yes
	Build Work Breakdown Structure	0%				6.25 days	Jan 23	-1.63 days	NA	Yes
	Document Project Assumptions	0%				5 days	Jan 22	4.63 days	NA	Yes
	Scope Document complete	*0%*				*0 days*	*Jan 23*	*-1.63 days*	*NA*	*Yes*
	·Procurement Plan	**0%**				**34.5 days**	**Mar 12**	**-1.63 days**	**NA**	**Yes**
	Determine Procurement Requirements	0%				2.5 days	Jan 27	-1.63 days	NA	Yes
	Define & Publish Subcontractor Scope	0%				5 days	Feb 3	-1.63 days	NA	Yes
	Identify Potential Subcontractors	0%				1 mon	Mar 12	-1.63 days	NA	Yes
	Identify Subcontract Type	0%				10 days	Feb 17	-1.63 days	NA	Yes
	Document Subcontractor Management P	0%				10 days	Feb 19	-9.63 days	NA	Yes
	Procurement Plan complete	*0%*				*0 days*	*Mar 12*	*-1.63 days*	*NA*	*Yes*
	·Risk Management Plan	**0%**				**12.5 days**	**Feb 3**	**7.56 days**	**NA**	**No**
	Identify Project Risks	0%				6.25 days	Jan 23	7.56 days	NA	No
	Analyze Project Risks	0%				3.13 days	Jan 28	7.56 days	NA	No
	Document Risk Management Plan	0%				3.13 days	Feb 3	7.56 days	NA	No
	Risk Management Plan complete	*0%*				*0 days*	*Feb 3*	*7.56 days*	*NA*	*No*
	Planning Phase complete	*0%*				*0 days*	*Mar 12*	*-1.63 days*	*NA*	*Yes*
	Light Rail Phase 2 complete	*0%*				*0 days*	*Mar 12*	*-1.63 days*	*Feb 13*	*Yes*

Figure WS.14 – Results of Process Status Updates

WORK SESSION #15 – PROCESS PROJECT CHANGE REQUEST

OBJECTIVE

Process an approved project change request and update the project baseline to include the approved changes

STEP 1   Add tasks to the schedule

Management has notified you that based on recommendations from the vendor, they approve you adding an additional task to your plan to review the project risks with the vendor to ensure adequate risk mitigation plans are in place. You negotiate with management that 16 hours will be required to complete this task. Insert this task into the plan prior to the 'Documentation of the Risk Management Plan', assign it to yourself and make the appropriate changes to the existing dependencies.

STEP 2   Obtain formal approval of schedule changes

Review and validate the impact this change has on the overall project plan and obtain final management approval of the changes.

STEP 3   Update Baseline

With Management approval of the change, add the new and changed tasks to the Project Baseline

EXPECTED RESULTS

	Task Mode	Task Name	Work Health	Baseline Work	Work	Work Variance	Schedule Health	Baseline Finish	Finish	Finish Variance
		Light Rail Phase 2 - Work Session 15		**325.6 hrs**	**358 hrs**	**32.4 hrs**		**Mar 16**	**Mar 12**	**-1.63 days**
✓		*Project Start*		*0 hrs*	*0 hrs*	*0 hrs*		*Jan 6*	*Jan 6*	*0 days*
		Planning		**325.6 hrs**	**358 hrs**	**32.4 hrs**		**Mar 16**	**Mar 12**	**-1.63 days**
		Scope Document		**64 hrs**	**86 hrs**	**22 hrs**		**Jan 26**	**Jan 23**	**-1.63 days**
i		Specify Deliverables and Acceptance Crite		8 hrs	30 hrs	22 hrs		Jan 8	Jan 15	4.63 days
i		Build Work Breakdown Structure		40 hrs	40 hrs	0 hrs		Jan 26	Jan 26	-0.63 days
i		Document Project Assumptions		16 hrs	16 hrs	0 hrs		Jan 15	Jan 22	4.63 days
		Scope Document complete		*0 hrs*	*0 hrs*	*0 hrs*		*Jan 26*	*Jan 23*	*-1.63 days*
		Procurement Plan		**216 hrs**	**216 hrs**	**0 hrs**		**Mar 16**	**Mar 12**	**-1.63 days**
i		Determine Procurement Requirements		8 hrs	8 hrs	0 hrs		Jan 29	Jan 27	-1.63 days
i		Define & Publish Subcontractor Scope		16 hrs	16 hrs	0 hrs		Feb 5	Feb 3	-1.63 days
▣ i		Identify Potential Subcontractors		128 hrs	128 hrs	0 hrs		Mar 16	Mar 12	-1.63 days
i		Identify Subcontract Type		32 hrs	32 hrs	0 hrs		Feb 19	Feb 17	-1.63 days
i		Document Subcontractor Management P		32 hrs	32 hrs	0 hrs		Mar 5	Mar 3	-1.63 days
		Procurement Plan complete		*0 hrs*	*0 hrs*	*0 hrs*		*Mar 16*	*Mar 12*	*-1.63 days*
		Risk Management Plan		**56 hrs**	**56 hrs**	**0 hrs**		**Feb 3**	**Feb 3**	**0 days**
▣ i		Identify Project Risks		20 hrs	20 hrs	0 hrs		Jan 14	Jan 21	5.56 days
i		Analyze Project Risks		10 hrs	10 hrs	0 hrs		Jan 19	Jan 26	5.56 days
i		Review Risks with SAS Vendor		16 hrs	16 hrs	0 hrs		Jan 29	Jan 29	0 days
i		Document Risk Management Plan		10 hrs	10 hrs	0 hrs		Feb 3	Feb 3	0 days
		Risk Management Plan complete		*0 hrs*	*0 hrs*	*0 hrs*		*Feb 3*	*Feb 3*	*0 days*
		Planning Phase complete		*0 hrs*	*0 hrs*	*0 hrs*		*Mar 16*	*Mar 12*	*-1.63 days*
◆		*Light Rail Phase 2 complete*		*0 hrs*	*0 hrs*	*0 hrs*		*Mar 16*	*Mar 12*	*-1.63 days*

Figure WS.15 – Change Request Processed

WORK SESSION #16 – PROJECT STATUS REPORTING

OBJECTIVE

Provide an accurate status of the project to project stakeholders.

STEP 1   Develop Project Timeline

Develop a project timeline suitable for submitting to management as part of a project status report.

(The remaining 3 steps are all performed in PWA – therefore if you are using Microsoft Project standalone, while we would expect that you would perform these three remaining steps, you would complete them as appropriate for the tools being used in your organization).

STEP 2   Review and Update Issues, Risks and Action items

Review and update all action items, issues and risks in preparation for reporting current project status

STEP 3   Update Project Home page

Review the Project Home page to validate currency and accuracy for status reporting

STEP 4   Distribute Project Status report

Produce Project Status report and distribute to project stakeholders.

EXPECTED RESULTS

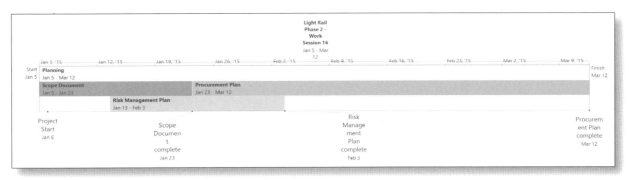

Figure WS.16 – Project Timeline

E

APPENDIX E:
Work Session Solutions

Sample files are available from the Download Area (See Appendix C) with our recommended solutions for each work session. We recommend you complete each session and then compare your results with our solutions after each work session. As each session builds on the previous, it is important to ensure that your results match ours for predictable results in future work sessions. Therefore, if necessary, refresh your environment with the appropriate results file following the directions provided in Work Session 2, Step 1 for loading a schedule into your environment.

WORK SESSION #1 SUBMIT A PROJECT PROPOSAL

STEP 1   Initiate a New Project Proposal

- Open Internet Explorer and go to your Project Web App (PWA) site.
- Click on 'Projects' and then from the 'Projects ribbon > Project section' select 'New'.
- Select the proper Enterprise Project Type (EPT), such as 'Software Development'.

STEP 2   Complete the Proposal Details

- Enter basic project information
  - Enter the name of the project – 'ZZ_<Your Name>_Light Rail Phase 2'.
  - Select the appropriate Investment Category.
  - Fill out all other fields that are known at this time.
  - It is recommended that the Problem Statement be filled in at this time. Although not required for the initial Business Case, the field is required once the Major Workflow is initiated. Required fields are marked with (*).
  - Click 'Save' and 'Close'.

STEP 3   Create the Resource Plan

- Select your proposal by clicking the row on the left hand side. From the 'Project ribbon > Navigate section' select 'Resource Plan'.
- To add generic resources to the Resource Plan from the 'Plan ribbon > Resources section' select 'Build Team'.

- From the 'Team ribbon > Data section' select the 'Generic Resources' view from the dropdown.
- Check the boxes for each generic resource (Project Manager, Business Analyst and Procurement Specialist) to be added to the project and then click 'Add'.
- Click 'Save & Close'.
- Set Resource Plan options
  - From the 'Plan ribbon > Resource Utilization section', from the 'Calculate from' list select 'Resource Plan'.
  - From the 'Plan ribbon > Resource Date Range section' change the 'Date Range' setting the start date (January 05, 2015) and the expected end date (March 27, 2015).
  - From the 'Plan ribbon > Display section' set the 'Work Units' to 'Full-time Equivalents' and 'Set the Timescale' to 'Months' (or however detailed you want to schedule).
- In the calendar area on the right enter a 1 for each month for the PM; a 1 for the first month for the Business Analyst and .5 for the next 2 months; and .5 for each month for the Procurement Specialist.
- From the 'Plan ribbon > Plan section' click 'Publish'.
- After the Resource Plan is published, click 'Close'.
- The project now has a resource plan and an estimated duration. Submit the proposal for formal approval.
- Ensure that the Proposal is 'Open for Edit' to enable 'Submit'.
- You will need to work with your PWA administrator to have your proposal moved through your organizational governance process to make it an approved project ready for plan development.

WORK SESSION #2 – PREPARE THE PROJECT SCHEDULE

STEP 1   Connect to Enterprise Environment and Load a Training Schedule

- Open Microsoft Project and login to your corporate environment
  - From the File menu, select 'Open' and browse to open the 'Light Rail Phase 2' MPP file that you have previously obtained from our download site.
  - Once the file is opened, go back to the File menu and select 'Save As' and select your corporate environment.

STEP 2   Complete Project Definition

- From the 'Project ribbon > Properties section' select 'Project Information' to launch the 'Project Information' dialog.
  - Set the Project Start Date to January 05, 2015.
  - Verify the project calendar is set to 'Standard'.
  - Complete all relevant Enterprise Custom Fields on the 'Project Information' dialog and press 'OK' when done.

STEP 3   Save and Check in the Plan

- Close and Check-in the Project schedule.

WORK SESSION #3 – COMPLETE THE WBS FOR THE PROJECT

STEP 1   Add Project Start Milestone

- Using 'Insert Milestone' command
  - Add a 'Project Start' milestone as the first line of the schedule.

STEP 2   Add new deliverable

- Add the additional 'Procurement Plan Deliverable' immediately below the 'Scope Document complete' milestone
  - Select the 'Risk Management Plan' summary task and use the Insert Task command from the 'Task ribbon > Insert section' to add the new deliverable and the supporting detailed tasks (as defined in the Work Session) into the schedule.
  - Use the Indent and Outdent from the 'Task ribbon > Schedule section' to create the appropriate structure. Select the first task 'Determine Procurement Requirements' and select Indent to make it a child of the Procurement Plan and make sure all subsequent tasks are on the same outline level.

STEP 3   Add completion milestones

- Using 'Insert Milestone', add the 'Planning Complete' milestone as the last line in the Planning group.
- Using 'Insert Milestone', add the 'Light Rail Phase 2 Complete' milestone as the last line of the schedule.

STEP 4   Add Task Notes

- Double click on a Task to open the 'Task Information' dialog, click on the 'Notes Tab' and enter relevant notes to provide further clarity to the task. Notes can be used to explain the purpose of the task, provide additional details to help complete the task, support estimating the work effort, or any other relevant information that can't be self-described with a meaningful task name.

WORK SESSION #4 – BUILD THE PROJECT TEAM

Project Web App Solution

STEP 1   Build the team

- This step applies only if you are using 'Enterprise Resources'. In Microsoft Project, from the 'Resource ribbon > Insert section' select 'Add Resources' and then 'Build Team from Enterprise'. The left-hand side of the dialog shows 'Enterprise Resources' available in the resource pool and the right-hand side of the view shows 'Project Resources'
  - Option A: Build Team by Role: To find resources by role, select the generic resource assigned from the template and press 'Match' to find suitable individuals in the resource pool. Then, select the individual and press 'Replace' to assign them to the project.
  - Option B: Build Team by Name: To find resources by name, select the individual in the 'Enterprise Resource' list on the left-hand side or start typing their first name to scroll quickly through the list. Then, press 'Add' to assign them to the project. With the named resource added, the generic resource would be deleted.

  Using one of these methods, replace the 3 generic resources with named resources.

Microsoft Project Standalone solution

STEP 1   Build the team

- If you are using Microsoft Project standalone, create 3 new resources using the 'B – Resource Sheet' by renaming the existing generic resources.

WORK SESSION #5 – ASSIGN RESOURCES

STEP 1   **Assign Resources to Tasks**

- Assign yourself to the following using the 'Resource ribbon > Assign section' to select the 'Assign Resources' dialog
  - Define Procurement Requirements – 40%
  - Define and Publish Subcontractor Scope– 40%
  - Identify Potential Subcontractors– 40%
  - Identify Subcontractor Type– 40%
  - Document Subcontractor Management Plan– 40%.
- Assign your colleague to Identify Potential Subcontractors at 40%.
- Please ensure that you follow the assignment percentages defined to ensure you obtain the same results in later exercises.

WORK SESSION #6 – ESTIMATE EFFORT

STEP 1   Add effort estimates to the plan

- Using the '05 – Planning Gantt' view enter 'Work' estimates for each task. Work estimates are directly entered into the 'Work' column on the '05 – Planning Gantt' view
  - Specify Deliverables and Acceptance Criteria – 8 hours
  - Build Work Breakdown Structure – 40 hours
  - Document Project Assumptions – 16 hours
  - Determine Procurement Requirements – 8 hours
  - Define and Publish Subcontractor Scope – 16 hours
  - Identify Subcontractor Type – 32 hours
  - Document Subcontractor Management Plan – 32 hours
  - Identify Project Risks – 20 hours
  - Analyze Project Risks – 10 hours
  - Document Risk Management Plan – 10 hours.

STEP 2   Add duration estimates to the plan

- Change the task type of 'Identify Potential Subcontractors' to 'Fixed Duration'. This can be done by double clicking on the task to launch the 'Task Information' dialog and then on the 'Advanced' tab setting the 'Task Type' to 'Fixed Duration'. Or, alternatively, you could have added the 'Type' column to the view and made the change in this column
  - Enter 1 month into the 'Duration' column for this task.
- Validate that the total effort for the project is 320 hours.

WORK SESSION #7 – CREATE DEPENDENCIES

 STEP 1   Add task dependencies

- Using the '03 – Dependencies' view, create the following dependencies. Dependencies can be created by multiple selecting the appropriate tasks and selecting the 'Link' icon from the 'Task ribbon > Schedule section' or the appropriate task line numbers can be directly keyed into the Predecessor or Successor columns in the view
    - Make the first task in the Scope Deliverable Finish-Start dependent on the 'Project Start' milestone (Line 4 should have a predecessor of 1).
    - For the Scope Document deliverable
        - Both the 'Build Work Breakdown Structure' and 'Document Project Assumptions' are Finish-Start dependent on 'Specify Delivery and Acceptance Criteria'. (Line 5 and 6 should both have a predecessor of 4).
        - The 'Scope Document complete' milestone is Finish-Start dependent on both the 'Build Work Breakdown Structure' and 'Document Project Assumptions'. (Line 7 should have a predecessor of both 5 and 6).
    - For the Procurement deliverable
        - The first task 'Determine Procurement Requirements' should have a Finish-Start dependency on the 'Scope Document complete' milestone (Line 9 should have a predecessor of 7).
        - The first two tasks 'Determine Procurement Requirements' and 'Define and Publish Subcontractor Scope' have a Finish-Start dependency on each other. (Line 10 should have a predecessor of 9).
        - The third task 'Identify Potential Subcontractors' has a Finish-Start dependency on 'Publish Subcontractor Scope', but there is 7 day lag before it can start. (Line 11 should have a FS + 7 predecessor of 10).
        - Create a Finish-Start dependency between 'Define and Publish Subcontractors Scope' and 'Identify Subcontractor Scope'. (Line 12 should have a predecessor of 10).
        - Create a Start-Start dependency between the last 2 tasks 'Identify Subcontractor Type' and 'Document Subcontractor Management Plan' with a lag of 2 days. (Line 13 should have a SS +2 predecessor of 12).
    - Create a Finish-Start dependency between 'Identify Subcontractor Scope', 'Identify Subcontractor Type' and 'Document Subcontractor Management Plan' and the 'Procurement Plan complete' milestone. (Line 14 should have predecessors of 11, 12 and 13).
    - For the Risk Management Plan deliverable
        - Create a serial Finish-Start dependency relationship where each task is dependent on the one immediately above it in the plan. (Line 17 should have a predecessor of 16, Line 18 should have a predecessor of 17 and Line 19 should have a predecessor of 18).
        - Create a Finish-Start dependency between the 'Project Start' milestone and the first task in the Risk Management Plan (Line 16 should have a predecessor of 1).

 STEP 2   Add milestone dependencies

- Make the completion of the three deliverables predecessors of the 'Planning Phase complete' Milestone. (Line 20 should have predecessors of 7, 14, and 19).

- Make the 'Light Rail Phase 2 complete' milestone a predecessor of the 'Planning Phase complete' milestone. (Line 21 should have a predecessor of 20).

STEP 3   Validate dependencies

- Use Filters '2a – Dependencies on summary tasks', '2b – No Predecessors on Detailed Tasks/Milestones' and '2c - No Successors on Detailed Tasks/Milestones' to validate the project dependencies.

WORK SESSION #8 –SET DEADLINES AND CONSTRAINTS

STEP 1   Add deadlines

- Using the '04 – Deadlines and Constraints' view enter a deadline of February 13, 2015 on the 'Light Rail Phase 2 complete' milestone by directly entering the date into the Deadline column.

STEP 2   Add Constraint

- Using the dropdown list on the 'Constraint Type' column change the constraint to 'Start no Earlier Than' and enter January 20, 2015 into the 'Constraint Date' column for the 'Identify Potential Subcontractors' task. An alternative solution is to double click on the task to open the 'Task Information' dialog and on the 'Advanced Tab' set both the 'Constraint Type' and 'Constraint Date'.

WORK SESSION #9 – RESOURCE WORKLOAD LEVELING

STEP 1   Set Max Units

- Set Max Units for all resources. Using the 'A – Resource Usage' view
  - Set the 'Max Units' for yourself to 80%.
  - Set the 'Max Units' for the Procurement Specialist and the Business Analyst resource to 40%.

STEP 2   Validate Assignment Units

- Continuing to use the 'A – Resource Usage' view, set the 'Assignment Units' for the Business Analyst Resource on the 'Build Work Breakdown Structure' task to 40%.

STEP 3   Validate Peak Assignment

- Continuing to use the 'A – Resource Usage' view, validate that no values in the 'Peak' field exceeds the 'Max Units' column. None should exist, step is included for completeness for other projects you will be managing.

STEP 4   Resolve over-allocations

- Using the '06 – Leveling Gantt' view, select Tasks 4, 6, 16, 17, and 18 and using the 'Assign Resources' dialog change the resource allocation to 40%. This change was required to adjust the individual assignments as a result of our previous change to reduce 'Max Units' from 100% to a more realistic 80%.

STEP 5   Level Resources

- From the 'Resource ribbon > Level section' select the 'Leveling Options' dialog
  - Select 'Manual' for 'Leveling calculations'.
  - Select 'Level entire project'.
  - Select the 'Clear leveling values before leveling' and click OK to close the 'Resource Leveling' dialog.
- Select 'Level All' to resolve the resource over-allocations. With the options we set, the leveling engine has the ability to reschedule any tasks needed to resolve the over-allocations. As a result, it selected the optimal set of tasks, based on its scheduling engine and the parameters provided and moved 'Document Subcontractor Management Plan' and changed its end date.

WORK SESSION #10 – CREATING THE PROJECT BUDGET

STEP 1   Add Cost Resources to track non-resource costs

- If your organization has Cost Resources defined, select and use the appropriate cost resources from the enterprise resources pool using the same process used to select enterprise work resources, otherwise, using the 'B – Resource Sheet' view, add a new cost resource called 'Training' and set the 'Type' to 'Cost'.
- Using the '05 – Planning Gantt', select the 'Build Work Breakdown Structure' task and from the 'Resource ribbon > Assignments section' select 'Assign Resources' to assign the 'Training' resource to the task with a cost of $5,000.

STEP 2   Add Budget Resources for the Project Budget

- Using the 'B – Resource Sheet' view, add two more 'Cost Resources' called 'Labor Budget' and 'Training Budget'
  - For each new resource, double click each new resource to open the 'Resource Information' dialog and select the 'Budget' checkbox.
  - Using the '05 – Planning Gantt', ensure that the "Project Summary Task' is showing ('Format ribbon > Show/Hide section – select checkbox for 'Project Summary Task').
  - From the 'Resource ribbon > Assignments section' select 'Assign Resources' and assign both 'Labor Budget' and 'Training Budget' to the 'Project Summary Task'.

STEP 3   Set Cost Type

- Using the 'B – Resource Sheet' set the 'Cost Type' to 'Labor' for all three named resources and the 'Labor Budget' cost resource.
- Set the 'Cost Type' to 'Training' for the Training resource and 'Training Budget' cost resource.

STEP 4   Create Project Budget

- Using the '02 Budget and Cost Planning' view, set the 'Budget Cost' for the 'Labor Budget' as the total of all the labor costs - $38,000. (Hint, in this case it's the total cost less the $5,000 Training cost, for larger projects, this can be determined from the 'A – Resource Usage' view by grouping the resources by 'Cost Type') .
- Set the 'Budget Costs' for the 'Training Budget' to $5,000 (or from larger projects from the total of the 'Training' group in the 'A – Resource Usage' view).

WORK SESSION #11 – SET THE ORIGINAL BASELINE AND PUBLISH THE PLAN

STEP 1   Set Project Baseline

- Using the '7 – Baselining' view, from the 'Project ribbon > Schedule section'
  - Select 'Set Baseline' to launch the 'Set Baseline' dialog.
  - Select 'Set Baseline' and 'Entire Project' options and click OK.

STEP 2   Preserve Original Baseline

- From the 'Project ribbon > Schedule section' select 'Set Baseline' to launch the 'Set Baseline' dialog
  - Select the 'Set Interim Plan' and copy from 'Baseline' to 'Baseline10' and 'Entire plan' options. This preserves a copy of the original Baseline into Baseline10 should you ever need to revert back to and/or report against the original project baseline.

STEP 3   Publish Project Plan

- Select 'File' and 'Publish Project Progress'. Once the publish is complete, 'Save' and 'Check In' your project, then close it.

STEP 4   Set Resource Utilization

- Launch PWA and select 'Projects'
  - Select your project from the project list.
  - From the 'Projects ribbon > Navigate section' select 'Resource Plan'.
  - From the 'Plan ribbon > Resource Utilization' section, select 'Project Plan' from the 'Calculate from' dropdown.

WORK SESSION #12 - SUBMITTING A TIMESHEET

Project Web App Solution

STEP 1   Create Timesheet

- In PWA, from the 'Quick Launch' select 'Manage Timesheets'. If you do not have PWA, alternate instructions are provided below for doing the same in Microsoft Project.
- Select the appropriate timesheet period (this will likely require you to change the view timeframe to show 'All Timesheets' to display timesheets for 2015). Select the timesheet which covers the first week of the project; January 05, 2015 to January 09, 2015.
- For the task 'Specify Deliverables and Acceptance Criteria'
   - Enter 4 hours for Monday
   - Enter 4 hours for Tuesday
   - Enter 2 hours for Wednesday.
- From the 'Timesheet ribbon > Submit section' select Save. This will save the changes and update the 'Remaining Work' to reflect the time just recorded.
- Update the Remaining Work for 'Specify Deliverables and Acceptance Criteria' to be 20
   - Enter the comment "5 new deliverables identified which will require 20 more hours" to explain the reason for the increased time on the task.
- Hit Save again to record the changes.

STEP 2   Submit Timesheet

- From the 'Timesheet ribbon > Submit section' select 'Send' and 'Turn in Final Timesheet'.

Microsoft Project Standalone solution

STEP 1   Create Timesheet

- Open the schedule in Microsoft project and select the 'A – Resource Usage' view.
- Scroll the calendar area of the view to display the first week of the project; January 5 2015 to January 9, 2015
   - If the 'Actual Work' field is not visible in the calendar view, right click anywhere in the calendar area and select 'Actual Work'.
- For the task 'Specify Deliverables and Acceptance Criteria' enter the time into the 'Actual Work' row
   - Enter 4 hours for Monday
   - Enter 4 hours for Tuesday
   - Enter 2 hours for Wednesday.
- Update the 'Remaining Work' for 'Specify Deliverables and Acceptance Criteria' to be 20.

WORK SESSION #13 – UPDATE PROJECT COSTS

STEP 1   Record Actual Costs

- Using the '09 – Cost Tracking' view, enter $3,000 actual costs for the 'Training' resource on the 'Develop Work Breakdown Structure' task
    - Scroll the calendar area to display the current status period (January 05, 2015 – January 09, 2015) and update the actual cost field.
    - If the 'Actual Cost' field isn't visible in the calendar area, right mouse click and select 'Actual Cost' to add it to the display.
    - Validate that the 'Remaining Cost' has been reduced to $2,000.

STEP 2   Review Budget performance

- Using the 'C – Cost Type' view, for each 'Cost Type' being tracked in your project, compare the 'Budget Cost' and the 'Cost' columns to validate the project's financial performance.

WORK SESSION #14 – PROCESS STATUS UPDATES

STEP 1   Confirm all timesheets have been entered

- In PWA, from the 'Quick Launch' in the Reports section, select 'Sensei Reports'
  - From the 'Report Area 5 – Project Status and Portfolio Reporting' select the 'Timesheet Compliance by Project Manager Report'.
  - Select your name from the list and ensure the appropriate timesheet date (January 05, 2015 – January 09, 2015) is selected.
  - Validate that all timesheets have been entered.

  If you are not using PWA, you can skip to Step 4 as timesheets have already been entered into Microsoft Project in the previous work session.

STEP 2   Review status update changes

- In PWA, from the 'Quick Launch' select 'Approvals' and review the schedule updates resulting from the timesheet data submitted. All schedule changes are shown in red to allow for ease of reviewing and understanding the impacts.
- Conduct a detailed review of the updates by clicking on the tasks in the 'Approval View' to launch the 'Task Details' screen to get a detailed description of the data provided on the Timesheet.
- Select the checkbox for the status updates you are accepting and then from the 'Approval ribbon > Actions section' select 'Preview Updates' to provide a full preview of the entire schedule with any changes as a result of the timesheet updates shown in blue.

STEP 3   Accept Status Updates

- In PWA, select the checkbox for the status update you are accepting and from the 'Approval ribbon > Actions section' select 'Accept'. This will accept the timesheet status updates and apply the changes in Microsoft Project the next time the plan is opened.

STEP 4   Update Status Date

- Open the plan in Microsoft Project and using the 'Project ribbon > Status section' select the 'Status Date' command to set the Status Date to January 11, 2015 (the Sunday at the end of the timesheet period – this is based on our timesheets period running from Monday thru Sunday – your organization may have a different weekly timesheet period).

STEP 5   Mark Milestones as complete

- Using the '10 – Project Status' view, select the 'Project Start' milestone, then from the 'Task ribbon > Schedule section' select the '100%' icon to complete the milestone.

STEP 6   Update KPIs

- From the 'Project ribbon > Properties section', select 'Project Information' to launch the 'Project Information' dialog

      □   Update the 'Project KPI' custom property to be 'On Track'. (Standalone Microsoft Project users will not be able to complete this step).

STEP 7   **Reschedule uncompleted work**

- From the 'Project ribbon > Status section', select 'Update Project' to launch the 'Update Project' dialog.
  - □ Select 'Reschedule uncompleted work to start after' and select January 11, 2015 from the calendar.

STEP 8   **Address schedule slippage**

- Following the technique to "Taking Corrective Action on the Critical Path"
  - □ Highlight the Critical Path, from the 'Format ribbon > Bar Style section' select the checkbox to show the 'Critical Tasks'. We also recommend using the 'Filter Feature' in the 'Critical' column to show only the tasks set to 'Yes'. The result is a sub-set of the complete project plan that we should focus on for trying to improve the project schedule, as only Critical Path tasks determine the project end date.
  - □ From the 'Format ribbon > Bar Style section', un-select the checkbox to show the 'Summary Tasks'.
  - □ From the 'View ribbon > Data section' select 'Sort', then 'Sort by' and select the 'Duration' field and 'Descending' order.
  - □ Investigate options for reducing the longest task 'Identify Potential Subcontractors'. After discussions with the procurement department, there are no options for change. We look at the next longest task 'Build Work Breakdown Structure' and we assign a new team member to this task to share the work equally with the original team member to improve the project finish date (but not enough to address all the schedule slippage). On investigation of the 'Specific Deliverables and Acceptance Criteria' task, we determine that we could add an additional resource and/or negotiate with Resource Management to increase the availability of the current resource. On further more careful examination, we determine that we have assigned ourselves to this task at only 40% and that since there is no other work assigned to us in this time period, we increase our resource availability to 80%. Activate the 'Task Form' and change the allocation to 80% on this task (or alternatively use the 'Assign Resource' dialog). This improves the project schedule, but still does not address all the slippage. Next, add a second resource to the 'Specific Deliverables and Acceptance Criteria' task by adding the resource assigned to the Business Analysis work to the task at 40%, and adjust the work per resource giving yourself 2/3 of the remaining work (80%) and the Business Analyst 1/3 of the remaining work (40%).
  - □ There is very little additional changes that can be done to improve the project schedule, so we return the view to display the full project plan by sorting by ID, and displaying the summary tasks and un-filtering the critical tasks.
  - □ With the non-critical tasks visible, we realize that we have over-allocated ourselves as we were in fact working on a non-critical task when we made the decision to increase our availability to 80%. From the 'Resource ribbon > Level section', select 'Level All' to have Project adjust the plan to resolve the resource over-allocation.
  - □ As there are no options to further crash the project schedule, so therefore go to management to report a project slippage and negotiate a change to the deadline.

WORK SESSION #15 – PROCESS PROJECT CHANGE REQUEST

STEP 1   Add tasks to the schedule

- Open the schedule in Microsoft Project and insert a new task 'Review Risks with SAS Vendor' between the 'Analyze Project Risks' and 'Document Risk Management Plan' tasks
  - Update the dependencies to have 'Analyze Project Risks' the predecessor to the new task and the 'Document Risk Management Plan' to be the predecessor to the new task. The most effective way to do this is using the '03 – Dependencies' view directly enter the IDs into Predecessor and Successor columns.
  - Using the 'Assign Resources' dialog, assign yourself to this task with a 'Work' estimate of 16 hours.

STEP 2   Obtain formal approval of schedule changes

- Select the new task and activate the Shortcut Menu with a right-mouse click and select 'Inactivate Task'. (In most instances, a Change Request would include multiple new lines added to the schedule, therefore, ensure that all new tasks are selected prior to inactivating them).
- With the new tasks still selected, select 'Inactivate Task' again to reactivate the tasks. This will result in change highlighting showing all tasks impacted by the Change Request.
- With change highlighting still visible, from the 'Task ribbon > Font section'
  - Select the Background Color and add a Blue background to the inserted tasks.
  - From the Background Color and add a Green background to all other project tasks where Change Highlighting is activated.
  - Using a Screen Capture tool, capture the screen(s) with all tasks where the Background Color has been set and obtain management approval of the overall impact that this change has on other tasks and milestones.

STEP 3   Update Baseline

- With all tasks with a 'Background Color' selected, from the 'Project ribbon > Schedule section' select 'Set Baseline' and set the baseline for only the 'Selected Tasks'.
  - With the baseline set, preserve this new baseline into the next available baseline (Baseline9) by again selecting 'Set Baseline', but this time selecting the 'Set Interim Plan' and copying the 'Baseline' into 'Baseline9'.
- Remove the 'Background Color' from all tasks.

WORK SESSION #16 – PROJECT STATUS REPORTING

STEP 1   Project Timeline

- Develop a project timeline suitable for submitting to management as part of a project status report
  - With the plan open in Microsoft Project, from the 'View ribbon > Data section', use the 'Outline' option to display 'Outline Level 1'. Select all these lines and then using a right-mouse click, activate the Shortcut Menu and select 'Add to Timeline'.
  - Expand your project plan to show all tasks using 'Outline – All Subtasks' and select the Milestones for each the project deliverables and also include them in the 'Project Timeline'.
  - Explore methods of improving the appearance of the Timeline. For example, change the Project Summary Task to 'Display as Callout' and add color to each bar to make them more distinct and move the locations of the milestone callouts to help make the 'Timeline' easier to read and understand.

STEP 2   Review and Update Issues, Risks and Action items

- Review and update all action items, issues and risks in preparation for reporting the current project status
  - In PWA, open the Project Site and review all action items, issues and risks to ensure that they are current and that work is being done to move the items to closure. From the 'Quick Launch' on the left, select 'Action Items', 'Issues' and 'Risks'.

STEP 3   Update Project Home page

- Review the Project Home page to validate currency and accuracy for status reporting
  - In PWA, open the Project Site and review and validate all the information displayed on the home page paying particular attention to the 'Timeline' 'Announcements' and 'Project Status' as these are the first items visible from the home page.

STEP 4   Distribute Project Status report

- Produce Project Status report and distribute to project stakeholders.
  - In PWA from the 'Quick Launch' menu, select 'Sensei Reports' and then from 'Report Area 5 – Project Status and Portfolio Reporting' select the 'Project Status Report'. From the selection area on the left, select your project and click Apply.
  - Review and validate the report and then distribute it to the appropriate Project Stakeholders.

INDEX OF TERMS

Sensei Proactive PPM Resources

As mentioned in the introduction, Proactive PPM is a philosophy and a set of best practices to help project managers and organizations be successful with Project and Portfolio Management (PPM) utilizing Microsoft Project, Project Server and Project Online.

In addition to this book, Sensei Project Solutions has developed an entire set of products, apps and solutions to help facilitate Proactive PPM and ensure adoption of the Microsoft PPM solution. Below is a brief description of these offerings.

Apps

The proliferation of apps on phones seems almost as if it occurred overnight. Now, with support for Apps in Microsoft Office, SharePoint, Windows 8, Windows Phone 8, iPad, iPhone and Android phones, project managers and executives have access to their PPM data from any device. Sensei offers a number of apps across devices. See www.senseiprojectsolutions.com for more details.

Training

Any change to existing processes and technology can be challenging for some people and organizations to adopt. Training end users in the context of their roles and processes is key to a successful deployment. Sensei offers a complete set of role-based and process-focused training classes to help communicate the business drivers behind the deployment as well as key benefits to users and detailed procedural instruction to perform on-going duties in the Microsoft PPM environment.

Report Packs

One of the most critical components of any PPM solution is the ability to extract data for reporting purposes. Sensei has developed a standard set of report packs aligned with PMI practice standards and Gartner recommendations to allow organizations to quickly apply world-class reporting to their existing Microsoft PPM environment.

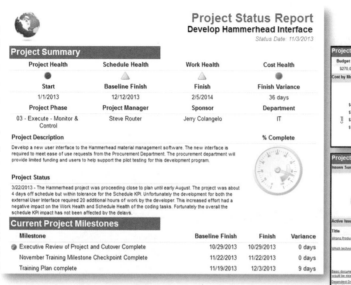
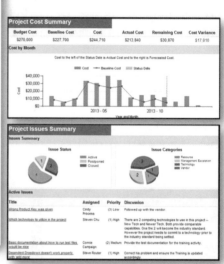

Jumpstart Solutions

Organizations new to Microsoft PPM or with limited processes in place can benefit greatly from a turn-key solution that is based on a proven solution and aligned with industry standards and best practices. Sensei's Jumpstart solution is aligned with the Project Management Institute's Practice Standards as well as PPM recommendations from Gartner. It provides a world-class Microsoft PPM configuration along with supporting processes, procedures and documentation. The Jumpstart Solution deploys in less than 3 weeks and provides an excellent starting point for anyone looking to get up and running quickly.

Jumpstart Solution				
Business Drivers	Key Performance Indicators	SharePoint Project Site Template	End User Procedures	Walkthrough
Timesheet	Enterprise Resource Pool	Enterprise Project Types (EPTs)	Business Case – Project Detail Pages	Governance Workflows
Project Server Base Installation	Project Pro views	PWA Views and Security	Report Packs	Schedule Templates